SPIRITUALITY AND MYSTICISM

THEOLOGY IN GLOBAL PERSPECTIVE SERIES

Peter C. Phan, General Editor
Ignacio Ellacuría Professor of Catholic Social Thought, Georgetown University

At the beginning of a new millennium, the *Theology in Global Perspective* series responds to the challenge to reexamine the foundational and doctrinal themes of Christianity in light of the new global reality. While traditional Catholic theology has assumed an essentially European or Western point of view, *Theology in Global Perspective* takes account of insights and experience of churches in Africa, Asia, Latin America, Oceania, as well as from Europe and North America. Noting the pervasiveness of changes brought about by science and technologies, and growing concerns about the sustainability of Earth, it seeks to embody insights from studies in these areas as well.

Though rooted in the Catholic tradition, volumes in the series are written with an eye to the ecumenical implications of Protestant, Orthodox, and Pentecostal theologies for Catholicism, and vice versa. In addition, authors will explore insights from other religious traditions with the potential to enrich Christian theology and self-understanding.

Books in this series will provide reliable introductions to the major theological topics, tracing their roots in Scripture and their development in later tradition, exploring when possible the implications of new thinking on gender and sociocultural identities. And they will relate these themes to the challenges confronting the peoples of the world in the wake of globalization, particularly the implications of Christian faith for justice, peace, and the integrity of creation.

Other Books Published in the Series

Orders and Ministry: Leadership in the World Church, Kenan Osborne, O.F.M.
Trinity, Anne Hunt
Eschatology: The Language of Hope, Anthony Kelly, C.Ss.R.

THEOLOGY IN GLOBAL PERSPECTIVE SERIES

SPIRITUALITY AND MYSTICISM

A Global View

JAMES A. WISEMAN

Maryknoll, New York 10545

Founded in 1970, Orbis Books endeavors to publish works that enlighten the mind, nourish the spirit, and challenge the conscience. The publishing arm of the Maryknoll Fathers and Brothers, Orbis seeks to explore the global dimensions of the Christian faith and mission, to invite dialogue with diverse cultures and religious traditions, and to serve the cause of reconciliation and peace. The books published reflect the opinions of their authors and are not meant to represent the official position of the Maryknoll Society. To obtain more information about Maryknoll and Orbis Books, please visit our website at www.maryknoll.org.

Manufactured in the United States of America.

Library of Congress Cataloging in Publication Data

Wiseman, James A., 1942-
Spirituality and mysticism : a global view / James A. Wiseman.
p. cm. — (Theology in global perspective)
Includes bibliographical references and index.
ISBN-13: 978-1-57075-656-6 (pbk.)
1. Spirituality. 2. Mysticism. I. Title. II. Series.
BV4501.3.W57 2006
248—dc22

2005029031

Contents

Foreword

by Peter C. Phan

Spirituality and Mysticism—words that conjure up things otherworldly and esoteric but also, as every publisher well knows, sell books! Although the latter goal is not beyond the wishes of Orbis Books, what this study shows is that Christian spirituality and mysticism are anything but esoteric and otherworldly. Rather, "spirituality," as James Wiseman argues along with many other contemporary theologians, means for Christians nothing more and nothing less than a striving for an intense union with God the Father through the Son Jesus Christ and by the power of the Holy Spirit. As for "mysticism," it is not to be contrasted with the "ordinary" way of Christian life and associated with extraordinary phenomena such as vision, ecstasy, levitation and the like. On the contrary, it is understood to refer to our consciousness of and reaction to the immediate presence of God that is in principle available to all Christians.

The ordinariness and everyday character of spirituality and mysticism do not mean of course that their articulation and explication throughout Christian history have been straightforward and unproblematic. Indeed, one of the great merits of Wiseman's book is a lucid and honest narrative of the twists and turns and ups and downs of this Christian river from the New Testament to our postmodern era, at times cascading from the heights of Neoplatonic speculations of such theologians as Origen of Alexandria, Gregory of Nyssa, and Augustine of Hippo; at times trickling into quiet rivulets of thinkers such as Dhuoda, Julian of Norwich, and Evelyn Underhill; at other times hurling into a torrent reminiscent of Francis of Assisi, Martin Luther, and Jonathan Edwards; and yet at other times overflowing its banks into fertile meadows and forests of theology such as those of Benedict of Nursia, Gregory of Palamas, and Karl Rahner; and at still other times merging with mighty rivers of thought such as that of Bede Griffiths, Kazoh Katamori, and Thomas Merton. Yet in this constant ebb and flow of Christian spirituality and mysticism, Wiseman keeps our eyes riveted on the gold nuggets that lie hidden in the works of this "cloud of witnesses."

In keeping with the ecumenical, intercultural, and interreligious character of this Theology in Global Perspective series, Wiseman is deeply aware of the global context in which the study of Christian spirituality and mysticism must be carried out. Within the narrow space allotted to his book, he deftly helps us not only to take a penetrating look at the Catholic, Protestant, Anglican, and Pentecostal spiritual and mystical traditions but also to extend our horizon to include Asia, Africa, and the Americas.

James Wiseman is not only a theoretician of Christian spirituality and mysticism with well-received publications in this field. A Benedictine monk, he knows experientially that whereof he speaks. A more trustworthy and sure-footed guide you cannot find. His humble hope that what he has learned in doing research for this book "will now be transmitted to readers in all parts of our shrinking globe" will be amply fulfilled.

Preface

"Globalization," a word not even found in dictionaries of the mid-twentieth century, is now heard in just about every place where English is spoken. The various meanings of the term provoke very different responses among those who hear it. For some, globalization primarily conjures up images of multinational corporations that are headquartered in Europe, North America, and Japan that cause economic hardship for people living in other parts of the world. Where this meaning prevails, we find public demonstrations and even riots protesting the policies of such corporations. For others, however, the word has a more positive meaning. For them, globalization refers above all to a growing sense of interconnectedness among all peoples and nations on earth, facilitated by rapid means of communication that promote a sharing of ideas and a broadening of intellectual and emotional horizons. It is this latter sense of the term that lies behind the publication of this and other volumes in the Orbis Books series entitled *Theology in Global Perspective.*

There was a time not many decades ago when it was simply assumed by authors in the North Atlantic region that works focusing on Christian spirituality would deal almost exclusively with figures and movements in Europe and North America. This assumption is no longer viable. It is estimated that by the year 2050 fully 75 percent of the world's Christians will live in Latin America, Africa, and Asia. The voices of Christians living on those continents must now be heard, not only for reasons of simple fairness but because they offer precious insights that are of benefit to all of us. Moreover, in both the Southern and Northern Hemispheres Christians are increasingly finding themselves in contact with members of other religious traditions, with whom dialogue is required for purposes of mutual understanding and enrichment. A book by Will Herberg that was published in the United States in the mid-twentieth century and that purported to describe the religious landscape in that country was entitled simply *Protestant, Catholic, Jew*. Nowadays, the title of any such book would have to be expanded at least threefold in order to take into account the increasing number of Hindus, Jains, Buddhists, Muslims, Sikhs, Daoists, and Baha'is now living in this country, not to mention Wiccans, Zoroastrians, practitioners of Native American religions, and many others. The situation is similar elsewhere.

It was with the intention of doing justice to this new, global context that the present book has been written. The relatively short length that characterizes all the volumes in this series means that the present treatment of Christian spirituality has had to be extremely selective. Rather than attempting to say just a bit about a great many persons and movements, I have gone into somewhat greater detail about a few of them. This inevitably means that some readers will lament the absence of one or more of their favorites. I can honestly join my lament to theirs, but I also hope that such readers will feel somewhat compensated by discovering new sources of insight and inspiration in some of the figures and topics about which they may be hearing for the first time. Works listed as "suggested readings" at the end of each chapter and ones included in the selected bibliography at the end of the book will provide leads for those who may wish to do some further exploration on their own.

The sequence of chapters in this book is quite straightforward. After looking at the meaning of spirituality and the related term "mysticism" in the opening chapter, I turn next to the spirituality of the Bible, the text that will always be foundational for Christian theology. The subsequent five chapters proceed chronologically. The third chapter takes up the spirituality of the early martyrs as well as of two very influential thinkers of late-second-century and early-third-century Alexandria (Clement and Origen), while the fourth chapter considers the beginning of the monastic movement, the fathers and mothers of the desert having regularly regarded themselves as the successors of the martyrs once the Roman persecutions ended. Chapter 5, focusing on the patristic era, treats several important authors from the Syriac tradition as well as individuals who wrote in Greek or Latin; it also looks at the work of one of the few Christian women from the first millennium of the church's history from whom we have something written by herself, and it then concludes with a section on the early Christian spirituality of Nubia and Ethiopia. The next chapter opens with a treatment of some of the most influential reform movements in the church of the Middle Ages—the Cistercians, Dominicans, and Franciscans—and goes on to consider the contributions of some important medieval women (the Beguines and Julian of Norwich) as well as a man who was himself influenced by the Beguines, Meister Eckhart. This chapter also examines the spirituality of the icons of the Eastern Church and concludes with a section on the hesychastic movement within that same church. The last of the strictly chronological chapters is the seventh, which discusses the spirituality of the sixteenth-century reformers, both Protestant and Roman Catholic, in each case showing how the work of those reformers has been reflected or carried forward by more recent figures in the history of Christian spirituality: Dietrich Bonhoeffer, Evelyn Underhill, Karl Rahner, and Thérèse of Lisieux.

Mindful of the global perspective of this book, even in these first seven chapters I have made numerous references to Christian spirituality as taught and practiced beyond the regions where Greek or Latin was the principal language of the people. Among other topics, these chapters accordingly include the consideration of (1) early Syriac spirituality as found in the *Odes of Solomon*, the *Book of Steps*, and the poetry of Ephrem the Syrian, (2) the prayer of the fourth-century Armenian missionary Gregory the Illuminator, (3) the life and teaching of the Coptic monastic founder Pachomius, and (4) the spirituality of the ancient Ethiopian liturgy. It was, however, mainly during and after the so-called Age of Discovery in the sixteenth century that Christianity spread in a very significant way to the continents of Asia, Africa, and South and North America. The final three chapters of the book focus exclusively on Christian spirituality as it developed on those continents.

Throughout the writing of this book I have been conscious of the fact that spirituality is manifested not only in written texts about traditional topics such as prayer and contemplation but also in visual and aural art and in such activities as liturgical worship and struggles to promote social justice. Some of these latter resources are discussed, for example, in the sections on the spirituality of the icon, the liturgical music and dance of African Christians, and the work of liberation theologians. I have also highlighted the important contributions of women by noting, from the first millennium, Perpetua and Felicity of Carthage, the Persian martyr Martha, Macrina the Younger, and the Frankish laywoman Dhuoda, and, from the second millennium, the Beguines (especially Marguerite Porete), Julian of Norwich, Teresa of Avila, Thérèse of Lisieux, Evelyn Underhill, Mary John Mananzan, and three North American women who are prominent Christian feminists.

Although the focus of this book is specifically on Christian spirituality, many of the figures studied have been heavily influenced by their contact with other religious traditions. This was especially true of Matteo Ricci, Roberto de Nobili, and Alexandre de Rhodes from the sixteenth and seventeenth centuries and of Henri Le Saux, Bede Griffiths, and Thomas Merton in more recent times. The particular slant of their spirituality will, I hope, prove to be particularly thought-provoking to many readers.

As noted above, many supplementary readings are suggested at the end of each chapter and in the bibliography at the end of the volume. When *Spirituality and Mysticism: A Global View* serves as a textbook in academic courses, it could be used in conjunction with readings from primary sources that are to be found in several useful anthologies. One of these, co-edited by Louis Dupré of Yale University and myself and entitled *Light from Light* (Paulist Press, 2001), contains fairly extensive selections from the following fifteen authors who are discussed in the present book: Origen, Gregory of Nyssa,

Augustine of Hippo, Bernard of Clairvaux, Francis and Clare of Assisi, Meister Eckhart, Gregory Palamas, Julian of Norwich, Ignatius of Loyola, Teresa of Avila, Jonathan Edwards, Thérèse of Lisieux, Evelyn Underhill, and Thomas Merton, as well as eight other authors who have not been discussed here simply for reasons of space: Pseudo-Dionysius, Bonaventure, Jan van Ruusbroec, the author of *The Cloud of Unknowing*, Catherine of Siena, John of the Cross, Francis de Sales, and Jeanne de Chantal.

The questions for reflection at the end of each chapter are intended to promote lively discussion, whether in the classroom or in study groups. Their very formulation should in many cases make it evident that on issues raised by the study of Christian spirituality there is often no unambiguously single right answer.

Of the various persons who have assisted me in the writing of this book, I would first like to thank my former research assistant Aaron Massey, who cheerfully and competently tracked down much helpful material in various libraries. I am also grateful to the students who have taken my courses in spirituality at The Catholic University of America over the years, for their questions often gave me new insights on how one or another topic might best be addressed; in this connection I think especially of the way I discuss the testing of Abraham (Gen 22:1-19) in my second chapter. Finally, I extend my sincere thanks to the general editor of this series, Peter Phan, for asking me to undertake this project in the first place. I learned a great deal simply by doing the necessary research and am hopeful that much of what I learned will now be transmitted to readers in all parts of our shrinking globe.

1

What Is Spirituality?

THE QUESTION THAT SERVES as the title for this opening chapter would seldom have been asked a century ago, for the term "spirituality" began to be frequently used only around the middle of the twentieth century. Since then it has become more and more common. One of the major publishing ventures of our time is a series entitled Classics of Western Spirituality, the first volume of which appeared in 1978. The response of the public to this series has been so enthusiastic that the editors have decided to leave it open-ended instead of stopping at a certain number of volumes, as originally planned. The last quarter of the twentieth century also saw the inauguration of another important new series, World Spirituality: An Encyclopedic History of the Religious Quest, which will consist of twenty-five volumes when complete.[1]

The generally positive response given to these two publishing ventures is just one indication of the widespread interest in spirituality today. Whereas the term "spiritual" was once often used in a negative sense to imply that a person was otherworldly or even irresponsible, today it is frequently used as a badge of honor, as when a person claims to be "very spiritual, though not religious." But people may well mean quite different things by such a phrase. As a first step toward clarifying how "spiritual" and "spirituality" will be understood in this book, it will be helpful to look at the root meaning of these two words.

THE ROOT MEANING OF SPIRITUALITY

Like so many English words, "spiritual" and "spirituality" have a Latin root. The Latin verb *spirare* means "to breathe," while the corresponding adjective *spiritualis* means "of *or* belonging to breathing *or* to air." We see at once that this word group has to do with life, for it is only through breathing that

1. The Classics of Western Spirituality are published by Paulist Press, while the series World Spirituality is published by Crossroad.

human beings can stay alive. In early Christian writings, there arose an important nuance to that literal meaning. When the Greek New Testament was translated into Latin by various writers in the second and third centuries of our era, a crucial term in St. Paul's letters, *pneumatikos*, was translated as *spiritualis*. What this word meant for St. Paul can best be understood by the context in which he used it near the beginning of his First Letter to the Corinthians, where he writes that he is speaking "in words not taught by human wisdom but taught by the Spirit, interpreting spiritual things (*pneumatika*) to those who are spiritual" (1 Cor 2:13). Spiritual persons are, then, those who are open to the Spirit of God. Paul contrasts these with persons who are "natural" (*psychikos*) and "fleshly" (*sarkinos*). It is clear that the point of the contrast is not between what is corporeal and what is noncorporeal. "Flesh" does not refer to the body as such but rather to creatureliness. To live "according to the flesh" means to live according to purely self-centered inclinations, which is inevitable in those who are immature in the faith. What Paul seeks is spiritual maturity, living according to the promptings of God's Spirit, whose fruit he describes in another of his letters as "love, joy, peace, patience, kindness, generosity, faithfulness, gentleness, and self-control" (Gal 5:22). For a follower of Christ to live in such a way is a preeminent mark of what Paul means by "a spiritual person." This brings us back to that root meaning of *spiritualis* as "pertaining to breathing" and hence to life, which is why Paul can very readily refer to God's Spirit as "the Spirit of life," as when he writes to the Romans that "the law of the Spirit of life in Christ Jesus has set you free from the law of sin and of death" (Rom 8:2).

On the basis of this root meaning of "spiritual" in the early Christian tradition, let us now look at the corresponding noun, "spirituality." The first certain appearance of this word in Christian literature dates from the fifth century, in a letter that was once ascribed to St. Jerome but is now considered to have been written by someone else. It is addressed to an adult who had recently been baptized and urges that person to live an authentic Christian life, always moving forward, avoiding all lukewarmness. The author writes that through "the new grace" received in baptism all cause for sorrow or tears has been removed. The newly baptized is urged to "act, be on guard, run, hasten. Act in such a way that you progress in spirituality (*in spiritualitate*)," that is, in life according to the Spirit that was given in baptism. This section of the letter concludes with the words, "While we have time, let us sow in the Spirit, that we may reap a harvest in spiritual things (*in spiritualibus*)."[2] Here, too,

2. Pseudo-Jerome *Epistle* 7, in *Patrologiae cursus completus: Series Latina*, ed. J.-P. Migne, 221 vols. (Paris: J.-P. Migne, 1844-55), 30:105-16, quoted by Aimé Solignac, *Dictionnaire de Spiritualité ascétique et mystique, doctrine et histoire* (1937; repr., Paris: Beauchesne, 1995), 14:1143, s.v. "Spiritualité."

there is no sense that living spiritually has anything to do with disdain for the body or for matter. It is, rather, a matter of living in accord with the promptings of the Spirit of God, as modeled by Jesus Christ's own manner of life as described in the Gospels.

By the early Middle Ages, however, this meaning of "spiritual" and "spirituality" was at times replaced by a more philosophical meaning in which the contrast was not with living according to merely human inclinations but rather with that which was bodily or material. Some reasons for this change will be discussed in the third chapter of this book, but the change itself can be seen, for example, in a work by a ninth-century German monk who contrasted *spiritualitas* with *materialitas* and *corporalitas*. Four centuries later the most influential of the medieval scholastic theologians, St. Thomas Aquinas, used the noun *spiritualitas* about seventy times, usually in the sense of life according to the Holy Spirit but fairly often in opposition to materiality or bodiliness.[3]

With the rise of vernacular languages in Europe, the Latin term gave rise to cognate terms in French (e.g., *spiritualité*) and English (*spirituality*). In both languages the Pauline meaning was often retained, though the noun also was used to refer to clerics exercising ecclesiastical jurisdiction, as contrasted with laypersons who exercised civil jurisdiction. The philosophical sense, contrasting the spiritual with the corporeal or material, sometimes appeared as well. In the late nineteenth and early twentieth century, writers like Swami Vivekananda and Annie Besant who sought to promulgate the values of Hinduism in the West regularly used the word "spirituality" to characterize Indian religion as being superior to rampant "materialism" in Western culture.[4] Beginning with the third decade of the twentieth century, however, there began to appear a number of books in English referring to Christian spirituality in their titles, one of the first being entitled simply *Christian Spirituality*, a translation of a four-volume French work by Pierre Pourrat. By the early twenty-first century the number of such titles has become legion. The words "spiritual" and "spirituality" are also used in the titles of journals (e.g., *Spiritual Life*) and in journal articles, workshops, conferences, and scholarly associations (such as the Society for the Study of Christian Spirituality). When used by Christians, the terms are normally related to that original Pauline sense of living according to the promptings of God's Spirit. Nevertheless, many precisions to the meaning of the terms have been offered in recent years, including nuances arising in non-Christian settings. We will

3. Walter Principe, "Toward Defining Spirituality," *Studies in Religion/Sciences Religieuses* 12, no. 2 (1983): 131.

4. Ibid., 133.

look briefly at three of the most significant of these, each somewhat different from the other two and yet arguably complementary.

THREE WAYS OF DESCRIBING OR DEFINING SPIRITUALITY

A number of writers regularly speak of spirituality in terms of self-transcendence. One of the most prominent of these is Sandra Schneiders, who notes in one of her numerous studies on the topic that the term "spirituality" has three interrelated references: first, to a fundamental dimension of the human being; second, to the lived experience that actualizes that dimension; and third, to the academic discipline that studies the experience.[5] Here, as well as in other studies she has published, Schneiders defines spirituality as "the experience of consciously striving to integrate one's life in terms not of isolation and self-absorption but of self-transcendence toward the ultimate value one perceives."[6] This accords with what we said earlier in this chapter about the kind of maturity that St. Paul sought to foster in the Corinthians and members of other churches to which he wrote. It is well known that infants or young children tend to assume that the entire world revolves around them, that they are the center of everyone's attention, and that their needs are the only ones that should be heeded. What we mean by "growing up" involves in large measure a transcending of this self-centered understanding of oneself and one's place in the world. When this self-transcendence is geared not merely toward a more comfortable adaptation to life in a family or society but toward what Schneiders calls "the ultimate value one perceives," then one may properly speak of spiritual experience or spirituality. Since we have used St. Paul's writings as an avenue of approach to the meaning of spirituality, some persons may feel it inappropriate to use the term outside of a Christian context. While it is important to beware of subtle ways of fostering a kind of Christian imperialism vis-à-vis other traditions, Schneiders's broad definition of spirituality in terms of transcendence "toward the ultimate value one perceives" makes it quite legitimate to speak, for example, of Hindu spirituality or Jewish spirituality. Indeed, since the ultimate value need not be perceived as a personal God (as it is not only in Christianity but also in Hinduism, Judaism, and other theistic religions), one could just as properly speak of Buddhist or Daoist spirituality, where there are clearly transcendent horizons

5. Sandra M. Schneiders, I.H.M., "Spirituality in the Academy," *Theological Studies* 50 (1989): 678.

6. Ibid., 684.

of ultimate value (the Buddha, nirvana, the Dao) even though none of these is understood to be a personal God. Indeed, the above-mentioned series World Spirituality even includes a volume entitled *Spirituality and the Secular Quest*. Although some might consider the phrase "secular spirituality" to be a contradiction in terms, there are good reasons to think that some forms of human experience can properly be identified in this way. This brings us to a second way in which spirituality has been understood in recent years.

In the introduction to that volume on secular spirituality, Peter Van Ness writes that "the spiritual dimension of life is the embodied task of realizing one's truest self in the context of reality apprehended as a cosmic totality. It is the quest for attaining an optimal relationship between what one truly is and everything that is."[7] This cosmic context, a sense of connectedness with all reality (and especially with every living thing on earth), is readily apparent in some of the works of Ursula Goodenough, a professor of biology who has written not only a best-selling textbook on genetics but also a widely read volume of reflections on the spiritual meaning that can be found at the heart of scientific endeavor. In this latter work, *The Sacred Depths of Nature*, she writes that although she finds herself unable to believe in a personal God, she revels in a sense of connectedness with other living beings that can only be described as sacred. Aware of sharing a common ancestor with all forms of life, Goodenough writes that we are connected "all the way down," and this connectedness is the source of what she calls her faith:

> For me, the existence of all this complexity and awareness and intent and beauty, and my ability to apprehend it, serves as the ultimate meaning and the ultimate value. The continuation of life reaches around, grabs its own tail, and forms a sacred circle that requires no further justification, no Creator, no superordinate meaning of meaning, no purpose other than that the continuation continue until the sun collapses or the final meteor collides. I confess a credo of continuation.[8]

Other writers go somewhat further by emphasizing that this sense of connectedness applies even to inanimate things. One of the best exemplars of this kind of "nature spirituality," even though he did not use the term, is the nineteenth-century American naturalist John Muir, who wrote in one of his many essays:

7. Peter H. Van Ness, "Introduction," in *Spirituality and the Secular Quest*, World Spirituality 22 (New York: Crossroad, 1996), 5.

8. Ursula Goodenough, *The Sacred Depths of Nature* (New York: Oxford University Press, 1998), 171.

> To lovers of the wild, these mountains are not a hundred miles away. Their spiritual power and the goodness of the sky make them near, as a circle of friends . . . You bathe in the spirit-beams, turning round and round, as if warming at a camp-fire. Presently you lose consciousness of your own separate existence: you blend with the landscape, and become part and parcel of nature.[9]

For someone like Muir, the wilderness itself would sometimes be described as a temple or church, while the animals he encountered there were recognized as his "brothers and sisters." This attitude is regularly referred to as "biocentrism," implying that the springs of personal vitality are to be found not in human beings alone ("anthropocentrism") but in everything that lives. Protecting and furthering the diversity of species on earth are accordingly two of the principal aims of persons whose spirituality follows this pattern of connectedness. Spirituality of this sort is certainly not opposed to spirituality defined in terms of self-transcendence. Indeed, Goodenough writes at one point that by becoming lost in something much larger than her own self she finds "the possibility of transcending my daily self."[10] The emphasis on connectedness with the realm of nature nevertheless allows us to see this at the very least as a special subset of spirituality understood as self-transcendence.

For a third and last example of how spirituality is sometimes described or defined today we turn to the work of the late Walter Principe, a Basilian priest who once served as president of the Catholic Theological Society of America. Basing his reflections on many earlier studies, Principe suggested that spirituality can best be defined if one keeps in mind three different though related levels. The first of these is the "real" or "existential" level, the way in which someone understood and lived a particular ideal. For Christians, this ideal will normally be described in trinitarian terms, such as "life in the Spirit as brothers and sisters of Jesus Christ and daughters and sons of the Father."[11] For other traditions, spirituality at this level will correspondingly be the way a person lives, within his or her particular historical context, that aspect of the tradition that one considers the highest and most conducive to leading to the ideal being sought. A second level is the formulation of a teaching about this lived reality. Often this formulation will be written by a person reflecting on his or her experience at the first level, though at other times it will be composed by someone familiar with that person's experience (such as a spiritual director or guide). Throughout the present work we will

9. John Muir, "Twenty Hill Hollow," in *Wilderness Essays: John Muir*, ed. Frank Buske (Salt Lake City: Gibbs-Smith, 1980), 88.

10. Goodenough, *Sacred Depths*, 102.

11. Principe, "Toward Defining Spirituality," 136.

see many examples of this kind of formulation, such as the treatises that St. Teresa of Avila composed as she reflected on her own journey toward what she called "spiritual marriage" with God. Finally, Principe's third level is what is being practiced in this book, namely, the scholarly examination of the first and second levels (especially the second level since the formulations will generally be more readily available to us than the lived reality of the first level, above all in the case of persons who have died). In an attempt to sum up the common elements in all three levels, Principe wrote toward the end of his article: "Spirituality, in this author's opinion, points to those aspects of a person's living a faith or commitment that concern his or her striving to attain the highest ideal or goal. For a Christian this would mean his or her striving for an ever more intense union with the Father through Jesus Christ by living in the Spirit."[12]

Principe's reference to "union" leads us to a consideration of another term that regularly crops up in the study of spirituality, namely, mysticism. In fact, when the persons responsible for launching the earlier-mentioned series Classics of Western Spirituality were pondering what to call the series, they gave serious consideration to calling it Classics of Western Mysticism. Their ultimate decision to go with the term "spirituality" was probably correct from a marketing standpoint since this term is much more common in everyday parlance than is "mysticism," but there is enough overlap in meaning that mysticism should also be discussed in this opening chapter.

WHAT IS MYSTICISM?

The way we began our consideration of spirituality—by looking at the etymology of the word—will also provide a useful entrée into our discussion of mysticism. The English word is derived ultimately from the Greek noun *mystērion* ("mystery") and the adjective *mystikos* ("mystical"), both related to the verb *myein*, which means "to close" (e.g., to close the eyes or lips) and accordingly conveys a sense of what is hidden or secret. There have been scholars who argued that the ancient mystery religions of the Greeks lie behind the New Testament's use of *mystērion*, but in fact the New Testament usage is best understood against a Semitic background as found in the Hebrew scriptures. The ancient Israelites thought of God as abiding above the solid firmament of the sky and joined there by a group of heavenly advisors sometimes called "the sons of God" (Job 1:6) or "the divine council" (Ps 82:1), similar to a civic governing body on earth. God would regularly con-

12. Principe, "Toward Defining Spirituality," 139.

sult with these beings before making final decisions, and for the most part these consultations were hidden from human beings. Some humans, however, were permitted access to the divine assembly. These were the prophets, who could then pass on the divine secrets to persons on earth who were willing to listen to them. A particularly clear instance of this is found early on in the Book of Daniel, where the prophet says: "There is a God in heaven who reveals mysteries, and he has disclosed to King Nebuchadnezzar what will happen at the end of days" (Dan 2:28).

In the New Testament Jesus himself regularly functions as a prophet of this sort, as when after narrating the parable of the sower he tells his disciples, "To you has been given the secret (*mystērion*) of the kingdom of God, but for those outside, everything comes in parables" (Mk 4:11). This and similar texts (e.g., Mt 11:25-27) are the Gospel counterparts to the much more frequent use of the term *mystērion* in the Pauline letters, where St. Paul writes that he and his fellow apostles are to be regarded as "servants of Christ and stewards of God's mysteries" (1 Cor 4:1) since they "speak God's wisdom, secret and hidden, which God decreed before the ages for our glory" (1 Cor 2:7). A central element in this mystery is that God wills all people to be saved, Gentile as well as Jew (Eph 3:4), while in the letter to the Colossians a note of personal intimacy with Christ is emphasized, for the Apostle's commission is "to make the word of God fully known, the mystery that has been hidden throughout the ages but has now been revealed," namely, "Christ in you, the hope of glory" (Col 1:26-27). These passages, along with sixteen other references to "mystery" in the Pauline literature, led the distinguished New Testament scholar Joseph A. Fitzmyer to write that *mystērion* is so central to Paul's thought that "it conveys for him the content of his gospel."[13]

When the great third-century theologian Origen of Alexandria reflected and wrote commentaries on various books of the Bible, he regularly tried to grasp what he called the "mystical sense" (*mystikos nous*) of the text, that is, the deeper meaning that God wanted to keep hidden from the prying eyes of the profane and even from immature Christians who were not yet able to grasp it. A similar use of the term "mystical" can be found in Origen's fellow Alexandrian of the preceding generation, Clement. Somewhat later, the term was likewise applied to the sacraments in order to convey the truth that the deeper reality of a sacrament was hidden from those who did not approach it with the eyes of faith. The eucharist, for example, was sometimes said to be not simple bread but "mystical bread," while the *Apostolic Constitutions* in the

---

13. Joseph A. Fitzmyer, "Pauline Theology," in *The New Jerome Biblical Commentary*, ed. Raymond E. Brown, S.S., et al. (Englewood Cliffs, N.J.: Prentice Hall, 1990), 1389.

late fourth century calls this sacrament "the mystical sacrifice of [Christ's] body and blood" (6.23.4).

Even these few references suffice to show that the meaning of "the mystical" in the Christian Scriptures and the early church was far removed from the sense that many people have given the term in more recent centuries, when mysticism has often had connotations of the unusual and exotic (visions, ecstasies, levitation, and similar phenomena). This is not to say, however, that the search for the mystical sense of scripture by someone like Origen was devoid of personal feeling. For example, in his *Commentary on the Song of Songs* he speaks as though from personal experience of one who "has burned with this faithful love for the Word of God" and "has been pierced with the lovable spear of His knowledge, so that he yearns and longs for Him by day and night, can speak of nought but Him, would hear of nought but Him, can think of nothing else, and is disposed to no desire nor longing nor hope, except for Him alone. . . ."[14]

In later centuries, this affective side of mystical writing became more and more pronounced, with the result that a common understanding of mysticism in recent centuries has held it to be a special state of consciousness surpassing ordinary experience through union with the transcendent reality of God. This was already the case in what the *Oxford English Dictionary* gives as the first recorded use of the word in this language, in Henry Coventry's *Philemon to Hydaspes* (1736). Coventry wrote: "How much nobler a Field of Exercise . . . are the seraphic Entertainments of Mysticism and Extasy than the mean and ordinary Practice of a merely earthly and common Virtue!" Here mysticism is clearly considered to be something extraordinary, akin to ecstasy and of an altogether different order from what is "mean," "earthly," and "common." Influential theologians and spiritual writers accepted this understanding, with the result that for many there was an essential distinction between mystical and ordinary Christian life, the former being an extraordinary way for those specially called to it (even though the best of these theologians, like Augustin-François Poulain, avoided an overemphasis on extraordinary experiences).[15]

More recently, however, and perhaps above all because of the Second Vatican Council's emphasis on the universal call to holiness, there has been a retreat from the distinction between an "ordinary" and a "mystical" way of Christian life. The change can be seen in the following passage from one of

14. Origen, *Commentary on the Song of Songs* 3.8, trans. R. P. Lawson, Ancient Christian Writers (Westminster, Md.: Newman, 1957; repr., New York: Paulist, n.d.), 198.

15. Augustin-François Poulain, *The Graces of Interior Prayer* (10th ed., 1922; repr., Westminster, Vt.: Celtic Cross Books, 1978).

Thomas Merton's best-known books, where he emphasizes not so much the differences among various stages of the spiritual journey as rather the basic continuity underlying them all:

> To reach a true awareness of [God] as well as ourselves, we have to renounce our selfish and limited self and enter into a whole new kind of existence, discovering an inner center of motivation and love which makes us see ourselves and everything else in an entirely new light. Call it faith, call it (at a more advanced stage) contemplative illumination, call it the sense of God or even mystical union: all these are different aspects and levels of the same kind of realization: the awakening to a new awareness of ourselves in Christ, created in Him, redeemed by Him, to be transformed and glorified in and with Him.[16]

A still more recent development should be noted as we conclude this introductory discussion of mysticism. In the passage just quoted, Merton speaks of "mystical union," and union has indeed been a term frequently associated with mysticism. However, one of the most prolific and respected scholars of mysticism in our own time, Bernard McGinn, has suggested that union is not the most essential characteristic of Christian mysticism, especially if such union is understood as a "union of absorption or identity in which the individual personality is lost."[17] His own extensive study of texts commonly regarded as mystical has led him to conclude that the term "presence" is a more useful category for describing the unifying characteristic in the various expressions of Christian mysticism. McGinn accordingly writes that "the mystical element in Christianity is that part of its belief and practices that concerns the preparation for, the consciousness of, and the reaction to what can be described as the immediate or direct presence of God."[18]

THE STUDY OF SPIRITUALITY

Having seen the basic meaning of spirituality and mysticism, we turn next to a consideration of how these interrelated subjects can best be studied. One helpful approach makes use of what Bernard Lonergan calls "intentional and conscious operations." In his important work *Method in Theology* as well as in

16. Thomas Merton, *Contemplation in a World of Action* (Garden City, N.Y.: Doubleday, Image Books, 1973), 175-76.

17. Bernard McGinn, *The Foundations of Mysticism*, vol. 1 of *The Presence of God: A History of Western Christian Mysticism* (New York: Crossroad, 1991), xvi.

18. Ibid., xvii.

some of his articles, Lonergan notes that in any endeavor we regularly and ineluctably move through various operations, corresponding to four different levels of consciousness. On the empirical or experiential level, we "sense, perceive, imagine, feel, speak, move." On the intellectual level, the level of understanding, we "inquire, come to understand, express what we have understood, [and] work out the presuppositions and implications of our expression." On the rational level, we "reflect, marshal the evidence, [and] pass judgment on the truth or falsity, certainty or probability, of a statement," and on the responsible level we "deliberate about possible courses of action, evaluate them, decide, and carry out our decisions."[19] His basic point is that in learning anything we move from data that we have gathered or experienced (the first level of consciousness) to the attempt to understand the data, from there to the judgment as to whether or not our understanding is correct, and finally to a decision about what this means for the way we conduct our lives, espouse certain values, and the like.

Even the youngest children move through these operations as they come to learn more and more about the world around them, but in the realm of scholarship one will regularly practice what Lonergan calls "functional specialties" in order to facilitate one's work in a particular field of study. He discusses eight such specialties in all, but the first four are particularly pertinent to the study of the past, which is the focus of this present study of Christian spirituality. These first four specialties are research, interpretation, history, and dialectic, and they correspond to the operations characteristic of the four levels of consciousness mentioned above. As we consider these four specialties one by one, an orderly way of undertaking the study of spirituality should become apparent.

Research

Research is the specialty by which we come into contact with and accumulate the data that are pertinent to our particular field of study. For the study of Christian spirituality, this will certainly include research into written texts. Some specialists in research seek out manuscripts that may have been gathering dust in libraries, caves, or bazaars for long periods of time. Others correlate the readings in disparate manuscripts of the same treatise, trying to determine the original text when the manuscripts have variant readings of certain words or phrases. Others painstakingly publish critical editions of

19. Bernard Lonergan, *Method in Theology* (New York: Herder & Herder, Seabury paperback, 1972), 9.

these treatises, offering the reader not only what they consider the most authentic text but also the variant readings in a critical apparatus so that other possibilities may be entertained, while still other scholars translate ancient texts into modern languages for the benefit of those who do not have the training to read the originals.

These are some of the ways in which primary research is done in the field of Christian spirituality. In recent decades it has led to highly acclaimed critical editions of the works of such important writers as St. Bernard of Clairvaux and Meister Eckhart. There is, however, the danger that one might conclude that research in spirituality, whether done by specialists or by students, is limited to texts. In fact, written texts comprise only a part of the material that is relevant. A fine article by P. Joseph Cahill discusses five "categories of symbolic expression" that illustrate the wide variety of materials that can contribute to the study of one or another field of theological or religious studies, including spirituality.[20] These five are (1) a body of literature, especially normative literature (which for Christians would be primarily the Bible); (2) theological formulations, including ones found in treatises of systematic theology but also stories, songs, legends, and expressions of popular wisdom; (3) visual art forms, such as painting, sculpture, and architecture; (4) aural art forms, usually but not exclusively sacred music; and (5) various historical formulations distinct from literature, such as popular forms of devotion, religious garb, and the development of formal institutions. The first of these five, the normative literature of the Bible, will be examined in some detail in the following chapter; here we will discuss the other four.

When one first hears the phrase "theological formulations" and wishes to apply it to the study of Christian spirituality, the temptation may be to think only of treatises of mystical theology like those of St. John of the Cross or that earlier-mentioned scholarly work by Poulain, *The Graces of Interior Prayer*, but Cahill rightly notes that theological formulations also include stories, songs, and legends. The entire realm of religious poetry opens up a vast field of study for students of spirituality. One need only think, for example, of the crucial role that George Herbert's poem "Love" had on the spiritual development of Simone Weil as she describes this in her spiritual autobiography.[21] So, too, as regards novels and short stories, and not just those with an explicitly religious theme. As David Tracy writes in one of his early theological works, "by redescribing the authentic possibilities of human existence . . . fictions open our minds, our imaginations, and our hearts to newly authentic

---

20. P. Joseph Cahill, S.J., "Theological Education: Its Fragmentation and Unity," *Theological Studies* 45 (1984): 334-42.

21. Simone Weil, *Waiting for God*, trans. Emma Craufurd (New York: Harper & Row, Colophon Books, 1973), 68. See also Leslie Fiedler's introduction to this book, 24-25.

and clearly transformative possible modes of being-in-the-world."[22] Thomas Merton was someone who sensed this and wrote about it movingly in his essays about the fictional works of writers like Albert Camus, William Faulkner, Flannery O'Connor, and Boris Pasternak.[23]

Visual art forms are also a treasure trove for research in Christian spirituality. Among the many books by the late Henri Nouwen was one entitled *Behold the Beauty of the Lord*, his reflections on four of the most revered icons of the Eastern Christian church.[24] Other authors have written more scholarly works that also help reveal the deep spirituality to be found in these images.[25] Titus Burckhardt writes at the very beginning of his foreword to one of these books, "The art of icons is a sacred art in the true sense of the word. It is nourished wholly on the spiritual truth to which it gives pictorial expression."[26] Similar words could be applied to some of the masterpieces of painting in the Western Christian church, whether Bonaventura Berlinghieri's scenes from the life of St. Francis of Assisi, Matthias Grünewald's powerful depictions of the crucifixion, or Georges Roualt's paintings of the face of Christ. Paintings from more recently founded Christian churches in Africa and Asia can reveal special characteristics of spirituality on those continents, such as reverence for one's ancestors, while the image of Our Lady of Guadalupe at the much-visited pilgrimage center outside Mexico City has deeply influenced Latino spirituality throughout South and North America.

Of course, visual art includes much more than painting. Works of sculpture, whether free-standing pietàs or carvings on the tympanums and side-walls of medieval churches, reveal much about the spirituality of particular epochs, as does the very architecture of the churches. Margaret Miles's *Image as Insight: Visual Understanding in Western Christianity* is especially fine in pointing out what the interiors of Catholic and Protestant churches at the time of the sixteenth-century Reformation tell us about the respective spiritualities of these two major traditions in Christianity.[27]

Aural art forms are another rich source for research in the history of Christian spirituality. Although Gregorian chant and the Latin texts for which it was composed are no longer widely used in the Catholic Church since the Second Vatican Council came to permit the use of vernacular lan-

---

22. David Tracy, *Blessed Rage for Order* (New York: Seabury, 1975), 207.
23. *The Literary Essays of Thomas Merton*, ed. Patrick Hart (New York: New Directions, 1981).
24. Henri Houwen, *Behold the Beauty of the Lord* (Notre Dame, Ind.: Ave Maria, 1987).
25. See, e.g., Leonid Ouspensky and Vladimir Lossky, *The Meaning of Icons*, 2nd ed. (Crestwood, N.Y.: St. Vladimir's Seminary Press, 1983).
26. Ibid., 7.
27. Margaret Miles, *Image as Insight: Visual Understanding in Western Christianity* (Boston: Beacon, 1985).

guages in the liturgy, there are still centers where it is sung; many persons testify to the way in which these monophonic pieces nourish their prayer life. At the beginning of the Protestant Reformation, Martin Luther promoted the singing of hymns in vernacular languages, composing some of them himself. The Catholic theologian and historian of spirituality Louis Bouyer, himself once a Lutheran pastor, pays rich tribute to this aspect of Protestant spirituality when he writes:

> We must not forget the most innovative aspect of all of Luther's Reformation—choral song. This was composed of the content of traditional hymns, sequences and anthems, strongly personalized . . . and vigorously rhymed, and surely remains a liturgical creation whose effects have never been anything but beneficial . . . What these songs were able to achieve in the diffusion of a surely evangelical piety cannot be overestimated.[28]

Of all the Germans who followed Luther, the one who some believe understood him best was not a theologian but the composer Johann Sebastian Bach, whose compositions have been expertly studied for their spiritual and theological depth by Jaroslav Pelikan and others.[29] Much more recently, rich forms of music sung in the vernacular have been composed in African countries. Even before the Second Vatican Council the *Missa Luba*, a folkloric setting of the Latin Mass using rhythms and instruments common in the Congo, quickly became known and appreciated throughout the Christian world, while the chants developed at the ecumenical monastery of Taizé in eastern France now nourish liturgical spirituality on every continent.

What Cahill calls "historical formulations distinct from literature" form a fifth broad area for possible research in spirituality. Popular forms of devotion can tell us much about the way a particular group understands its search for a nourishing spiritual life. For example, the way in which the Toba/Qom people in the Gran Chaco of northern Argentina have brought elements (especially dance) from their ancestral religion into liturgical services led by Mennonite missionaries has resulted in what one of those missionaries calls a "healthy syncretism." According to him, this has allowed members of that indigenous ethnic group to be engaged in "constructing their own theology and expressing that theology through a spirituality and a church that are unique. It is the celebration of this very uniqueness that gives hope."[30] Simi-

---

28. Louis Bouyer, *Orthodox Spirituality and Protestant and Anglican Spirituality*, vol. 3 of *A History of Christian Spirituality* (New York: Seabury, 1969), 75.
29. Jaroslav Pelikan, *Bach among the Theologians* (Philadelphia: Fortress, 1986).
30. Willis G. Horst, "Spirituality of the Toba/Qom Christians of the Argentine Chaco," *Missiology: An International Review* 29, no. 2 (April 2001): 182.

lar statements could be made about indigenous ethnic groups in other parts of Latin America and in Africa and Asia; specific examples of this kind of "healthy syncretism" will be given in later chapters of this book.

The development of formal institutions is another aspect of this fifth category of symbolic expression. One of the most significant instances of this would be the rise of various religious orders in the Catholic Church. Numerous religious orders and congregations have developed particular ways of living according to the gospel that have influenced not only those who are actually members of these orders but also laypersons who are affiliated with them as "associates" or members of "Third Orders." One of the most important recent publications in the field of Christian spirituality, *The New Dictionary of Catholic Spirituality*, has numerous and fairly lengthy articles describing some of these spiritualities, including ones proper to Augustinians, Benedictines, Carmelites, Cistercians, Dominicans, Franciscans, Jesuits, and Salesians.[31]

Interpretation

Having seen some of the areas in which research can be done by students and scholars of Christian spirituality, we may turn more briefly to the other three functional specialties that are at play when we confront the past in any field of study. The first of these three is called "interpretation," a challenge that will necessarily arise as soon as any thoughtful person comes into contact with a text, image, musical composition, liturgical service, or institution not previously familiar. Here the challenge can be daunting. One may have to acquire skill in one or more foreign languages, skill that is advanced enough to pick up nuances of meaning that will not be apparent merely with the help of a dictionary. Symbolic elements in the paintings or sculpture of another culture and era may remain puzzling for months on end, only to become clear when one has the chance to speak with someone from that culture and finally be able to exclaim, "Oh yes, now I understand!" Specialists in the art of interpretation regularly publish monographs and commentaries in order to make known their findings, allowing students to increase their own understanding by consulting such works and, perhaps, coming up with alternative interpretations of their own. To give just one example, which will be considered more fully in a later chapter, the first Dominican ever to be charged with heresy was the fourteenth-century German mystic Meister Eckhart. In defending him-

31. Michael Downey, ed., *The New Dictionary of Catholic Spirituality* (Collegeville, Minn.: Liturgical Press, 1993).

self at his first trial, he insisted that his accusers had misunderstood him by taking his statements out of context and, among other things, understanding in temporal categories what Eckhart intended as eternal.[32] For someone today properly to interpret texts by someone who lived long ago in another culture and perhaps holding quite different presuppositions can be challenging indeed. Specialists in late medieval thought still today debate the correctness of the judgment pronounced against Eckhart.

History

Because of this potential difficulty in coming to a correct understanding of a particular point, Lonergan writes that the subsequent operation will be that of judging, specifically judging whether one's first attempt at understanding was correct. However, in what may appear to be a certain jump in logic, he calls the corresponding functional specialty "history" on the grounds that history "judges and narrates what occurred."[33] In any case, a student of spirituality is called to know not only something about this or that figure or movement over the past twenty centuries of Christian history but also what was "going forward" during all this time. What were the influences of one epoch on another? What developments occurred over these centuries? Who were the major players and how did the later ones themselves regard their most influential predecessors? These are just some of the questions that arise when one attempts to grasp something of the entire flow of Christian spirituality, a flow that has in fact occasionally been imaged as a river with all sorts of side tributaries making their particular contributions to the ever widening and deepening stream. Some specialists will attempt to write histories of Christian spirituality as a whole, while others will produce histories of a particular movement or period; some of these works are listed in the bibliography of the present work. Students, on the other hand, are challenged to become reasonably familiar with the basic historical works, always striving to make sure that they learn a reasonable number of details without losing a sense of the overall development over the past twenty centuries. One ought not "lose the forest for the trees." The purpose of this study of history is not simply to become learned about an often fascinating topic. Josef Weismayer,

---

32. Thus, Eckhart said his judges were mentally weak if not openly blasphemous "when they say God created the world in another now than in the now of eternity, although every action of God is his substance, which is eternal" ("Response to the List of Fifty-nine Articles," in *Meister Eckhart: The Essential Sermons, Commentaries, Treatises, and Defense*, trans. Edmund Colledge, O.S.A., and Bernard McGinn, Classics of Western Spirituality [New York: Paulist, 1981], 76).

33. Lonergan, *Method*, 134.

an Austrian historian of Christian spirituality, expressed the ideal motivation when he wrote that we study such history not only to learn how things once were but also in order to grasp something of the multiplicity of the Holy Spirit's work, for the Spirit of God has always opened up new understandings of the message of salvation and new ways of accepting that message.[34]

Dialectic

When one studies this history, and with reference to the above-mentioned image of a river, it soon becomes obvious that the stream has not always been flowing smoothly. There have been floods, whirlpools, logjams, and many other obstacles arising because not everyone proposes or advocates mutually complementary ideas or practices. Mention was already made of the fact that a famous Dominican was, over his protests of innocence, condemned for heresy back in the fourteenth century. In much more recent times, other Catholics who have been professedly or at least tangentially involved in the teaching of Christian spirituality have fallen into one or another degree of disfavor with the Vatican, including Pierre Teilhard de Chardin, Anthony de Mello, and Willigis Jäger. Despite what one might think at first, Christian spirituality is a field containing a number of theological land mines. A student of the subject will therefore inevitably be challenged to engage in the fourth functional specialty, which Lonergan calls "dialectic." Of the terms used for these first four specialties, this one may seem the most difficult to understand, for, as Lonergan acknowledges, the word "has been employed in many ways." However, he adds at once that the sense he intends "is simple enough," for dialectic "has to do with the concrete, the dynamic, and the contradictory."[35] In other words, this functional specialty focuses precisely on the specific, conflicting viewpoints—the positions and counterpositions—that history reveals. Anyone practicing this specialty, whether a specialist or a student, is faced with the need to determine as accurately as possible those cases in which the conflicts and differences are irreconcilable or where, on the other hand, they can be seen as complementary truths within a larger whole. The controversy surrounding the writings of Meister Eckhart has already been mentioned as one case in which conflict arose. Another was the controversy over Quietism in seventeenth-century France, with the major adversaries being two bishops, Jacques-Bénigne Bossuet and François Fénelon.

---

34. Josef Weismayer, "Spirituelle Theologie oder Theologie der Spiritualität?" in *Spiritualität in Moral*, ed. Günter Virt (Vienna: Wiener Dom-Verlag, 1975), 72.

35. Lonergan, *Method*, 129.

Four Further Functional Specialties

It should be obvious that merely ordering the opposing positions in their significant similarities and differences is not enough. This brings us beyond dialectic to a whole new set of functional specialties proposed by Lonergan: foundations, doctrines, systematics, and communications. These need not concern us at such great length because they are less directly involved with the study of the past, the main focus of this book, but something should be said about each. The link between dialectic and foundations is tight. In Lonergan's own words, "Dialectic brings to light oppositions in appreciative and evaluative interpretation and history, in the history of movements, in determining the meaning of texts, and in the special research performed in the prosecution of the foregoing tasks. Foundations takes sides: it selects as its stand some coherent set out of the array of opposing positions."[36] In other words, having come to realize the existence of various positions and counterpositions, a student of spirituality should, after due reflection, take a stand, either claiming that the opposition is only apparent and can be overcome by approaching the question from a different viewpoint or else rejecting one position and espousing the other. Here one is called to a personal faith decision, which has its own risks but at least allows one to avoid the charge of irrelevantly remaining ensconced in an ivory tower away from the turmoil of the real world.

If one takes that stand, one moves on to the next functional specialty, doctrines, by which Lonergan means not expertise about the doctrines of the past but rather the ability to make explicit one's personal stand in language that will express as clearly as possible what one holds as a Christian believer, however mysterious this may be. The study of history will reveal how people like St. Augustine or St. Teresa of Avila did this in their own time and in their own society and culture. Many of their terms and categories are still viable, but one must always be careful to avoid simply repeating the way earlier Christians expressed themselves, whether in words, images, or musical tones. Ideally we are called to do in our own context what those in earlier ages did in theirs.

Having done this for particular issues, one is next challenged to work out what Lonergan calls "appropriate systems of conceptualization" through the practice of the functional specialty of systematics. However adroitly one may have expressed one's stance on particular issues in the practice of the preceding specialty, doctrines, there may be inconsistencies among the expressions

36. "Bernard Lonergan Responds," in *Foundations of Theology: Papers from the International Lonergan Congress 1970*, ed. Philip McShane, S.J. (Dublin: Gill & Macmillan, 1971), 229.

developed on a variety of topics. The exercise of this seventh specialty is intended to remove any such inconsistencies so that the overall presentation of one's spirituality will be coherent. Otherwise one may rightly be charged with holding mutually contradictory positions.

With this resolved, there remains the need to communicate to others what one holds and believes. As Lonergan once wrote, "If one is to hearken to the word, one must also bear witness to it . . . If one assimilates tradition, one learns that one should pass it on."[37] One might even argue that this last specialty, communications, is the most significant of all for Christians, who have, after all, received the solemn charge from the Lord not to leave their light under a bushel basket but to set it upon a lampstand so that it may give light to all in the house (Mt 5:15). In our day, this requires a certain level of expertise not only in verbal, visual, and aural expression but also in contemporary means of communication, including radio, television, motion pictures, and the Internet. It also requires a more-than-superficial familiarity with other religious traditions and with the most important secular movements, for as Christianity becomes a world church and no longer a Eurocentric one, dialogue with persons of other persuasions is absolutely necessary. Later chapters of this book will offer examples of how some others have done this already (for example, Matteo Ricci, Roberto de Nobili, and Bede Griffiths), but such examples should be taken less as models than as spurs to one's own creative thinking about how to do this even better.

With this introduction to the nature of Christian spirituality and mysticism and to how one might best approach the study of such material, we are ready to turn in the next chapter to that one aspect of Joseph Cahill's categories of symbolic expression that was only briefly mentioned above, namely, the normative literature of the Bible. Whatever else might characterize Christian spirituality at its best, it will always have to be a scriptural spirituality if it is to be judged authentic.

QUESTIONS FOR REFLECTION

1. What are the implications of someone's claiming to be "spiritual but not religious"? Is such a distinction well grounded? What might be some potentially negative effects of traditional religious practice on one's spiritual growth?
2. Have there been any particular experiences in your own life that gave you some insight into what you might understand by the term "spiritual experience"?
3. Of the various ways of describing or defining spirituality treated in this chapter, which makes most sense to you? Would you argue for a still different way of defining the term?

---

37. Lonergan, "Functional Specialties in Theology," *Gregorianum* 50 (1969): 492.

4. In the light of what was said in this chapter, how would you yourself define mysticism? What do you take to be the relationship between mysticism and spirituality?
5. To what extent do you find Bernard Lonergan's notion of eight functional specialties helpful as a way of facilitating the study of spirituality?

SUGGESTIONS FOR FURTHER READING AND STUDY

On the Description or Definition of Spirituality

McGinn, Bernard. "The Letter and the Spirit: Spirituality as an Academic Discipline." *Christian Spirituality Bulletin* 1, no. 2 (Fall 1993): 1-10.

Principe, Walter. "Toward Defining Spirituality." *Studies in Religion/Sciences Religieuses* 12, no. 2 (1983): 127-41.

Schneiders, Sandra. "Religion vs. Spirituality: A Contemporary Conundrum." *Spiritus: A Journal of Christian Spirituality* 3 (2003): 163-85.

———. "Spirituality in the Academy." *Theological Studies* 50 (1989): 676-97.

On the Description or Definition of Mysticism

McGinn, Bernard. General Introduction to *The Foundations of Mysticism: Origins to the Fifth Century*, xi-xx. Volume 1 of *The Presence of God: A History of Western Christian Mysticism.* New York: Crossroad, 1991.

Wiseman, James A. "Mysticism." In *The New Dictionary of Catholic Spirituality*, ed. Michael Downey, 681-92. Collegeville, Minn.: Liturgical Press, 1993.

On the Study of Spirituality

Cahill, P. Joseph, S.J. "Theological Education: Its Fragmentation and Unity." *Theological Studies* 45 (1984): 334-42.

Lonergan, Bernard. *Method in Theology.* Toronto: University of Toronto Press, 1990. See especially chapter 1, "Method" (pp. 3-25), and chapter 5, "Functional Specialties" (pp. 125-45).

Miles, Margaret R. "Vision and the Sixteenth-Century Protestant and Roman Catholic Reforms." In *Image as Insight: Visual Understanding in Western Christianity and Secular Culture*, 95-125. Boston: Beacon, 1985.

Nouwen, Henri. *Behold the Beauty of the Lord.* Notre Dame, Ind.: Ave Maria, 1987.

Pelikan, Jaroslav. *Bach among the Theologians.* Philadelphia: Fortress, 1986.

Saliers, Don. "Sound Spirituality: On the Formative Expressive Power of Music for Christian Spirituality." *Christian Spirituality Bulletin* 8, no. 1 (Spring/Summer 2000): 1-5.

2

Biblical Spirituality

An anecdote from the life of Barnabas Ahern, one of the most important Scripture scholars of the twentieth century, provides a useful way of introducing the topic of this chapter. At a symposium near Chicago in the 1960s he had given a paper entitled "The Biblical Way of Life," which he then reworked for a conference in Minnesota. Unbeknownst to him, the organizers of this latter conference publicized his paper under a different title, "The Spirituality of the Bible." In his opening remarks, he expressed uneasiness and concern over this new title on the grounds that it could lead a person to conclude that there are other things in the Bible beside spirituality. On the contrary, he said, "Scripture is all spirituality. There is nothing in it except the tracing of God's relation to man and man's relation to God. So St. Paul meant, I think, when he said to Timothy that all scripture is inspired by God and profitable for teaching, for correcting, for rebuking, and for instructing in justice, that the man of God may be perfect (see 2 Tim 3:16)."[1]

It may be that Ahern was overly fussy about the implications of the title assigned to his paper, but if one grants that he was basically correct in claiming that "scripture is all spirituality" and if one further keeps in mind not only the length of the Bible but also the thousands of books and articles that have been written on biblical topics down through the centuries, then it does become obvious that treating biblical spirituality in a single chapter of a book like this will have to be done very selectively. Accordingly, we will limit the treatment to two major points: an overview of some of the most basic themes of biblical spirituality and an exemplification of ways in which one important scriptural text has been interpreted at various periods in church history, together with reflections about the kind of spiritual teaching that could naturally arise from each of these ways.

Before looking at the basic themes, something should be said about terminology. In Christian usage, the two main divisions of the Bible have tradi-

1. Barnabas M. Ahern, C.P., "The Biblical Way of Life/The Spirituality of the Bible," in *Protestants and Catholics on the Spiritual Life*, ed. Michael Marx, O.S.B. (Collegeville, Minn.: Liturgical Press, 1965), 3.

tionally been called the Old Testament and the New Testament. The former of these two terms has recently been called into question, primarily on the grounds that for many persons it sounds offensive to call something "old" (with the possible nuances of "outdated," "superseded," and the like). For this reason, many contemporary authors have begun using other terms, such as "the Hebrew Scriptures" or "the Jewish Bible." However, this newer usage raises its own difficulties, not least because the books of the Bible that are considered divinely inspired by the Catholic Church include a number that are not included by Jews in their Bible, such as the books of Tobit, Judith, Sirach, and First and Second Maccabees. In addition, there are many Jews who do not at all take offense at the term "Old Testament" inasmuch as "old" also has the connotations of "foundational," "worthy of reverence," and so forth. As a way out of a dilemma that seems to have no perfect solution at the present time, this book will use the terms "First Testament" and "New Testament," the former term including those books of the Bible fully accepted by Catholics but regarded by Jews and Protestants as apocryphal or deuterocanonical.

It is already of the greatest significance to note that about three-fourths of the written work that is foundational for Christian spirituality includes what is also part of Scripture for the Jewish people. This means that however much Christians rightly want to be open to and learn from the spirituality of any of the world's religious traditions, there is a unique tie with the Jewish people, despite the sad fact that relations between Christians and Jews have often been tense if not outright hostile. We will therefore look first at some of the major themes of spirituality as found in the First Testament before turning to the New.

THE SPIRITUALITY OF THE FIRST TESTAMENT

Even though, as noted in the opening chapter, one could rightly speak of the secular spirituality of persons who do not believe in God, and even though some Jews are atheists and value their Jewishness for its ethnic rather than its religious significance, the spirituality of the First Testament is decidedly centered on God and God's relationship to human beings and the rest of creation. The introduction to the volume on Jewish spirituality in the earlier mentioned series World Spirituality begins with a quotation from several verses of Psalm 27 about "seeking the face of God," followed by these remarks by the editor of the volume: "Seeking the face of God, striving to live in His presence and to fashion the life of holiness appropriate to God's presence—

these have ever been the core of that religious civilization known to the world as Judaism . . . Life in the presence of God . . . is perhaps as close as one can come to a definition of 'spirituality' that is native to the Jewish tradition and indeed faithful to its Semitic roots."[2]

That author's reference to "Semitic roots" calls for one further distinction in terms. Strictly speaking, the term "Jewish" is applied only after the Babylonian exile of the sixth century B.C.E. Prior to that, the people were more properly called Israelites, that is, those who traced their ancestry to a remote ancestor named Israel (= Jacob) and ultimately to the great patriarch Abraham. What forged their identity as a people, however, was not so much blood relationship as rather the conviction that their ancestors had been delivered by God from slavery to the Egyptians, an event that occurred probably in the thirteenth century B.C.E. During their many years of wandering in the desert under the leadership of Moses, the Israelites are said to have entered into a covenant at Mount Sinai with this liberating God, whom Moses revealed to them as having the name Yahweh, a mysterious term that may originally have meant something like "the one who causes to be." The covenant itself, a solemn ritual agreement that included the people's being sprinkled with the blood of a sacrificial animal (Ex 24:8), brought with it responsibilities for both parties. The people were to observe various ordinances, including but by no means limited to the Ten Commandments, and they understood that faithfulness to these ordinances would keep them in God's favor and indeed enable them to share in God's holiness. As is said in the Book of Leviticus, "The Lord spoke to Moses, saying: Speak to all the congregation of the people of Israel and say to them: You shall be holy, for I the Lord your God am holy" (Lv 19:1-2).

The chapters in the Pentateuch that follow the account of the covenant at Sinai often recount the distress that Moses felt when he found the people backing away from their covenant commitment. Still later books of the First Testament, especially those recounting the activity of one or another of the great Israelite prophets, are likewise scathing in their denunciation of departures from the challenge to let God's holiness be reflected in the conduct of one's own life. Whereas the earliest prophets, such as those we read about in the time of King Saul, were for the most part persons who would readily fall into states of religious ecstasy (see 1 Sm 10:1-13), not long thereafter there arose prophets like Elijah and Nathan, who courageously called political leaders to task for their failure to live up to the holiness required of them. The

---

2. Arthur Green, introduction to *Jewish Spirituality: From the Bible through the Middle Ages*, World Spirituality 13 (New York: Crossroad, 1994), xiii.

ingenious way in which Nathan confronted King David over his commission of murder and adultery—by telling a parable apparently about someone else and then showing that it applied to the king himself (2 Sm 12:1-15)—is one of the high points of early prophecy in Israel.

The response of David to the prophet's rebuke reveals another crucial aspect of Israelite spirituality, for he acknowledged his crimes, repented of them, and became the most loved king in Israelite history. It is impossible to know how many of the psalms may actually have been composed by him, but the well-known Fifty-first Psalm, one of the traditional penitential psalms, said to have been composed by David after Nathan's rebuke, is one of the Bible's best examples of what could be called a spirituality of repentance, as in the lines:

> Create in me a clean heart, O God,
> and put a new and right spirit within me.
> Do not cast me away from your presence,
> and do not take your holy spirit from me.
> Restore to me the joy of your salvation,
> and sustain in me a willing spirit. (Ps 51:10-12)

When that same psalm goes on to say that the sacrifice acceptable to God is not a burnt offering of some sacrificial animal but rather "a broken and contrite heart" (v. 17), it enunciates a theme especially common in those who are sometimes called "the writing prophets," that is, those who have books of the Bible named after them. Whereas earlier prophets like Nathan and Elijah were primarily concerned with the behavior of individual leaders, prophets like Amos, Micah, Isaiah, and Jeremiah turned their attention to the behavior of the society as a whole, calling the people to adhere to a higher standard than was often in evidence. It would be quite wrong to say that these prophets disdained the ritual sacrifices of the temple, but they were very clear that sacrifices of that sort were useless before God if not accompanied by an upright and devout way of life.

Representative of this vein of prophecy is the entirety of the rather short Book of Micah, a prophet whose life spanned the turn from the eighth to the seventh century B.C.E. He denounces greed in the sharpest terms, as when he says:

> Alas for those who devise wickedness
> and evil deeds on their beds!
> When morning dawns, they perform it,
> because it is in their power.

They covet fields, and seize them;
houses, and take them away;
They oppress householder and house,
people and their inheritance. (Mi 2:1-2)

He and his fellow prophets did not limit themselves to pronouncing God's doom upon evildoers, however, for they regularly taught how one ought to live so as to be holy even as God is holy. In words that have often been engraved on the façades of houses of worship, courthouses, and law schools, the same prophet proclaimed:

He has told you, O mortal, what is good;
and what does the Lord require of you
But to do justice, and to love kindness,
and to walk humbly with your God? (Mi 6:8)

Although it would be an exaggeration to say that this verse summarizes Israelite spirituality, it certainly encapsulates much that has been of lasting significance in it: living in a way that respects the rights of others, treating them with kindness and compassion (elsewhere in the First Testament this is often mentioned in connection with kindness to strangers and aliens, on the grounds that the Israelites were themselves in that condition before entering the Promised Land from Egypt—see, e.g., Dt 10:19), and humbly recognizing one's own creatureliness vis-à-vis the sovereignty of the Lord.

With so much injustice and suffering in Israelite society before, during, and after the Babylonian exile, it is not surprising that many of the people became despondent and hopeless. Psalm 137 is the particularly poignant lament of an exile sitting by the rivers of Babylon and feeling unable to sing at the bidding of his captors. In this situation, hope was engendered not by calculations of success wrought by human beings but rather by the expectation of a powerful act of God at least equal to the Israelites' deliverance from slavery in Egypt centuries earlier. This hope is called "messianic," derived from a Hebrew word meaning "anointed." Just as kings and priests were anointed with sacred oil upon assuming office, it was now proclaimed by Isaiah, Jeremiah, and other prophets that another anointed one, greater than any in the past, would appear to restore salvation (= wholeness) to the society. This messiah would be a figure of the line of King David and in the minds of some would therefore come from David's own native place, Bethlehem, as announced in still another important passage from the prophecy of Micah:

> But you, O Bethlehem of Ephratha,
> who are one of the little clans of Judah,
> From you shall come forth for me
> one who is to rule in Israel,
> Whose origin is from of old,
> from ancient days. (Mi 5:2)

This messianic hope was by no means uniform at all periods or among all groups in Israel's history. Some believed that a powerful human being deputed by God would bring about a new order, while others thought that God would intervene directly. Some held that the grandeur of the former Davidic monarchy would be restored, while others looked forward to a utopia far different from anything in the past, a state of affairs possibly ushered in by an apocalyptic cataclysm quite discontinuous with previous history. Even today a bedrock conviction among the majority of Jews is that the messiah is still to come. This, of course, is a major difference between that mother religion and its sometimes disdainful daughter, Christianity. Against the background of this cursory depiction of some of the main lines of the spirituality of the First Testament, we turn to that of the New.

THE SPIRITUALITY OF THE NEW TESTAMENT

One often hears the expression that Jesus proclaimed the kingdom and what came about was the church. Although often understood in a pejorative sense, the statement is not only true but altogether open to a positive interpretation. It is all too obvious in a world marked by the destitution of millions of people, the ongoing prevalence of warfare and other acts of violence, and the frequent need for any human being to admit with St. Paul that "I do not do the good I want, but the evil I do not want is what I do" (Rom 7:19), that the kingdom preached by Jesus has by no means arrived in its fullness. The church itself is in constant need of renewal, and yet it is also—and always has been—a sign of hope, especially when its members acknowledge that whatever in them genuinely reflects the life and teaching of Jesus is ultimately due to the grace of God. For this reason, the spirituality of the New Testament may be called an ecclesial spirituality of discipleship, provided that this is understood as a calling that is unmerited and, in its actual realization, never fully attaining its ideal.

This ideal can be expressed in various ways, but a few crucial verses from the New Testament provide indispensable clues for grasping what real discipleship entails. In the sermon of St. Peter recounted in the second chapter of the Acts of the Apostles, delivered on what is often called the birthday of the church, the first Christian Pentecost, this leader of the Twelve said: "Let the entire house of Israel know with certainty that God has made both Lord and Messiah this Jesus whom you crucified" (Acts 2:36). At this stage in the church's history there was not yet any precise clarity about just what this Lordship entailed or what it meant as regards Jesus' relationship to the one he called Abba, Father. Nevertheless, Peter's sermon clearly marked the early church's conviction that the messianic era that Israel had been expecting since the time of the great eighth- and seventh-century prophets had now been inaugurated. But not only that. In what is without doubt the most significant of all Christian claims about their Lord, Peter and the other early disciples proclaimed that this crucified Jesus had been raised up to new life by God, not just in the sense that we might claim that a deceased person lives on in our hearts and minds but in the sense that he had been truly raised from the dead and had appeared to many of the disciples over an extended period of time.

If, as mentioned earlier, life in the presence of God is about as close as one can come to a definition of spirituality that is native to the Jewish tradition, one could say something similar about a core aspect of Christian spirituality. The Christian belief that the Lord Jesus is truly alive means that for many Christians nothing could be more desirable than living in his presence. This is why St. Paul, the most energetic and widely traveled of all the early apostles, could write as follows to one of his favorite communities, the church at Philippi: "To me, living is Christ and dying is gain. If I am to live in the flesh, that means fruitful labor for me; and I do not know which I prefer. I am hard pressed between the two: my desire is to depart and be with Christ, for that is far better; but to remain in the flesh is more necessary for you" (Phil 1:21-24). He goes on to say in that passage that he is convinced that it is right for him to remain for the time being in this life, helping the churches he founded to progress in their faith, but it is clear that this sense of relative absence from Christ is a hardship for him.

What made the hardship bearable was not simply Paul's conviction that it was God's will for him but also his belief that living in a certain way made it possible already in this life to be "with Christ" or "in Christ," even if not to the extent that he expected to occur after his death and his own resurrection. He specifies in various passages from his letters just what this way of life entails, as in the following verses from his longest and most influential letter, that to the Romans, written around the year 57: "Owe no one anything, except to love one another; for the one who loves another has fulfilled the law.

The commandments, 'You shall not commit adultery; You shall not murder; You shall not steal; You shall not covet'; and any other commandment, are summed up in this word, 'Love your neighbor as yourself.' Love does no wrong to a neighbor; therefore, love is the fulfilling of the law" (Rom 13:8-10).

In writing thus, Paul was reflecting the teaching of Jesus himself as found in the Gospels. One of the best-known passages in the New Testament occurs in the twenty-fifth chapter of Matthew's Gospel, which teaches that the criterion of judgment that will determine the salvation or damnation of any human being is how one treated "the least" of Jesus' followers, either coming to their aid when they were hungry, thirsty, naked, or imprisoned or else neglecting to do so. This passage, in turn, spells out in some detail what Jesus is shown teaching earlier when asked about the greatest commandment in the Jewish Law; in reply, he joins together the command to love God with all one's heart, soul, and mind with the command to love one's neighbor as oneself (Mt 22:34-40; cf. Dt 6:5 and Lv 19:18).

Elsewhere in the Gospels this kind of love and concern is exemplified in Jesus' very activity. As is evident from even the most cursory reading of the Gospels, his activity was to a large extent centered on healing persons afflicted in various ways. It is sometimes said that the evangelists depict so much of this healing activity primarily to show that the final age of the kingdom of God was breaking in, but it is important to note that the motivation regularly ascribed to Jesus himself is simple compassion for those in need. When Matthew writes of Jesus' healing of two blind men on the outskirts of Jericho, after recounting the conversation Jesus has with them the evangelist concludes with these words: "Moved with compassion, Jesus touched their eyes. Immediately they regained their sight and followed him" (Mt 20:34). Near the very beginning of Mark's Gospel we find something similar. A leper approaches Jesus and says, "If you choose, you can make me clean." Mark continues: "Moved with pity, Jesus stretched out his hand and touched him, and said to him, 'I do choose. Be made clean'" (Mk 1:40-41). This same motive is attributed to Jesus still elsewhere in the Gospels, whether it be for those already sick (Mt 14:14) or for those about to faint from hunger after following him for three days in a deserted part of the countryside (Mt 15:32). If anything, John sharpens the teaching of the other three evangelists about love of others when he includes in his account of Jesus' discourse at the Last Supper a "new commandment"—not simply to love one's neighbor as oneself but rather, "Just as I have loved you, you also should love one another" (Jn 13:34).

The centrality of love of others as the hallmark of Christian spirituality is also evident in descriptions of life in the early church as found in some of

Paul's letters and in the Acts of the Apostles. The latter work, which is really Luke's continuation of his Gospel, includes descriptions of life in the Christian community at Jerusalem that are no doubt to some extent idealized but that nevertheless highlight this ideal of love of others. Luke writes, for example, that in those first halcyon days "the whole group of those who believed were of one heart and soul, and no one claimed private ownership of any possessions, but everything they owned was held in common . . . There was not a needy person among them, for as many as owned lands or houses sold them and brought the proceeds of what was sold" (Acts 4:32-34; cf. 2:44-45). More realistic is what Paul wrote to the Corinthians. Like the other communities that he founded, the Corinthians would come together regularly to celebrate the Lord's Supper, in accordance with the command Jesus had given to the Twelve when he gathered with them for a final meal before his arrest and crucifixion: "Do this in remembrance of me" (Lk 22:19; cf. 1 Cor 11:24-25). However, Paul had heard that when the Corinthians came together to celebrate this central act of Christian liturgical life, greed and stinginess had gained the upper hand over that sentiment of concern for others depicted in Acts: "Now in the following instructions I do not commend you, because when you come together it is not for the better but for the worse . . . When you come together, it is not really to eat the Lord's supper. For when the time comes to eat, each of you goes ahead with your own supper, and one goes hungry and another becomes drunk" (1 Cor 11:17-21).

In the very next chapter of this letter, Paul goes into considerable detail to express the theological foundation for his teaching about love. His key assumption is that a Christian is not an independent, self-contained entity but rather a member of a larger body, with Christ as head. Just as in the case of anyone's physical body the various parts "have the same care for one another," so that "if one member suffers, all suffer together with it," so too in the case of the body that is the church: "You are the body of Christ and individually members of it" (1 Cor 12:25-27). Not everyone has the same calling within this body, some being apostles, others prophets, still others teachers, and so forth, but all are called to the practice of the most excellent way of all, which Paul goes on to describe in his well-known paean to love in the thirteenth chapter of the letter, where he lists some of the most prominent characteristics of Christian love: it is patient, kind, not envious or boastful; it rejoices not in wrongdoing but in the good, bears all things, believes all things, hopes all things, endures all things, and—in sum—is the greatest of what came to be called the theological virtues of faith, hope, and love.

From what has been said already in this chapter it should be clear that Christian spirituality is deeply rooted in Israelite/Jewish spirituality. The First Testament regularly depicts God as a loving redeemer who will not abandon the people even after their repeated backslidings (e.g., Hos 14:4-7), just as Jesus assures his followers that his Father loves them with an abiding love (Jn 16:26-27). The joy that the Israelites found in living in God's presence, strikingly evoked in the psalms of praise (e.g., Pss 148-150), is mirrored in the joy that some of the earliest Christians expressed even in the midst of their hardships (Col 1:24). And although the Sermon on the Mount in Matthew's Gospel draws some sharp distinctions between the teaching of Moses and that of Jesus, above all concerning the treatment of those regarded as one's enemies, even here the opposition is not complete, for there are striking passages also in the First Testament that are fully in accord with Jesus' teaching, such as the following: "When you come upon your enemy's ox or donkey going astray, you shall bring it back. When you see the donkey of one who hates you lying under its burden and you would hold back from setting it free, you must help to set it free" (Ex 23:4-5).

There is, however, a larger issue related to biblical spirituality that has not even been hinted at thus far in this chapter. Most of what was said up to this point has been altogether positive in tone, which could imply that there is nothing in Scripture that might be of questionable value in providing sure guidelines for the practice of Christian spirituality. Indeed, this was a common assumption in the earliest centuries of the church's history and is still assumed by many to be the case today. However, things are not so simple. The final half of this chapter will accordingly look at some of the major ways in which the Bible has been interpreted over the past two millennia, including some recent ways that are quite critical of certain aspects of Scripture. To provide a clear structure to this presentation, we will be focusing on one particular scriptural passage precisely in order to see the different ways it has been interpreted at various times, together with the implications these ways might have for one's understanding and practice of Christian spirituality.

THREE PARADIGMS FOR INTERPRETING THE BIBLE

The scriptural passage chosen for this purpose is the well-known account of the testing of the patriarch Abraham as found in Genesis 22. Having finally had a son, Isaac, born to him and his wife Sarah after they had long given up hope of having any children, Abraham is here put to the severe test of being told by God to take his son on a journey of several days to the land of Moriah and slay him as a burnt offering, a holocaust, on a mountain that would be pointed out to him. Drawing near the place, Abraham places the wood for the offering on the shoulders of his son while he himself carries the fire and the knife. To Isaac's question about the whereabouts of the lamb that the boy expected to be sacrificed, Abraham replies that God will provide the lamb. Having reached the top of the mountain, Abraham builds an altar, binds Isaac, lays him on top of the wood, and takes the knife to kill the boy when a voice from heaven tells him to stop, "for now I know that you fear God, since you have not withheld your son, your only son, from me" (Gn 22:12). Instead, Abraham offers a ram that he sees caught in a nearby thicket, after which the Lord in the guise of an angel speaks to him a second time, promising that because of his obedience God will bless him and make his offspring as numerous as the stars of heaven and the sand of the seashore.

As one would expect, there have been numerous ways of interpreting this story in both Judaism and Christianity. In the latter religion, three general paradigms or approaches may be singled out: the premodern and precritical paradigm that prevailed for roughly the first seventeen centuries of our era, the modern or critical paradigm whose roots lie in the European Enlightenment, and the postmodern or postcritical paradigm that characterizes much (though certainly not all) scriptural interpretation in our own time. The very choice of merely these three categories may appear dubious both because there is so much variety within any one of the three and because few recent interpreters of the Bible could be said to exemplify only one of these approaches to the total exclusion of the other two. Nevertheless, the following examples of different ways of understanding the account of the testing of Abraham reflect such distinctive characteristics that the use of these categories does seem warranted.

The Premodern Paradigm

David Klemm, in the introduction to the two volumes on hermeneutical inquiry that he edited, writes that in the premodern paradigm that prevailed during the patristic and medieval periods of church history, the biblical text was treated not as an object of dispassionate analysis but as a vehicle for the disclosure of divine truth.[3] The two testaments were seen as the integrally related parts of a single whole, the revealed word of God. As found in the First Testament, this revealing word in one way or another looked forward to Christ, the incarnate Word. For a particularly clear representative of this premodern approach to the Bible we will look at the way Origen of Alexandria,

3. David E. Klemm, introduction to *Hermeneutical Inquiry*, vol. 1, *The Interpretation of Texts*, AAR Studies in Religion 44 (Atlanta: Scholars Press, 1986), 9.

one of the most prolific theologians of any century, commented on the testing of Abraham in his eighth homily on the book of Genesis.

As noted in the preceding chapter of this book, Origen regularly sought the "mystical" or "spiritual" sense of a biblical text. If the text were from the First Testament, he sought to show how the deeper meaning of the passage prefigured something in the New, especially something about the life of Christ. In this particular homily on the testing of Abraham, preached at Caesarea in Palestine sometime between the years 238 and 244, Origen goes through the passage verse by verse, commenting on each in turn. His most frequent references to Christ begin with the sixth verse, which speaks of Abraham's placing the wood for the holocaust on his son Isaac. This leads Origen to comment as follows: "That Isaac himself carries on himself 'the wood for the holocaust' is a figure, because Christ also 'himself carried his own cross,' and yet to carry 'the wood for the holocaust' is the duty of a priest. He himself, therefore, becomes both victim and priest."[4] Grammatically speaking, "he himself" in that final sentence is Isaac, but the words refer simultaneously to Christ, who is prefigured in Isaac, the "type" (or prototype) of Christ. Each, therefore, is both priest and victim.

This becomes abundantly clear a bit later in the homily when Origen comments on the ram caught by its horns in a thicket. Just as he had earlier said that Isaac, who is not slain, represents Christ, Origen now says that the ram, which is slain, likewise represents him. This is so because each represents a different aspect of Christ: Isaac represents the Word of God "from above," Christ "according to the spirit" who remains "in incorruption," while the ram prefigures the "Word made flesh" who suffered and endured death "in the flesh." "For this reason," says Origen, Christ himself "is both victim and priest. For truly according to the spirit he offers the victim to the Father, but according to the flesh he himself is offered on the altar of the cross, because just as it is said of him, 'Behold the Lamb of God, behold him who takes away the sin of the world' [Jn 1:29], so it is said of him, 'You are a priest forever according to the order of Melchisedech' [Ps 110:4]."[5]

There is another christological reference in this homily that should also be noted. The passage in Genesis says that Abraham was blessed because he did not withhold or spare his only son, which leads Origen to relate this verse to the line in the Letter to the Romans where Paul writes that "God did not spare his own Son, but gave him up for all of us" (Rom 8:32). God, says Origen, is here contending with humans in magnificent liberality: "Abraham

---

4. Origen, *Homily 8 on Genesis*, in idem, *Homilies on Genesis and Exodus,* trans. Ronald E. Heine, Fathers of the Church 71 (Washington, D.C.: The Catholic University of America Press, 1982), 140-41.

5. Ibid., 145.

offered God a mortal son who was not put to death; God delivered to death an immortal son for men."[6] This divine liberality causes Origen to conclude his homily with the exhortation to be generous in what one offers God, who will not be outdone in generosity. The homilist's final words are: "Do you see what it means to lose something for God? It means to receive it back multiplied. But the Gospels promise you something even more, 'a hundred-fold' is offered you, besides also 'life eternal' in Christ Jesus our Lord, to whom belongs glory and sovereignty forever and ever. Amen."[7]

In addition to this closing exhortation to generosity, which is a straightforward example of the spiritual teaching that Origen drew from this passage in Genesis, there is a further aspect of this homily that is very significant for the study of Christian spirituality. Toward the beginning of this chapter we noted that the proclamation of Christ's resurrection was pivotal in the preaching of the earliest disciples, but little was said there about his suffering and death. Origen's reflection on the latter in this homily is just one of countless references to Christ's death in the literature of Christian spirituality. The fact that he had died so shameful a death made it incumbent upon the members of the early church to make sense of this, and they did so largely by searching the writings of the First Testament in order to show that the Messiah was meant to undergo an ignominious death. Several texts in particular stood out, such as Psalm 69 and the four Songs of the Suffering Servant in the Book of Isaiah. Whether or not the mysterious servant in Isaiah originally referred to a single individual or to Israel as a whole, the early church saw in the servant a prefiguring of Christ, who was led "like a lamb to the slaughter" (Is 53:7) and so became the one who would "make many righteous" and "bear their iniquities" (Is 53:11). With the passing of centuries and in certain parts of the Christian world, Christ came to be regarded more or less exclusively as "the Man of Sorrows," whose saving activity was so tightly linked to his crucifixion that the redemptive nature of the entire paschal event, including therefore the resurrection, was neglected. Among other things, this led many to conclude, in practice if not also in theory, that the following or imitation of Christ could best be effected through one's own suffering, suffering that could rightly be sought out and not simply endured when it occurred willy-nilly. This teaching is found already in Origen, for in the concluding lines of his first homily on the Book of Leviticus he writes of the desirability of "being conformed to the image of the sacrifice of Christ," and he elsewhere expounds on this in greater detail:

6. Origen, *Homilies on Genesis and Exodus,* 144.
7. Ibid., 147.

> Often in prayer we say, "Almighty God, give us the lot of the Prophets, give us the lot of the Apostles of Christ so that we may be found also with Christ himself." But when we say this, we do not realize what we pray. For in effect we are saying this: "Let us suffer what the Prophets have suffered, let us be hated as the Prophets were hated, give us the kind of words for which we will be hated, let befall us the kind of misfortunes which befell the Apostles."[8]

As we will see later in this book, this desire to suffer so as to be more closely conformed to Christ was taken much farther by some figures in late medieval and early modern spirituality.

The Modern Paradigm

Origen's consistent search for the deeper, spiritual meaning of passages in the Bible was continued and expanded in succeeding centuries by writers like Sts. Ambrose, Augustine, and Bonaventure. Even though the major Protestant Reformers Martin Luther and John Calvin rejected this approach and appealed instead to the literal or grammatical meaning as being usually identical with the text's subject matter, even they remained basically within what David Klemm has called "the premodern openness to God's word directly or indirectly manifest in Scripture."[9] The change to a new paradigm had to await the coming of the Enlightenment in Europe, with its radical questioning of whether what appears to be the case is really so, the kind of questioning adumbrated in René Descartes' methodical doubt. Within the field of scriptural interpretation the modern, critical paradigm was most clearly manifested in the rise of the historical-critical method, sometimes called "the higher criticism." As practiced by the eighteenth-century exegete Johann Semler, a rigid separation was made between "the contents" of the Bible, which are the word of God, and "the writings themselves," which are relatively fallible and are to be considered authoritative only to the extent that they promote the moral improvement of the human race. According to Semler, what is "canonical" for one generation would not necessarily be so for another. Through careful analysis of the meanings and references of words in a biblical text, this scholar identified individual authors of the various books

8. Origen, *Homily 14 on Jeremiah*, in idem, *Homilies on Jeremiah; Homily on 1 Kings 28*, trans. John Clark Smith, Fathers of the Church 97 (Washington, D.C.: Catholic University of America Press, 1998), 149.

9. Klemm, introduction, 11.

of Scripture and showed how these books belonged to different social contexts and periods of history.

This set the stage for an increasingly rationalist approach to the Bible, a situation that led the leaders of the Catholic Church to be very suspicious of the historical-critical method itself. Their suspicion gradually abated, until finally in the middle of the twentieth century Pope Pius XII's groundbreaking encyclical *Divino Afflante Spiritu* encouraged Catholic Scripture scholars to try to determine the character and circumstances of the biblical authors, the times in which they lived, their written and oral sources, and the like. With this kind of encouragement, Catholic exegetes quickly made up for lost ground. One of them, Bruce Vawter, became a highly respected commentator on the Book of Genesis. The way he approached the account of the testing of Abraham is an excellent example of how the historical-critical method can be applied to this text in a manner quite different from Origen's quest for a spiritual, christological meaning.

Vawter notes that human sacrifice, especially child sacrifice, was widely practiced by Israel's Semitic neighbors and indeed by Israelites themselves, who at times regarded it as compatible with their worship of God. He goes on to surmise that it would be strange if no record at all remained of the change that came about as the Israelites arrived at a new insight into the nature of God and God's requirements. The account of Abraham's testing would then be such a record, showing that whereas a man of proven religious sensitivity had once thought that God required him to sacrifice his only heir in service of some greater good, this same man subsequently came to a new conception of what pleases God and, indeed, to a new conception of God. Vawter concludes:

> Surely something more than trivial change of fancy and whim is being insinuated here . . . Israel did, after all, almost alone of its compeers raise its eyes to a vision of God and religion that relegated the otherwise respectable institution of human sacrifice to the dank backwaters of superstition and barbarism. It ought not seem strange that its great forefather Abraham should have been thought to anticipate this enlargement of the human spirit even as he has anticipated so much else that is Israelite in the pages of Genesis.[10]

Like most practitioners of the historical-critical method, Vawter does not here go on to exhort his readers to a certain kind of behavior in the way Ori-

---

10. Bruce Vawter, *On Genesis: A New Reading* (Garden City, N.Y.: Doubleday, 1977), 256.

gen and other premodern authors regularly did, but the spiritual import of his way of approaching the passage of Abraham's testing is nevertheless clear. Anyone who believes that the Bible is divinely inspired will be led to concur with this "new insight" into God's nature, the realization that God does not want to be placated by violence done to innocent human beings. Rather, God wishes human beings to flourish, and it is the responsibility of those who would call themselves God's servants to promote that flourishing in whatever ways possible, including in a special way the protection and nurturing of children. (It would, of course, take further centuries before people came to the additional insight that God does not desire the slaying of sacrificial animals either.)

Whereas Vawter primarily practiced historical criticism of the Bible, there are refinements of this method that came to be associated with it, including source criticism, form criticism, and redaction criticism. There is no need to go into the details of these methods here, but it would be helpful to look at a fourth such refinement, literary criticism, not least because the Genesis account of Abraham's testing was brilliantly analyzed in the very first chapter of one of the most influential works of literary criticism in the past hundred years, Erich Auerbach's *Mimesis*. In this chapter, "Odysseus' Scar," Auerbach contrasts the way in which Homer recounts the scene of Odysseus's return home in book 19 of the *Odyssey* with the way in which the biblical author describes the scene of Abraham's testing in Genesis. In Homer, everything is narrated in leisurely fashion, with well-articulated descriptions of implements, ministrations, and gestures. All this is in accord with the "basic impulse of the Homeric style: to represent phenomena in a fully externalized form, visible and palpable in all their parts, and completely fixed in their spatial and temporal relations."[11] The same is true of psychological processes: Homer's personages regularly express their inmost thoughts in speech, and when they do not, the reader is informed of what is going on in their minds.

The genius of this particular style, Auerbach observes, becomes all the more apparent if contrasted with an equally epic style from a different setting, that of the Bible. To spell out the comparison, he goes through the account of the testing of Abraham point by point, noting how nothing is said in Genesis about where God and Abraham are to be found, nothing about why God is tempting Abraham so terribly, nothing about the deliberations that must have taken place in the divine heart. So, too, when the story itself begins, it unrolls with no discrete episodes, no description of the landscape

---

11. Erich Auerbach, *Mimesis: The Representation of Reality in Western Literature*, trans. Willard Trask (Garden City, N.Y.: Doubleday, Anchor Books, 1957), 4.

through which the travelers passed, no details about the servants or pack animals that accompanied Abraham and Isaac. It would be difficult, writes Auerbach, to imagine styles more contrasted than these two. For the Homeric characters, delight in physical existence is everything, whereas the sole concern of the biblical stories is moral and religious, their human author being obliged to write exactly what the truth of the tradition demanded of him. "The Scripture stories do not, like Homer's, court our favor, they do not flatter us that they may please us and enchant us—they seek to subject us, and if we refuse to be subjected we are rebels."[12] These stories, in other words, speak of the claim of a hidden, mysterious God upon chosen human beings, whose formation "proceeds gradually, historically, during the earthly life of him upon whom the choice has fallen. How the process is accomplished, what terrible trials such a formation inflicts, can be seen in our story of Abraham's sacrifice."[13]

No more than the historical critic Vawter does the literary critic Auerbach express exhortations for his readers of the sort that are frequent in a premodern author like Origen, but the main import of his analysis for spirituality is not difficult to surmise. For anyone who believes that the Bible expresses God's call to human beings to live in a certain way, the uncompromising starkness of the divine address—whether to Abraham on Mount Moriah, to Isaiah in the Jerusalem Temple, or to Saul on the road to Damascus—may readily lead readers to consider the possibility, even the likelihood, that they themselves have been or may be addressed in a similar way. To be thus addressed by God does not mean that a person is especially gifted or holy. As Auerbach writes, all of these biblical figures "are bearers of the divine will, and yet they are fallible, subject to misfortune and humiliation—and in the midst of misfortune and in their humiliation their acts and words reveal the transcendent majesty of God."[14] The misfortunes and humiliations that any of us experience can likewise be bearers of God's transcendent majesty, provided only that they are not denied or ignored.

The Postmodern Paradigm

When practiced by religious believers, explanatory methods like historical or literary criticism assume that the basic message of the Scriptures, however interpreted, is basically life-giving. The intent is to determine as fully as

12. Auerbach, *Mimesis*, 12.
13. Ibid., 14.
14. Ibid., 15.

possible what this vital text has to say to us today. A common term for this way of proceeding is "the hermeneutics of retrieval." It was clearly expressed some decades ago by Markus Barth when he wrote that even though the biblical records do not claim to give exhaustive information, "they have clearly been proved to contain sufficient clarity, poignancy, and exemplification to instruct one generation after another in all that pertains to the communion between God and man . . . Here the only trustworthy testimony of the eyewitnesses of God's full revelation is set down in writing."[15] Over against this position, there has arisen in the course of the last century the suspicion that even within the Bible there may be systemic distortions that have to be faced forthrightly. This "hermeneutics of suspicion" is part of the postmodern paradigm. The Enlightenment ideals of clarity and rationality are no longer revered by thinkers influenced by Nietzsche, Marx, and Freud, the three most prominent "masters of suspicion." In the words of David Tracy, "the basic developments in the postmodern hermeneutic tradition have been . . . explicitly geared to formulating various critical theories forged to expose the latent meanings of texts—especially those latent meanings that enforce not mere error but illusion, not occasional difficulties but systematic distortions."[16] Elsewhere, Tracy specifies what this kind of exposure means for the text of Scripture itself:

> To claim the ancient Israelites as our predecessors is an honor. But that claim also forces us to face the patriarchal nature of their society. We cannot forget what the Israelites did to the Canaanites and what their prayers against the children of their enemies might mean. To cherish the Christian scriptures as a charter document of liberation is entirely right. Yet we must also face its anti-Judaic strands, strands that reach us with the full history of the effects of centuries of Christian "teaching of contempt" for the Jews. And we have just begun to face the centuries of subjugation of women in Christian history—indeed, in all Western history.[17]

Of the various postmodern, postcritical approaches to scriptural interpretation, the one to which Tracy alludes at the very end of that passage—feminist hermeneutics—has become widely practiced in recent decades. Feminist theologians and Scripture scholars do not suppose that the biblical authors were free of hidden interests, interests possibly hidden even from themselves

---

15. Markus Barth, *Conversation with the Bible* (New York: Holt, Rinehart, and Winston, 1964), 196.

16. David Tracy, "Theological Method," in *Christian Theology: An Introduction to Its Traditions and Tasks*, ed. Peter C. Hodgson and Robert H. King, rev. ed. (Philadelphia: Fortress, 1985), 43.

17. David Tracy, *Plurality and Ambiguity: Hermeneutics, Religion, Hope* (San Francisco: Harper & Row, 1987), 68-69.

because they unwittingly imbibed patriarchal assumptions of their society. A feminist scholar such as Elisabeth Schüssler Fiorenza will scan the scriptural text carefully, reading between (or behind) the lines in search of what she calls "rhetorical clues and allusions that indicate the reality about which the texts are silent."[18] Nor surprisingly, among the texts that have been studied in this way is the account of Abraham's testing. Phyllis Trible, professor of sacred literature at Union Theological Seminary in New York City, spoke at length about her reading of this story when interviewed by Bill Moyers as part of a televised series about the Book of Genesis. Her search for "clues" about which the text is silent became evident when she said in her opening remarks that when she began looking at the story from a feminist perspective some years ago she found no evidence in the preceding chapters that Abraham was really attached to Isaac; his attachment was rather to Ishmael, his son by the slave woman Hagar. Trible then asked herself, "Who has the attachment to Isaac?" and concluded that it was Sarah. In the preceding chapters of Genesis it is always Sarah, never Abraham, who says, "My son, Isaac." Trible further observes that the last words that come from Sarah's lips are her command to Abraham to cast out Hagar and her son so that Sarah's son, Isaac, will alone have the inheritance. Not long thereafter Sarah dies, "without being healed of *her* attachment to Isaac, which led her to be tyrannical, malicious, and mean-spirited," all because she, like Hagar, was

> trapped in patriarchy. And patriarchy has only two places for women. One is the pedestal, and the other is the doormat or gutter. Hagar occupies one of those two places, and Sarah occupies the other . . . Now if, instead of Abraham, Sarah had been the chief character, she would have been healed of this attachment to Isaac. By offering to sacrifice him, she would have become capable of nonattachment, and God would have said, "Now I know you fear God." This healing would then have opened up the possibility of a healing between Sarah and Hagar.[19]

Once more, as was the case with the interpretations of Vawter and Auerbach, Trible makes no explicit attempt to draw spiritual teaching from her reflections on the Genesis account, but feminist scholars would have little difficulty doing so. Perhaps the greatest single theme in Christian feminist literature is that a male-centered, patriarchal mind-set is damaging to the

18. Elisabeth Schüssler Fiorenza, "Remembering the Past in Creating the Future," in *Feminist Perspectives on Biblical Scholarship*, ed. Adela Yarbro Collins, SBL Centennial Publications, Biblical Scholarship in North America 10 (Chico, Calif.: Scholars Press, 1985), 60.

19. Phyllis Trible, quoted in Bill Moyers, *Genesis: A Living Conversation*, ed. Betty Sue Flowers (New York: Doubleday, 1996), 237-38.

human and spiritual growth of both women and men. In Trible's words, men have regularly placed women either on a pedestal or in the gutter, to the detriment not only of men but of both kinds of women: the one kind has the impossible task of trying to live up to an unrealistic ideal, the other becomes afflicted with a sense of worthlessness that stunts emotional and spiritual growth to maturity, and both become blocked from having wholesome relationships with each other as well as with men. Spiritual maturity will become possible only if the patriarchal assumptions are brought to consciousness and rejected, although feminists (a group that includes men as well as women) debate among themselves over the degree of aggressiveness that will most effectively achieve their aims.

Personal Readings of Scriptural Texts

As we come to the end of this overview of various ways in which scholars from the time of Origen in the third century up to the present have interpreted the account of Abraham's testing, one may well feel at something of a disadvantage, as though it would be rash to attempt to interpret a passage from Scripture without first having become quite thoroughly familiar with all the various types of scriptural interpretation. Granted that there is much to be gained from such familiarity, it would be wrong to conclude that such attempts at understanding should be reserved to experts. Kathleen Fischer gave excellent advice when she wrote in one of her first books that the vast amount of learning that scholars have accumulated on the Bible across the centuries ought never deter persons from trusting their own reading of a biblical text. Being believed by Christians to be the locus of revelation, the Bible "is not simply information; it is a relationship in which we are called to participate. We enter into a dialogue with the text, bringing our questions to it and allowing the biblical questions to address us: 'Whom do you seek?' 'Do you love me?' 'Who do you say that I am?'"[20]

In accord with that advice, it would be appropriate to conclude this chapter by referring to a particularly moving account of personal encounter with the story of Abraham's testing, known in Hebrew as the *Aqedah.* The account is by Elie Wiesel, whose imprisonment in Auschwitz when he was a child was powerfully described in his book *Night*. Having survived the death camp and eventually reaching the United States, he has written a number of books on biblical themes. In one of these, he tells how as a child he would read and

---

20. Kathleen Fischer, *The Inner Rainbow: The Imagination in Christian Life* (New York: Paulist, 1983), 35.

reread the tale of the *Aqedah*, a sense of dark apprehension coming over him as he tried to understand the three characters: the strangeness of a merciful God asking so inhuman a deed of Abraham, the unfathomable willingness of the patriarch to accede to this request, and the disturbing meekness of Isaac's submission. To Wiesel as a child, the *Aqedah* was a deep mystery, something to be relived, if not solved, by every generation of Jews. Of all the biblical tales, he writes, this one may be the most timeless and most relevant to our generation. In his words:

> At the end of time, say our sages, God will tell Abraham: Your children have sinned. And Abraham will reply: Let them die to sanctify Your name. Then God will turn to Jacob and say: Your children have sinned. And Jacob will reply: Let them die to sanctify Your name. Then God will speak to Isaac: Your children have sinned. And Isaac will answer: My children? Are they not also Yours? Yours as well?
>
> It will be Isaac's privilege to remain Israel's Melitz-Yosher, the defender of his people, pleading its cause with great ability. He will be entitled to say anything he likes to God, ask anything of Him. Because he suffered? No. Suffering, in Jewish tradition, confers no privileges. It all depends on what one makes of that suffering. Isaac knew how to transform it into prayer and love rather than into rancor and malediction. This is what gives him rights and powers no other man possesses. His reward? The Temple was built on Moriah. Not on Sinai.[21]

QUESTIONS FOR REFLECTION

1. What do you judge to be the principal themes of First Testament spirituality? Were any indispensable themes left out in this chapter?
2. Christianity is sometimes reproached for advocating love without adequately teaching just how love is to be practiced. To what extent might this be a just criticism?
3. The church has regularly taught the unity of the two testaments of the Bible, but some have held that significant differences between the two are too readily glossed over. How do you understand the relationship between the First Testament and the New?
4. Of the three paradigms of scriptural interpretation treated in this chapter, which seems to offer the most promise for nourishing your own spirituality? How do you yourself interpret the account of the testing of Abraham?

---

21. Elie Wiesel, *Messengers of God: Biblical Portraits and Legends* (New York: Random House, 1976), 96-97.

SUGGESTIONS FOR FURTHER READING AND STUDY

On Biblical Spirituality

Green, Arthur. Introduction to *Jewish Spirituality: From the Bible through the Middle Ages*, edited by Arthur Green, xiii-xv. World Spirituality 13. New York: Crossroad, 1994.

Schneiders, Sandra. "Scripture and Spirituality." In *Christian Spirituality: Origins to the Twelfth Century*, edited by Bernard McGinn and John Meyendorff, 1-20. World Spirituality 16. New York: Crossroad, 1985.

On Various Approaches to Scriptural Interpretation

Auerbach, Erich. "Odysseus' Scar." In *Mimesis: The Representation of Reality in Western Literature*, 1-20. Garden City, N.Y.: Doubleday, Anchor Books, 1957.

Fitzmyer, Joseph A., S.J. "Historical Criticism: Its Role in Biblical Interpretation and Church Life." *Theological Studies* 50 (1989): 244-59.

Klemm, David E. Introduction to *Hermeneutical Inquiry*. Vol. 1, *The Interpretation of Texts*, 1-53 (esp. 1-24). AAR Studies in Religion 44. Atlanta: Scholars Press, 1986.

Moyers, Bill. "The Test." In *Genesis: A Living Conversation*, edited by Betty Sue Flowers, 219-47. New York: Doubleday, 1996.

Origen. *Homily 8 on Genesis*. In *Homilies on Genesis and Exodus*, translated by Ronald E. Heine, 136-47. Fathers of the Church 71. Washington, D.C.: Catholic University of America Press, 1982.

Schüssler Fiorenza, Elisabeth. "Remembering the Past in Creating the Future." In *Feminist Perspectives on Biblical Scholarship*, edited by Adela Yarbro Collins. SBL Centennial Publications, Biblical Scholarship in North America 10. Chico, Calif.: Scholars Press, 1985.

———. "Toward a Feminist Critical Hermeneutics." In *In Memory of Her: A Feminist Theological Reconstruction of Christian Origins,* 3-40. 2nd ed. New York: Crossroad, 1994.

Steinmetz, David. "The Superiority of Pre-Critical Exegesis." In *The Theological Interpretation of Scripture*, edited by Stephen E. Fowl, 26-38. Cambridge, Mass.: Blackwell, 1997.

Tracy, David. "Theological Method." In *Christian Theology: An Introduction to Its Traditions and Tasks*, edited by Peter C. Hodgson and Robert H. King, 35-60. Rev. ed. Philadelphia: Fortress, 1985.

Vawter, Bruce. *On Genesis: A New Reading*. Garden City, N.Y.: Doubleday, 1977. Esp. 253-58.

Wiesel, Elie. "The Sacrifice of Isaac: A Survivor's Story." In *Messengers of God: Biblical Portraits and Legends*, 69-97. New York: Random House, 1976.

3

Martyrs and Other Witnesses in the Early Church

ACCORDING TO ST. LUKE, the very last words spoken by Jesus to his chosen apostles were these: "You will be my witnesses in Jerusalem, in all Judea and Samaria, and to the ends of the earth" (Acts 1:8). The Greek word here translated as "witnesses" is *martyres*, which has given us the English term "martyr," usually referring to someone who has given his or her life in testimony to the truth of the Christian faith. However, it was only in the post-apostolic church that the word came regularly to be used in this specific sense. In the Bible a martyr is, more broadly, anyone who bears witness, often in a juridical way, as during a criminal trial. That the word soon came to mean someone who died for the faith was almost inevitable, given the fierce opposition that Christian witness frequently provoked, but in the present chapter we will begin by using the term in its original, broader sense to refer to those who bore witness to Jesus "to the ends of the earth."

These were, of course, in the first instance those whom the Gospels name "the Twelve," but there were other important witnesses as well: not only St. Paul, often called "the Apostle to the Gentiles," but also countless other missionaries in the early centuries of the Christian era, including some of Paul's own associates. Our focus will be not only on their evangelizing work as such—especially on what they taught about how Christians should live—but also on how their words led to particular forms of spiritual practice in the communities that they addressed. We will, in other words, be looking at what Walter Principe called the first two levels in his description of "spirituality": the existential level (the way some of the early Christians and their communities actually lived the faith), and the formulation of teachings about this lived reality in texts that have come down to us. Not surprisingly, these texts will normally advocate or describe an ideal that may have been followed only quite imperfectly by many early Christians. This helps explain why the existential level regularly includes expressions of repentance for not having measured up to the ideal.

THE SPIRITUALITY OF THE EARLY CHRISTIAN COMMUNITIES

In the previous chapter we referred to St. Luke's description of life in the first Christian community in Jerusalem, where he said the whole group of believers held everything in common. Those who owned lands or houses sold them and allowed the Twelve to distribute the proceeds to any of the community who were in need (Acts 4:34-35). Earlier in the same book of Acts, Luke writes that those who entered the community through baptism "devoted themselves to the apostles' teaching and fellowship, to the breaking of bread and the prayers" (Acts 2:42). Since there was as yet no break from Judaism, the common prayers to which he referred included ones prayed in the Jewish Temple. Others were offered when the newly baptized met in their homes for "the breaking of bread" (Acts 2:42, 46), a common term for what we normally call the eucharist. However idealized this picture may be, Luke's description encapsulates practices and attitudes that have remained central in Christian spirituality ever since: (1) non-possessiveness with regard to material goods (and a concomitant generosity toward persons in need), (2) attentiveness to the teaching of those recognized as leaders of the community, (3) a sense of fellowship, and (4) the practice of common prayer, centered above all on the celebration of the eucharist. Some or all of these four points will regularly appear in other texts of the first few centuries of the church's history that will be examined later in this chapter.

The nascent period of peace during which Luke says the Christians enjoyed "the goodwill of all the people" (Acts 2:47) was short-lived. The evangelist writes that the preaching of Stephen, who was severely critical of his fellow Jews, so enraged his hearers that he was stoned to death, thereby becoming the first Christian martyr in the narrower sense of one who gave up his life for bearing witness. Luke adds that on the very day of Stephen's death, a severe persecution broke out against the church in Jerusalem, with the result that many in the community went elsewhere, witnessing to the gospel as they went. Philip first went north to Samaria and later traveled southwest of Jerusalem to Gaza (Acts 8:5, 26), while Peter preached to non-Jews for the first time in Caesarea along the Mediterranean coast (Acts 10). Unnamed others went as far as Cyprus and Antioch (Acts 11:19). From that last-named city, Paul, always with one or more companions, began his missionary journeys throughout the Mediterranean area, proclaiming Jesus to be the risen savior to both Jews and Gentiles in major cities of Asia Minor, Greece, and eventually Rome. Momentous as Paul's work was, its very importance has had the unfortunate effect of severely overshadowing the spread of

Christianity to other parts of the world. If this present work is to be faithful to the aim of presenting spirituality "in global perspective," it is imperative to note how Christian faith and practice spread in all directions from Jerusalem and Antioch and not only to the north and west as a result of Paul's journeys.

Several hundred miles to the northeast of Antioch lay the trading center Edessa, situated along the Silk Road between the Euphrates and Tigris rivers in northern Mesopotamia. We do not know exactly when missionaries first brought the gospel to this part of the world, but an early tradition noted by Eusebius at the end of book 1 of his *Ecclesiastical History* claims that this occurred already in the first century and at the request of a king of Edessa. In any case, the fact that Edessa was the location of the first public building ever identified as a church (in the year 201) indicates that Christians in that city were allowed to live in peace with their religiously diverse neighbors. Most inhabitants of the city and the surrounding region spoke Syriac, a dialect of Aramaic, the language that Jesus himself spoke, although Greek was the language of the upper classes. Some of the most important documents from the first three centuries C.E., whether originally written in Greek or Syriac, have come to us in whole or in part from Syria and provide a precious glimpse into the practice of Christian spirituality there.

One of these texts, known as the *Odes of Solomon*, is a collection of forty-two hymns, a number of them probably composed in either Edessa or Antioch near the beginning of the second century. In some of these hymns we find the Syriac Christian tradition's predilection for using feminine images of God, something already present in certain parts of the First Testament but not prominent in the Western church until the Middle Ages. The nineteenth *Ode,* for example, begins with the following lines:

> A cup of milk was offered to me,
> and I drank it in the sweetness of the Lord's kindness.
> The Son is the cup,
> and the Father is he who was milked,
> and the Holy Spirit is she who milked Him.[1]

Even more important than these *Odes* is the *Teaching of the Twelve Apostles*, commonly known by the first word of its Greek title, the *Didache*. Discovered only in 1873, this document falls into two parts. The first is a code of Christian morals presented in the form of the "Two Ways"—one of life, the other of death. This part is generally thought to have originated in or near

---

1. *Odes of Solomon*, in *The Old Testament Pseudepigrapha*, vol. 2, ed. James H. Charlesworth (Garden City, N.Y.: Doubleday, 1985), 726.

Alexandria and will be discussed later in this chapter when we turn to the spirituality of that part of the world. Part 2 of the *Didache* is a manual of church order, that is, a set of regulations about church life that seems to have originated in rural parts of Syria late in the first century. This part provides one of our earliest descriptions of Christian sacramental practice, particularly as regards baptism and the eucharist. The section on baptism specifies a trinitarian formula to be spoken while the candidate is immersed in running water or has water poured three times over the head, while the section on the eucharist emphasizes not only the theme of thanksgiving to God the Father "for the life and knowledge which you made known to us through Jesus your child" but also that of the communion to be experienced by those who partake of the sacrament: "As this broken bread was scattered upon the mountains but was brought together and became one, so let your Church be gathered together from the ends of the earth into your kingdom, for yours is the glory and the power through Jesus Christ forever."[2] The members of the community are also told to pray the Lord's Prayer three times each day (ch. 8). Subsequent chapters of the *Didache* give instructions about how to treat "apostles and prophets" who arrive in a community. The author says that if their teaching is in accord with what he himself has written and so promotes "the increase of righteousness and knowledge of the Lord," then the visitors are to be given a gracious welcome, but even then they are not to stay more than two or three days unless they are willing to work for their living (chs. 11-12). If they do remain and prove to be honest workers, then they should be gifted with the firstfruits of the winepress, threshing floor, and flocks of sheep and oxen; in other cases, these firstfruits are to be given to the poor (ch. 13). After this interlude about visitors, the text returns to the celebration of the eucharist, specifying that the community is to come together on the first day of the week, "the Lord's Day," with no one allowed to participate who has not first been reconciled with another after a quarrel (ch. 14). The sixteenth and final chapter of the *Didache* is a call to vigilance, warning against false prophets and urging the readers to be "frequently gathered together seeking the things which are profitable for your souls" as they await the return of their Lord. One readily sees in this short document a reference to each of those elements of Christian spirituality singled out by Luke in the second and fourth chapters of the Acts of the Apostles: concern for the poor (although without Luke's emphasis that all possessions were held in common, for the practice of strict communism soon fell into abeyance), attentiveness to the

---

2. *Didache* 9, in *Readings in World Christian History*, vol. 1, *Earliest Christianity to 1453*, ed. John W. Coakley and Andrea Sterk (Maryknoll, N.Y.: Orbis Books, 2004), 15.

teaching of those who had shown themselves to be genuine "apostles and prophets," the fostering of fellowship by the text's insistence on reconciliation and on frequent gatherings for mutual support, and the practice of prayer, especially the central prayer of thanksgiving that is the eucharist.

A further feature of early Syriac spirituality, at least in the few works that have come down to us before the fifth century, was its relatively severe asceticism. The word "asceticism" itself refers to training, of the sort that athletes undergo in order to compete successfully. This imagery was already used by Paul in urging the Corinthians to be diligent in their practice of the faith: "Athletes exercise self-control in all things; they do it to receive a perishable wreath, but we an imperishable one" (1 Cor 9:25). Moreover, the Gospels regularly speak of the need for followers of Christ to avoid the accumulation of riches (as in the parable of the rich fool [Lk 12:13-21]) and to be prepared to fast when the bridegroom is no longer with them (Mt 9:15 and parallels). Perhaps most significant of all, Luke adds the word "daily" to Jesus' call for his disciples to take up their cross and follow him: "If any want to become my followers, let them deny themselves and take up their cross daily and follow me" (Lk 9:23; cf. Mt 16:24; Mk 8:34). Such passages, together with the invitation to embrace celibacy for the sake of the kingdom (Mt 19:10-12), were among the most influential inducements to the practice of voluntary asceticism throughout the early Christian world. Ascetic practices were undertaken with particular strictness by groups in Syria known as "sons and daughters of the covenant," who lived within the larger Christian community in small, informal groups that may be considered precursors of formal monastic communities. The fourth-century Syriac author Aphrahat tells us that these groups consisted of two categories of people: virgins, and married persons who had "sanctified themselves" in the sense that they abstained from sexual intercourse. The motivation for such abstinence was not disdain for the body but rather an understanding that baptism allowed one to enter a quasi-paradisal state in which marriage was not itself rejected but only postponed until the eschaton, the final age, when a wedding feast with Christ the Bridegroom would take place.[3] More will be said of early Syriac asceticism when we turn to the monastic movement proper in the next chapter.

North of Edessa lay the semi-independent kingdom of Armenia. Although the Armenian church has a tradition that the Gospel was first brought to that land by the apostle Bartholomew, the first historical record of a mission is that of Gregory the Illuminator, who was born in Armenia in the

3. Sebastian Brock, introduction to *The Syriac Fathers on Prayer and the Spiritual Life*, Cistercian Studies 101 (Kalamazoo, Mich.: Cistercian Publications, 1987), xxv.

last half of the third century, converted to Christianity while living in Asia Minor, and returned to his native land around the year 300. Tradition has it that he was imprisoned for some years for refusing to sacrifice to an Armenian deity but that upon release he was made a bishop in 314 and proceeded to establish the church in Armenia. Among the writings ascribed to him is a "prayer for times of trouble" in which one of the common themes of all Christian (and Jewish) spirituality—repentance for not having lived fully in accord with God's will—is prominent, as seen in the following short excerpt:

> Have mercy on me, God, who have power over all,
> And grant the grace of tears to my sinful soul,
> So that I may wash away the multitude of my sins;
> . . . .
> Receive me into paradise with the perfectly just.
> Receive the prayers of this your sinful servant
> By the intercession of the saints who are pleasing to you,
> Jesus Christ, our Lord.[4]

Around this time a new script was developed for the Armenian language, primarily for the purpose of translating the Bible into Armenian. Christianity quickly became a crucial part of the Armenian national identity, so much so that this became the first country to adopt Christianity as its state religion. Christological controversies in the fourth and fifth centuries led many in the west to label the Armenian church heretical, but today it is generally recognized that the differences in terminology are semantic rather than strictly doctrinal. The rich spirituality that subsequently found expression in the liturgical prayers of this church and its sisters in what are usually called the Oriental Orthodox churches remains a precious resource for all Christians.

Further to the east lay the vast subcontinent of India. Oral traditions hold that the apostle Thomas first brought the gospel to the Malabar coast (modern-day Kerala) and that he was later martyred and buried near Chennai (Madras). Although there is no historical proof of his missionary work in India, it is certainly possible that he went there, for the ships of Greco-Roman traders regularly plied the waters between Egyptian ports on the Red Sea and India at this period.

More definite is the early arrival of Christianity in Egypt. As already mentioned, the first part of the *Didache* is generally thought to have originated in Alexandria, then one of the most important cities in the Mediterranean

4. *Prayers from the East: Traditions of Eastern Christianity*, ed. Richard Marsh (Minneapolis: Fortress, 2004), 10-11.

world. This part of the treatise, dating from sometime in the second century, may itself be a late form of an original catechism into which the author inserted some passages from the Gospels of Matthew and Luke and other early Christian texts. The spirituality of the Sermon on the Mount is evident in the *Didache*'s call to pray for one's enemies, to turn the other cheek, and to go the second mile. Generosity to those in need, so prominent in Luke's description of the early church at Jerusalem, is commanded several times, both in chapter 1 ("Give to everyone that asks you, and do not refuse, for the Father's will is that we give to all from the gifts we have received") and in chapter 5 ("You shall not turn away the needy, but shall share everything with you brother, and shall not say that it is your own, for if you are sharers in the imperishable, how much more in the things which perish?").[5] An honest recognition of one's failings, similar to what we saw earlier in the prayer of St. Gregory the Illuminator, concludes the *Didache*'s teaching on "the way of life" and hints at what would later become a more strictly organized regime of public penance for transgressions: "In the congregation you shall confess your transgressions, and you shall not betake yourself to prayer with an evil conscience. This is the way of life" (ch. 4).

THE SPIRITUALITY OF THE EARLY MARTYRS

If the first part of the *Didache* was indeed written in Alexandria, it was apparently composed prior to any persecution of Christians living there, for it contains no reference to such activity. Over the course of the first four centuries of the church's history, however, there were a number of government-sponsored persecutions, not only in the Roman empire but also in the Persian empire under the Sassanid rulers, who came to power there in the third decade of the third century. The persecutions were often local rather than empire-wide and were frequently directed not against all Christians indiscriminately but only against those who were prominent, whether as leaders of the community or as new converts. There was no one reason uniformly advanced by civil rulers to justify the persecutions, but a common one in the Roman empire was the refusal of Christians to demonstrate their loyalty to the state by sacrificing to its gods, often joined with a suspicion that members of the church were guilty of secret crimes. Such reasoning is evident in a famous letter that the Roman senator Pliny the Younger sent from the province of Bithynia in Asia Minor to the emperor Trajan around the year

5. In *Readings in World Christian History*, 1:13-14.

113. Pliny was seeking guidance from the emperor about how he should deal with persons suspected or accused of being Christians: whether, for example, unsigned papers giving the names of alleged Christians should be honored, and whether any allowance should be made for age. In the course of his letter Pliny described succinctly the procedure he followed with those accused of being Christians: "I asked at their own lips whether they were Christians, and if they confessed, I asked them a second and third time with threats of punishment. If they kept to it, I ordered them for execution; for I held no question that whatever it was that they admitted, in any case obstinacy and unbending perversity deserve to be punished." Then, at the end of his letter, he commented on what he saw as the danger in the Christian religion and the success that his own policy was beginning to have: "The contagion of that superstition has penetrated not the cities only, but the villages and country; yet it seems possible to stop it and set it right. At any rate it is certain enough that the almost deserted temples begin to be resorted to [and] that long disused ceremonies of religion are restored. . . ."[6]

The revival of devotion to the Roman gods to which Pliny refers is but one indication that many Christians did abandon the faith under threat of execution. This became even more evident in the persecution under the emperor Decius in the middle of the third century when, in the words of one historian, "Vast numbers lapsed forthwith. Many denied ever having been Christians. The Church was only saved from ruin by the constancy of a few individuals, coupled with the authorities' lack of organization and means to press home their initial advantage."[7] The very fact that not all members of the church proved courageous enough to die for their faith made the martyrs all the more significant as models held up for imitation, many of them being honored with special devotions on the anniversary of their death. Although there is no consensus among historians about how many were killed during the early persecutions (estimates range from ten thousand to a hundred thousand), we do have important literature by and about some of the most prominent martyrs and can thereby gain a direct insight into their spirituality. One of the earliest such documents was a letter written by a bishop being transported to his death in Rome.

Ignatius, the second bishop of Antioch in Syria, was arrested around the year 110 and taken by ten soldiers (whom he called "leopards") to Rome to be killed by wild beasts in the Colosseum. While traveling overland through

---

6. Pliny the Younger to Trajan, in *Readings in World Christian History*, 1:23-24.
7. W. H. C. Frend, *Martyrdom and Persecution in the Early Church: A Study of a Conflict from the Maccabees to Donatus* (Oxford: Basil Blackwell, 1965), 409.

Asia Minor he wrote seven letters, most of them addressed to Christian communities in that region urging them to promote church unity through obedience to their bishops and opposition to heresy. Altogether different in content and tone was the letter he sent ahead to the Christians in Rome, for this missive was his attempt to dissuade them from doing anything to have him pardoned and so miss the opportunity of quickly attaining the full union with Christ for which he longed. In the previous chapter we saw St. Paul telling the Philippians that his desire was "to depart and be with Christ, for that is far better." If anything, Ignatius's desire for such departure was even more ardent and insistent. In words that have struck some readers as extravagant but that did in fact inspire and encourage many subsequent martyrs to remain firm in their faith, he wrote:

> I am writing to all the churches and assuring them that I am truly in earnest about dying for God—if only you yourselves put no obstacles in the way . . . I am His wheat, ground fine by the lions' teeth to be made purest bread for Christ ...
>
> This is the first stage of my discipleship, and no power, visible or invisible, must grudge me my coming to Jesus Christ. Fire, cross, beast-fighting, hacking and quartering, splintering of bone and mangling of limb, even the pulverizing of my entire body—let every horrid and diabolical torment come upon me, provided only that I can win my way to Jesus Christ.[8]

Among the seven letters that Ignatius wrote while still on his way to Rome was one addressed not to a particular Christian community but to an individual, Polycarp, at that time the young bishop of Smyrna in Asia Minor. About a half-century later Polycarp himself, then in his mid-eighties, was himself arrested during a flaring up of violence against Christians in that city. The *passio,* or account of his death, written in the form of a letter sent from the church at Smyrna to a sister community in Phrygia and containing the request that it be sent on to still other churches, is the earliest surviving account of a martyrdom outside the New Testament. Since Christ himself is called "the faithful martyr [or witness]" in the Book of Revelation (Rev 1:5 and 3:14) and since the early church often designated him as "the first martyr," it is not surprising that the *passio* describing Polycarp's suffering and death should have a number of parallels with details of the final days of

8. Ignatius of Antioch, *The Epistle to the Romans*, in *Early Christian Writings*, trans. Maxwell Staniforth (London: Penguin, 1968), 87.

Christ's life as described in the Gospels: the person who betrayed Polycarp's whereabouts to the civil authorities was a member of his own household, the official who was resolved to have him put to death was named Herod, and he was taken to the city mounted on an ass, even as Christ entered Jerusalem a few days before his own passion (Mk 11:7). Even more significant is the prayer that Polycarp is said to have uttered while bound to the stake in the arena, for it seems to mirror the eucharistic prayer that he would have said each Sunday, the elderly bishop himself now being the offering in place of the bread and wine consecrated at the eucharist:

> O Lord God Almighty, Father of your blessed and beloved Son Jesus Christ, through whom we have been given knowledge of yourself, you are the God of angels and powers, of the whole creation, and of all the generations of the righteous who live in your sight. I bless you for granting me this day and hour that I may be numbered among the martyrs, to share the cup of your Anointed and to rise again to life everlasting, both in body and soul, in the immortality of the Holy Spirit. May I be received among them this day in your presence, a sacrifice rich and acceptable, even as you did appoint and foreordain and do now bring to pass, for you are the God of truth and in you there is no falsehood. For this, and for all else besides, I praise you, I bless you, I glorify you, through our eternal High Priest in heaven, your beloved Son Jesus Christ, by whom and with whom be glory to you and the Holy Spirit, now and for all ages to come. Amen.[9]

After Polycarp had been executed and the centurion had had his body burned, some members of the church gathered up his bones and laid them in a suitable place (left unnamed in the *passio* for security reasons) where the congregation could later assemble for prayer, especially on the anniversary of his death, here for the first time called the saint's *natalis,* or heavenly birthday. Such reverence for the saint's bodily remains developed into the custom of regularly having relics of martyrs encased in the altars used for the celebration of the eucharist. The author of Polycarp's *passio* also alludes to the exemplary nature of his death, saying that "he was a martyr without peer, and one whose martyrdom all aspire to imitate, so fully does it accord with the Gospel of Christ."[10]

Whereas the persecution that led to Polycarp's death was localized, a broader persecution broke out toward the beginning of the third century, dur-

---

9. *The Martyrdom of Polycarp* 14, in *Early Christian Writings,* 129-30. Translation slightly modernized.

10. Ibid., 19.

ing the reign of the emperor Septimius Severus, this one directed especially against new converts in order to discourage still other persons from embracing the Christian faith. Among those arrested in the North African city of Carthage was a young noblewoman named Perpetua, along with her slave, Felicity, and several male catechumens. The account of their martyrdom is a collection of various documents, including a passage written by Perpetua herself, one of the very few surviving first-person narratives written by a woman in the first Christian millennium. She recounts in some detail the various attempts by her pagan father to have her renounce the faith for both his sake and that of her infant son. Despite her grief at his anguish, she refused to offer sacrifice for the well-being of the emperors, nor would Felicity. The latter woman, eight months pregnant, feared that she would not be able to be executed with the others since Roman law forbade such punishment in the case of pregnant women, but her child was delivered a month prematurely and entrusted to the care of her sister, allowing both Felicity and Perpetua to be martyred on the same day. The two women were first attacked in the arena by a wild heifer, and when that did not kill them they were put to the sword, first embracing one another "that they might consummate their martyrdom with the kiss of peace . . . Perpetua, that she might taste some pain, being pierced between the ribs cried out loudly, and she herself placed the wavering right hand of the youthful gladiator to her throat."[11] These penultimate lines of the *passio* are followed by a concluding sentence espousing the hope that this new account of Christian bravery might serve "for the edification of the Church not less than the ancient ones, so that new virtues also may testify that one and the same Holy Spirit is always operating even until now . . ."

Hundreds of miles to the east and a century and a half later, a persecution of Christians broke out in the Sassanid empire of Persia, brought on by the government's suspicion that Persian Christians were disloyal to the state and its officially Zoroastrian regime. One of those killed was King Shapur II's master craftsman, Posi. Subsequently his daughter Martha was also arrested and threatened with the same fate. The account of her martyrdom places on her lips sentiments akin to those of Perpetua but with more explicitly trinitarian references, as in the prayer she uttered just before her execution by the sword:

> At your hands, Jesus, the true High Priest, may I be offered up as a pure, holy, and acceptable offering before the glorious Trinity of the hidden Being, in whose name you taught us to be instructed and baptized. Visit,

11. *The Martyrdom of Perpetua and Felicity*, trans. R. E. Wallis, in *The Ante-Nicene Fathers*, vol. 3 (Buffalo: Christian Literature Co., 1885), 706.

> Lord, your persecuted people; preserve them in true faith in the midst of their enemies, and may they be found like pure gold in the furnace of persecution that has been erected against your people; may they be strengthened in the worship of your majesty, fearlessly worshipping and confessing Father, Son, and Holy Spirit, now and always and for eternal ages. Amen.[12]

Such accounts of martyrdom unquestionably strengthened the resolve of many early Christians when faced with the threat of execution by the state. But whether or not the church was undergoing persecution at a particular time or in a particular locale, there was also need for another kind of edification, sound teaching, including that of how a Christian could best live out the Pauline ideal of being "in Christ." Since Alexandria with its famous library was in these early Christian centuries a preeminent center of learning, it is fitting that two of the most influential spiritual teachers of the second and third centuries—Clement of Alexandria and Origen—should have done much of their work in that city. We will conclude this chapter by looking at their accomplishment.

CLEMENT OF ALEXANDRIA AND ORIGEN

Clement, born around the middle of the second century, is especially remembered for his three treatises: the *Protrepticus* (Exhortation to the Greeks), the *Paedagogus* (The Instructor), and the *Stromata* (Miscellanies). One of his major aims was to of combat the Gnostic doctrines that had sprung up in that part of the world and had by the second century been systematized by teachers such as Basilides and Valentinus. Although there were major differences among the myths taught in the various Gnostic systems, they had in common a severe dualism according to which the material world was believed to have been created by an inferior deity or demiurge. Salvation was accordingly understood as escape from the material realm, a liberation attainable through knowledge (*gnōsis*) of one's essentially spiritual nature. Clement sought to show that true *gnōsis* was to be found not in any of these systems but in the New Testament teaching about the mystery of God's saving will revealed in Jesus Christ. He accordingly taught that "if the Lord is 'truth' and the 'wisdom and power of God,' as indeed he is, it is shown that the real gnostic is

12. *The Martyrdom of Martha, Daughter of Posi, Who Was a Daughter of the Covenant*, in *Holy Women of the Syrian Orient*, ed. and trans. Sebastian P. Brock and Susan Ashbrook Harvey (Berkeley: University of California Press, 1987), 71.

the one who knows him and knows the Father through him."[13] Although this emphasis on knowledge might seem to imply that genuine Christianity is restricted to a certain elite, those who were "in the know," Clement was actually making the realistic assumption that relatively few persons make the effort seriously to deepen their faith. He also helped guard himself against any charge of intellectualist elitism by insisting on the centrality of love in the life of a Christian gnostic, as when he wrote: "God is love and is knowable (*gnōstos*) to those who love Him . . . We must enter into His intimacy by the divine love (*agapē*) so that we can contemplate the like by the like" (*Strom.* 5.1).

More questionable in Clement's spiritual teaching was the way he spoke of passionlessness (*apatheia*), especially in the later books of the *Stromata*. Being one of the most learned and widely read scholars of his day, Clement knew well the writings of the Stoic philosophers, one of whose major themes was *apatheia*. When understood as referring to a way of life in which the various desires or passions are harmoniously ordered to a noble end, *apatheia* is a fully acceptable way of describing one of the goals of Christian spirituality. There are, however, passages in Clement that go considerably beyond this, as when he writes that whereas the Christian gnostic is subject only to the desires needed for the maintenance of the body, such as those for food and drink, the Savior did not even experience these but ate and drank only so that those who were with him would not think that he did not have a real body at all. Rather, "he was entirely impassible (*apathēs*), not liable to any movement of feeling, whether pleasure or pain" (*Strom.* 6.9). In like manner the apostles, having already mastered the feelings of anger, fear, and lust through the Lord's teaching while he walked among them, were after his resurrection not liable even to those affections that otherwise seem good, such as courage or joy: courage would be pointless since nothing could any longer inspire fear in them, nor could they feel joy, since they no longer fell into any pain, being persuaded that all things happen well (ibid.).

One obvious difficulty with what Clement here says about Christ is its incompatibility with the way the Gospels portray him as a man of deep and wide-ranging feelings. Jesus regularly became angry with those who were hypocritical or hard of heart, as on the occasion when he cured a man with a withered hand on the Sabbath and some of the onlookers saw this only as an opportunity to accuse him of breaking the Mosaic Law. Mark writes: "He looked around at them with anger; he was grieved at their hardness of heart"

13. Clement of Alexandria, *Stromata* 2.11, in idem, *Stromata*, books 1-6, ed. Otto Stählin and Ludwig Früchtel, 3rd ed. (Berlin: Akademie-Verlag, 1960). My translation.

(Mk 3:5). Later in the same Gospel, when Jesus went with his disciples to the Garden of Gethsemane shortly before his arrest, he took three of his closest followers farther into the garden and there "began to be distressed and agitated. And he said to them, 'I am deeply grieved, even to death; remain here, and keep awake'" (Mk 14:33-34). Clement of Alexandria's portrayal of a savior "not liable to any movement of feeling, whether pleasure or pain" does not begin to do justice to the profound humanity of Jesus conveyed by those Gospel passages, or by the one in which he rejoiced at the way his Father revealed his deepest secrets not to the learned and clever but to the merest children (Mt 11:25).

Even though Clement's depiction of Jesus and of the ideal Christian gnostic found an echo among some later Christian writers, there were some early objections to an excessively Stoic understanding of the passions. Lactantius, a fourth-century author whose *Divine Institutes* are the first systematic Latin account of the Christian attitude toward life, protested in the strongest terms against the teaching of those who considered feelings like pity, desire, or fear to be signs of a flawed spirituality. "Who," he asked, "is able not to grieve if pestilence has emptied his country, or if an enemy has destroyed it, or if a tyrant has oppressed it? Can anyone not grieve if he sees his liberty taken away, if his nearest relatives, friends, or good persons are done away with or most cruelly slaughtered? Only he [could not grieve] whose mind has been so hardened that all feeling has been snatched away from him."[14]

Clement himself would have experienced events similar to those named by Lactantius, for early in the third century the empire-wide persecution that led to the martyrdom of Perpetua and Felicity in Carthage also broke out in Alexandria, leading Clement to flee the city. Among those killed in Alexandria during this persecution was a certain Leonides, the father of Origen. Eusebius writes in his *Ecclesiastical History* that Origen, then in his teens, himself sought martyrdom on that occasion and would have followed his father had not his mother hidden his clothes to force him to stay indoors! Soon thereafter he became qualified to teach grammar as a way of supporting the now fatherless family, and several years after that he began teaching Christian doctrine to certain pagans who came to him with the request to learn more about the faith. Before long he dropped the teaching of grammar altogether and devoted all his energies to catechesis. That he was able to do so while the persecution was continuing under a succession of prefects is probably best explained by the fact that only Christians of the higher classes were then being hunted down. Origen's father seems to have been among

14. Lactantius, *Divinae institutiones* 6.15, in idem, *Opera Omnia*, 2 vols. (Paris, 1748), 1:476. My translation.

them, but if Origen's mother was an Egyptian, her son would have shared his mother's lower status and thereby avoided serious harassment by the police.

Origen's taking over the leadership of the catechetical school in Alexandria was but the first step in a career that has led some to call him the church's first great theologian. We have already seen in the first two chapters of this book that in his commentaries and homilies on Scripture Origen regularly sought what he called "the spiritual sense," as when he found Christ prefigured in various ways in the account of Abraham's testing in Genesis 22. In much greater detail, Origen likewise saw Christ prefigured in one of the shortest books of the First Testament, the Song of Songs. Originally a collection of love poems between a man and a woman, this book was regularly understood by the Jewish rabbis as a dialogue between God and his bride, the people of Israel. This approach was adopted and modified by St. Hippolytus of Rome in the early third century by taking the bride to be the church. While retaining this interpretation, Origen was the first Christian writer to see the text as referring also to the love between Christ and the individual soul. He thereby became the first in a long line of Christian spiritual writers to approach the Song of Songs in this way, some of his best-known successors being Gregory of Nyssa, Bernard of Clairvaux, Teresa of Avila, and John of the Cross.

Another important aspect of Origen's *Commentary on the Song of Songs* is his treatment of the way this book of the Bible deals with what he calls contemplation (*theōria*). The influence of Greek, especially Platonic, philosophy is evident here, as when he speaks in the prologue of contemplation as the activity by which we know "something of divine and heavenly things and gaze at them with the mind alone," but there are other passages in the prologue that make it clear that this contemplative gaze is not severely intellectual but is also a matter of love. He spells this out at some length and with more than a hint of his own personal love of Christ, when, in the commentary itself, he writes as follows on the verse "I have been wounded by love" (Sg 2:5):

> If there is ever anyone who at any time has burned with this faithful love for the Word of God; if there is anyone who, as the Prophet says, has received the sweet wound of him who is the "chosen dart"; if there is anyone who has been pierced with the lovable spear of his knowledge so that he sighs and longs for him day and night . . . and is not disposed to desire, seek, or hope for anything other than him; then such a soul truly says, "I have been wounded by love."[15]

15. Origen, *Commentary on the Song of Songs* 3.8, in idem, *The Song of Songs: Commentary and Homilies*, trans. R. P. Lawson, Ancient Christian Writers 26 (Westminster, Md.: Newman Press, 1957), 198. Translation slightly modernized.

In another of his spiritual works, the treatise *On Prayer*, which he wrote at the request of his friend and patron Ambrose of Alexandria, Origen offered not only general reflections on this central practice of Christian devotion but also one of the earliest commentaries on the Lord's Prayer. Two points in the treatise are of special interest. First, like many later writers in the Christian tradition, he considered how one might fulfill St. Paul's injunction to the Thessalonians, "Pray without ceasing" (1 Thess 5:17). Origen distinguished between prayer in the narrow sense of addressing certain words to God and prayer in the broad sense of the way one lives: That person prays without ceasing "who unites prayer with the deeds required and right deeds with prayer. For the only way we can accept the command to 'pray constantly' as referring to a real possibility is by saying that the entire life of the saint taken as a whole is a single great prayer. What is customarily called prayer is, then, a part of this prayer."[16] Most persons today would probably agree that this interpretation of the verse from First Thessalonians is more in accord with St. Paul's own thinking than are those interpretations that recommend the frequent repetition of a short prayer formula as a way of praying "without ceasing."

Surely more questionable for persons reading Origen today are some of his comments on petitions in the Lord's Prayer. To be fair to Origen, it should be noted that he did not in any way regard matter as evil, but there is nevertheless in his work a pronounced dualism between spirit and matter. Human beings, for example, are essentially "rational beings" (*logika*) or "minds" (*noēs*), created from all eternity and originally intended to remain in constant contemplation of their Creator.[17] In book 1 of his important treatise *On First Principles* Origen claims that almost all of these beings voluntarily and culpably fell away from this contemplation. Those who sinned least became angels; those who sinned most became demons; and those rational beings or *noēs* who sinned to an intermediate degree became human souls (*psychai*), bound to a body and placed in this terrestrial world as a place of correction so that by living holy lives they might, after death, return to the heavenly realm—clothed now with a "resurrection body"—and once more enjoy the bliss of contemplating the divine Beauty.

This view of the corporeal and material, seeing it not as evil but as definitely of much lower worth than the spiritual, is evident in the way Origen

16. Origen, *On Prayer* 12.2, in *Origen: An Exhortation to Martyrdom, Prayer* [and other works], trans. Rowan A. Greer, Classics of Western Spirituality (New York: Paulist, 1979), 104.

17. In fact, Origen's teaching about the preexistence of souls, as well as his tendency to subordinate the Son to the Father and certain other teachings, led to his later being declared a heretic. In 543 the emperor Justinian ordered his works destroyed. Many survived, at least in Latin translation, but the emperor's decree did result in the loss of a great body of work by a monumental Christian thinker.

comments on the verse about requesting "our daily bread" in the Lord's Prayer. Whereas many writers today, especially liberation theologians, see this petition as integrally connected with the call to provide healthy food to the poor and undernourished of this world, Origen moves in a very different direction, asking: "How can the One [Jesus] who says we must ask for heavenly and great things have us ask for bread to be given for our flesh, since that is not a heavenly thing nor is the request for it a great thing? It would be as though He had forgotten His own teaching and ordered us to offer supplication to the Father for an earthly and small thing" (*On Prayer* 27.1; Greer p. 137). Throughout this volume we will come across similar sentiments in other writers who had much less appreciation of the body than most Christians today would find appropriate.

Among Origen's many other works, which include hundreds of homilies that have come down to us either in the original Greek or, more often, in Latin translation, was a second work that he composed for Ambrose of Alexandria, the *Exhortation to Martyrdom*. At one point Ambrose and a priest named Protoctetus were arrested and were facing martyrdom for their faith. To encourage them to remain steadfast, Origen drew on many passages from the Bible, including the description of the seven sons put to death before their mother's eyes in the seventh chapter of 2 Maccabees. Origen urges his two friends to be just as brave as those young men and so attain liberation from the fetters of this life. Near the end of this treatise he sums up his argument in a way that clearly refers to his understanding of the human person as essentially a "rational being" or "mind," for he writes:

> the mind preserves a relation to what is intelligible and to God, who transcends the intelligible order. Therefore, why do we hang back and hesitate to put off the perishable body, the earthly tent that hinders us, weighs down the soul, and burdens the thoughtful mind? Why do we hesitate to burst our bonds and to depart from the stormy billows of a life with flesh and blood? Let our purpose be to enjoy with Christ Jesus the rest proper to blessedness, contemplating Him, the Word, wholly living. (*Exhortation to Martyrdom* 47; Greer p. 76)

Origen himself would later have a chance to heed his own exhortation, for in the middle of the third century, while he was living in Caesarea in Palestine, he was arrested and tortured in the general persecution launched by the Roman emperor Decius. The tortures inflicted on Origen are described in excruciating detail by the historian Eusebius, and he would likely have died on the rack had not the persecution ended when Decius was killed in battle.

It is generally believed that Origen lived only a short while longer, dying about the year 253. Persecutions would break out from time to time during the next six decades, but with the accession of Constantine to the throne and the proclamation of the Edict of Milan in 313, extending rights and toleration to Christians, the period of imperial opposition to the church came to an end. In the words of W. H. C. Frend, for all the harm that persecution had done to the church, in the end it "had failed as a policy . . . The pagan world had had enough, enough of bloodshed, enough of the butchers' shop in service to the gods, enough of the deaths of men known to be upright, learned and brave. As the killing went on, so more turned to Christ . . . for pagans wanted to know more about this belief which men were prepared to defend to the death, and having learnt, accepted it themselves."[18]

It was at this time that the monastic movement began to flourish. Sometimes called "the white martyrdom," it provided another way to witness to the faith now that the red martyrdom of the Roman persecutions had come to an end. To this other form of witness we will turn in the next chapter.

QUESTIONS FOR REFLECTION

1. What role do you think asceticism should play in the practice of Christian spirituality? What criteria would most effectively help keep ascetical practices from becoming excessive?
2. Do you find Ignatius of Antioch's ardent desire for martyrdom to be inspirational or inordinate? How would you justify your position?
3. What motivations do you think would be most conducive for helping a person facing martyrdom to stand firm in his or her resolve?
4. Do you consider *apatheia* an ideal toward which Christians should strive? Why or why not?
5. How did Origen's understanding of the essential nature of human beings affect his appreciation of the body? How might your understanding differ from his?

SUGGESTIONS FOR FURTHER READING AND STUDY

On the Spirituality of the Early Christian Communities

The Didache. In *Readings in World Christian History*, vol. 1, *Earliest Christianity to 1453*, edited by John W. Coakley and Andrea Sterk, 12-16. Maryknoll, N.Y.: Orbis Books, 2004.

---

18. Frend, *Martyrdom and Persecution*, 520-21.

Brock, Sebastian, ed. *The Syriac Fathers on Prayer and the Spiritual Life*. Cistercian Studies 101. Kalamazoo, Mich.: Cistercian Publications, 1987. See especially the chapter on Aphrahat (pp. 1-28), which contains his "Demonstration IV: On Prayer."

McGinn, Bernard, John Meyendorff, and Jean Leclercq, eds. *Christian Spirituality: Origins to the Twelfth Century*. World Spirituality 16. New York: Crossroad, 1985. See especially the essays by John Zizioulis, "The Early Christian Community" (pp. 23-43), and Roberta Bondi, "The Spirituality of Syriac-Speaking Christians" (pp. 152-61).

On the Spirituality of the Early Martyrs

Coakley, John W., and Andrea Sterk, eds. *Readings in World Christian History*. Volume 1, *Earliest Christianity to 1453*. Maryknoll, N.Y.: Orbis Books, 2004. See especially "Correspondence of Pliny and Trajan" (pp. 23-24), "The Martyrs of Lyons (Letter of the Churches of Lyons and Vienne, ca. 177)" (pp. 24-30), "The Martyrdom of Perpetua and Felicity" (pp. 30-37), and "The Martyrdom of Martha, Daughter of Posi, Who Was a Daughter of the Covenant" (pp. 110-12).

Early Christian Writings: The Apostolic Fathers. Translated by Maxwell Staniforth. London: Penguin, 1968. See especially Ignatius of Antioch's *Epistle to the Romans* (pp. 83-89) and *The Martyrdom of Polycarp* (pp. 125-35).

On Clement of Alexandria and Origen

Clement of Alexandria. *Stromateis: Books One to Three*. Translated by John Ferguson. Fathers of the Church 85. Washington, D.C.: Catholic University of America Press, 1991. See especially book 2, chapter 20, "Indispensable Role of Asceticism" (pp. 226-40).

Osborn, E. F. *The Philosophy of Clement of Alexandria*. Cambridge: Cambridge University Press, 1957.

Origen. *An Exhortation to Martyrdom; Prayer; First Principles: Book IV; Prologue to the Commentary on the Song of Songs; Homily XXVII on Numbers*. Translated by Rowan A. Greer. Classics of Western Spirituality. New York: Paulist, 1979.

Crouzel, Henri. *Origen: The Life and Thought of the First Great Theologian*. Translated by A. S. Worrall. San Francisco: Harper & Row, 1989. See especially part 3, "Spirituality" (pp. 85-149).

4

The Beginnings of the Monastic Movement

THERE IS NO SINGLE REASON why the "white martyrdom" of the monastic movement expanded rapidly in the fourth century, but one reason certainly arose out of the fact that when Christianity came to be tolerated by the Roman government after the Edict of Milan in 313 and eventually became the state religion, it became advantageous for social reasons for persons to embrace it. Many of these converts were lax in their religious observance, leading more fervent Christians to conclude that it would be better to withdraw to settings where they would not be exposed to the influence of their less devout co-religionists. These early monastics[1] often looked to the martyrs as their exemplars, as noted by an anonymous author of the life of the Egyptian monk Pachomius: "When those who . . . had become monks had seen the struggles and patient endurance of the martyrs, they began to renew their life . . . [They looked] not only to Christ crucified but also to the martyrs, whom they had seen take up the struggle as they had."[2] Some others no doubt took up the monastic way of life in order to avoid conscription into the army or other hardships imposed on citizens of the Roman empire. It has also occasionally been said that all that is needed to explain the rise of monasticism in any part of the Christian world is the presence of Scripture. Whatever merit one might ascribe to this claim in other contexts, it can certainly be argued in the case of the man sometimes called "the father of monasticism," Antony of Egypt (also known as Antony the Great or Antony of the Desert), who embraced the monastic life while persecutions were still going on. A survey of major themes in his life and teaching will serve as a helpful introduction to the monastic life as a whole.

---

1. Since there were both men and women who followed the monastic way of life, in recent years the term "monastic" has come to be used as a noun, thereby avoiding the need to use the two nouns "monks" and "nuns" to refer to these persons.

2. *The First Greek Life of Pachomius*, in *Pachomian Koinonia*, vol. 1, trans. Armand Veilleux, Cistercian Studies 45 (Kalamazoo, Mich.: Cistercian Publications, 1980), 298.

ANTONY OF EGYPT

Antony was born of Christian parents in Middle Egypt around the year 251, when Origen was being tortured in the Decian persecution. In the *Life of Antony*, written in Greek and traditionally ascribed to St. Athanasius, bishop of Alexandria, we read that while still in his late teens Antony, now an orphan, one day entered a church as the Gospel was being read. The passage included Jesus' words to the rich young man: "If you wish to be perfect, go, sell your possessions and give the money to the poor, and you will have treasure in heaven; then come, follow me" (Mt 19:21). Having been raised a Christian, Antony would have heard these words before, but on this occasion he felt they were being directed specifically at him. This reading, together with a similar passage on a subsequent day, led him to sell all that he had and give the proceeds to the poor. Entrusting his younger sister to the care of a community of virgins, he determined to learn all he could from the various male ascetics who lived in the vicinity. The author of the *Life* writes that Antony observed the graciousness of one, the earnestness in prayer of another, the kindheartness of one and the physical austerity of another, but "in one and all alike he marked especially devotion to Christ and the love they had for one another."[3]

For the next two decades Antony lived primarily in solitude, first at a place near his former home, then in an empty burial vault, and subsequently in a deserted fort at Pispir on the east bank of the Nile, with food brought to him at intervals by some of his friends, but eventually those who wished to learn from his holiness persuaded him to leave his solitude. Now in middle age, Antony is said to have emerged from the fort sound in mind and body. For the rest of his life he maintained a rhythm of withdrawal to a wilderness retreat at the "Inner Mountain" about seventy-five miles east of the Nile, followed by regular return to populated areas along the river, whether to give instruction to other monks, encourage prisoners awaiting martyrdom in Alexandria, or rebut persons espousing the Arian heresy. In these ways, the author of the *Life* shows Antony as modeling the kind of love and concern for others that he had earlier observed in all of the ascetics living near his native village. He writes that God gave Antony "charm in speaking, and so he comforted many in sorrow, and others who were quarreling he made friends. He exhorted all to prefer nothing in the world to the love of Christ. And when in his discourse he exhorted them to be mindful of the good things to

3. Athanasius, *The Life of Saint Antony* 4, trans. Robert T. Meyer, Ancient Christian Writers 10 (New York: Newman Press, 1978), 21.

come and of the goodness shown us by God . . . he induced many to take up the monastic life" (*Life* 14; Meyer pp. 32-33).

It is this latter phrase that has given Antony the sobriquet "father of Christian monasticism," and there is no doubt but that he did inspire many to embrace a life of strict poverty and celibacy. The term ought not, however, be understood as though Antony was introducing some entirely new way of life. The *Life* itself indicates that there were already some persons called monks at the time Antony retreated to the desert, and it seems certain that the lifestyle of these monks was in strict continuity with that of all those persons who, from the very beginning of the Christian movement, had taken quite seriously Jesus' words about giving up one's possessions and making oneself a eunuch for the sake of the kingdom of heaven (Mt 19:10-30). These ascetics or "renunciants" (*apotaktikoi*) withdrew from the normal round of social life and obligations, but at the beginning most of them remained in an urban setting. One of today's principal historians of early monasticism, James E. Goehring, points out that "Antony's innovation lay not in the idea of withdrawal per se, but in its translation from an ethical to a physical plane . . . through [his] flight to ever more remote retreats."[4]

There is no doubt that Antony's way of life, especially in his solitary retreat at the Inner Mountain, was rigorous by any standards, but the author of the *Life* makes much of the fact that Antony's strict regime of prayer and fasting did not in any sense break his health or depress his spirits. On the contrary, he writes that if Antony were present in a gathering of monks and someone with no previous acquaintance with him wished to see him, he could at once pick Antony out of the crowd, not because of his stature but because of his settled character and the purity of his soul, which "was imperturbed, and so his outward appearance was calm. The joy in his soul expressed itself in the cheerfulness of his face, and from the body's behavior one saw and knew the state of his soul, as Scripture says: 'When the heart is glad, the face is radiant'" (*Life* 67; Meyer p. 77).

Elsewhere in the *Life* there is a long discourse attributed to Antony, dealing mostly with the fearlessness with which the monks ought to deal with demonic temptations. There is no way of knowing exactly how much of such teaching goes back to Antony himself and how much is to be attributed to his biographer, but this ambiguity is not of the greatest moment as regards our understanding the spirituality of early Christian monasticism, for both Antony and his biographer were deeply devoted to the monastic ideal and wished to promote it. Indeed, the prologue to the *Life* expresses the desire to

4. James E. Goehring, *Ascetics, Society, and the Desert: Studies in Early Egyptian Monasticism* (Harrisburg, Pa.: Trinity Press International, 1999), 25.

present Antony as a model that others would want to emulate. This desire definitely came to fruition, for the work became one of the first Christian best-sellers, already being read in Latin translation in distant Gaul less than twenty years after it was written. It served as the literary model for St. Jerome's lives of the early monks Paul and Hilarion and, as we will see, was described by St. Augustine in his *Confessions* as one of the crucial factors in his own conversion.

If one had to single out two short passages in the *Life* as best encapsulating the spirit that animated Antony, they would very likely be ones already quoted above: first, the passage noting that what the young Antony found in each and every ascetic whom he visited before going off into solitude himself was their "devotion to Christ and the love they had for one another"; and, second, the passage describing Antony's exhortation to his friends when he emerged from the solitude of the deserted fort, urging them "to prefer nothing in the world to the love of Christ." Love of God (here transposed into terms of the love of God incarnate in Jesus Christ) and love of neighbor were the two great commandments enunciated in the Gospel and were surely in the background of St. Paul's teaching that love is the fulfillment of the law (Rom 13:10). Even though some later monks were motivated largely by an urge to outdo others in feats of asceticism, at its best the monastic movement had love as its driving force. Apart from this, the movement would not even have begun, nor would it have flourished. This will become ever more evident as we continue this survey.

PACHOMIUS

Around the time that Antony was in Alexandria in the year 311 in order to give encouragement to Christians undergoing persecution there, a young pagan Copt named Pachomius was conscripted into the Roman army and billeted in the city of Thebes in Upper Egypt, about six hundred kilometers south of Alexandria. Some Theban Christians mercifully brought food and drink to the conscripts, who were under heavy guard lest they try to escape. Pachomius's later biographers, whose lives of the saint have come down to us in Greek as well as in various Coptic dialects, state that upon learning that his benefactors were Christians, he prayed to the Christian God, promising that he would one day serve his fellows in the same way. Upon being discharged from the army, he received instructions in the Christian faith, was baptized, and after several years adopted a strictly ascetic life under the guidance of an elderly hermit named Palamon. One day, while praying near the deserted village of Tabennesi, Pachomius heard a voice telling him to build a monastery there and prepare to receive many monks into that new community. With Palamon's consent he did so and soon began to receive numerous disciples. Eventually, his followers are said to have numbered as many as three thousand, divided into nine affiliated monasteries of men and two of women, one of the latter being presided over by his own sister. These foundations have often led historians to call Pachomius the father of cenobitic monasticism (that is, monks living in community rather than in solitude as hermits), but this is misleading. In his day there were already some cenobitic monasteries that he had not founded. His innovation was of a somewhat different nature, for he was responsible for the system of affiliated monasteries, the *koinōnia*, which became the forerunner of later congregations or federations of monastic communities.

In the course of time, Pachomius provided written legislation for the governance of these communities, the first instance in Christian history of a written monastic rule. It is not for this, however, nor for the system of affiliation that he is most significant for Christian spirituality. As his modern biographer Philip Rousseau has written,

> Specific advice—on prayer, for example, or on the day-to-day conduct of community life—was certainly necessary and was committed to writing at an early stage, but it was Pachomius himself who was the "rule" in the fullest sense. The personal example of his service, the fruit of his own experience, above all his insight into scripture, conveyed in frequent catechesis: those were the indispensable keys to his enduring influence. It is leadership we are dealing with, more than legislation.[5]

That term "leadership" has many connotations. For some, it conjures up images of someone who quite ruthlessly pursues his own vision of how things should be, drawing after him those who are of the same mind and simply abandoning those who see things differently. A "strong leader" may imply someone who will not be pushed around, who never yields on any point. This was not Pachomius's way, and it was not his way because he did not see leadership of this sort in his own model, Jesus Christ. A passage in one of the early lives of Pachomius brings this out with all possible clarity. His monasteries being so large, Pachomius divided each one into a group of "houses," with each house comprising twenty or so monks under their own housemaster. The text in question says that Pachomius himself humbly submitted to

---

5. Philip Rousseau, *Pachomius: The Making of a Community in Fourth-Century Egypt* (Berkeley and Los Angeles: University of California Press, 1985), 106.

the master of the house in which his own individual cell was located. Even though he was especially adept at expounding the Scriptures and at the beginning of the *koinōnia* had attracted many persons to the monastic way of life through his reputation as a gifted and holy speaker, at the hour of catechetical instruction in that particular house he would stand listening with all the other monks as the housemaster spoke. "For more than the eternal tortures," the text concludes, "he feared becoming estranged from the humility and the sweetness of the Son of God, our Lord Jesus Christ."[6]

Other passages in the lives of Pachomius recount stories in which he treated recalcitrant monks with great gentleness, but one should not infer from such accounts that Pachomius was excessively lenient. He could at times be very strict, especially with those who he felt would profit from harsh reprimands, but whether gentle or harsh his goal was always the same: a community built on mutual respect and mutual support, the fulfillment of Jesus' new commandment as given in John's Gospel: "Love one another as I have loved you." In Rousseau's words, Pachomius

> fully accepted responsibility as a teacher, anxious always for individuals, in all their variety, and never content merely to create or transmit an abstract and beautiful view of the cosmos . . . The confidence of [his] early disciples sprang not from a sense of arrival, but from recognizing new possibilities in themselves and from seeing in Pachomius a man who would lead them "straight to God" . . . The *delectatio* [joy] that came from prayer and companionship, the sense of "feasting in heaven," the desire for enduring contact with "the humility and sweetness" of Jesus himself: those were not experiences that a rule could impose . . . They had to be discovered and recognized by each monk personally, often in moments of unexpected loneliness and silence.[7]

Much more could be said about Pachomian monasticism—references to the kinds of work the monks did, the times of day at which they gathered to pray and to have their meals, the nature of the catechetical instruction and common discussion that took place on a regular basis. All that is far from unimportant, but the heart of this early form of cenobitic monasticism lies rather in the person of Pachomius himself, a living rule for his monks. For that reason, and as one might expect, at his death there was a crisis of leadership, and the whole enterprise gradually declined in both spirit and numbers. This has led one monastic scholar, Adalbert de Vogüé, to ask whether

6. *The First Greek Life of Pachomius* 110, in *Pachomian Koinonia*, 1:374.
7. Rousseau, *Pachomius*, 148.

those early cenobites of Upper Egypt were deceiving themselves as to their communities' chances of survival. In one sense they were, for the rules and traditions, the organization and hierarchy, the buildings and congregation all but disappeared. There is another way of looking at it, however, which is the way de Vogüé takes in writing that "in truth, the *Koinonia* of the sons of Pachomius has not ceased to exist. It is found wherever brothers gather together in the love of Christ to live in total sharing, perfect charity, and the renunciation of self-will 'under a rule and a father.'"[8]

THE SAYINGS OF THE DESERT FATHERS AND MOTHERS

Among those who imbibed some of the wisdom of Antony once he emerged from the deserted fort were a number of persons who themselves became monastic leaders, monks like Hilarion, who helped spread the monastic way of life in Palestine; Macarius the Elder, spiritual father to several thousand monks in the desert of Scetis in Lower Egypt; and Amoun, founder of monasticism at Nitria, just north of Scetis. Even as these leaders had once learned from Antony and other elders, so too did younger disciples start coming to them for advice. There were also important women monastics; these generally resided in or near cities and towns, although some lived farther out in desert areas like most of the monks.

At first, the sayings of those reputed for their monastic wisdom were passed on orally, but after several generations written collections of these sayings began to be made. Several such collections have come down to us, some arranged thematically, others alphabetically according to the name of the speaker. Rather frequently they begin with some such line as this: "A young monk came one day to an elder and said, 'Father, give me a word by which I may live.'" In other words, what was sought was wise guidance of a very personal sort, which means that some of the sayings in these collections sound inconsistent with others since the advice pertinent for one disciple might differ radically from the advice another needed to hear. There are, however, a number of these texts that have a more universal applicability and that go far toward capturing the fundamental spirit of these early monastics. We will look at a few of these.

In any group and in any era, it is most discouraging when some of those who once joined with great enthusiasm decide to leave and take up another way of life. Such departures can even become infectious. It is therefore not

8. Adalbert de Vogüé, foreword to *Pachomian Koinonia*, 1:xxiii.

surprising that some of the sayings of the desert deal with this issue. One of these, which has close links with what we have seen as a fundamental motivation behind Antony's monastic calling, is the following: One day a young monk asked an elder how a fervent brother could avoid being shocked and discouraged upon seeing others giving up their monastic practice and returning to their former way of life. The elder advised the young monk to consider the case of a dog that has seen a wild hare and begins pursuing it. Soon other dogs start following the first one, but since these others have not seen the hare, they run after the first dog for only a short time and then give up, returning to where they had been resting before. "Only the one who has seen the hare follows it till he catches it, not letting himself be turned from his course by those who give up, and not caring about ravines, rocks, and undergrowth. So it is," continued the elder, "with him who seeks Christ as Master: Ever mindful of the Cross, he cares for none of the obstacles that stand in his way until he reaches the Crucified."[9]

These desert monastics did not often speak openly of their piety. Many of their sayings do not mention Christ or God at all, but deal in a very down-to-earth manner with all sorts of practical matters like obedience, discernment, humility, fasting, vigilance, and the like. That very reticence makes a saying like the one just quoted all the more striking, since it so clearly highlights the love of Christ which led them to undertake the life in the first place and to persevere in it. They were also very clear that such love could never be separated from love of one another. Living alone or in small groups, they may indeed have had relatively little scope for practicing what the Bible calls love of neighbor, but there are nevertheless numerous sayings that illustrate the centrality of mutual love in their life. One reads as follows:

> It was said of a brother that, having made some baskets, he was putting on the handles when he heard his neighbor saying, "What can I do? Market day is near and I have no handles to put on my baskets." Then the former took the handles off his own baskets and brought them to the brother, saying, "Here are these handles which I have over; take them and put them on your baskets." So he caused his brother's work to succeed by neglecting his own.[10]

Another saying on the same general topic of mutual love shows that those who set down this material did, for all their seriousness of purpose, have a gentle sense of humor as well:

---

9. *The Wisdom of the Desert Fathers:* Apophthegmata Patrum *from the Anonymous Series*, trans. Sr. Benedicta Ward (Oxford: SLG Press, 1975), 24. Translation slightly amended.

10. Ibid., 59.

> Two elders had lived together for many years and had never fought with one another. The first said to the other, "Let us also have a fight like other people do." The other replied, "But I do not know how to fight." The first said to him, "Well, look. I'll put a brick between us, and I will say it's mine, and you say, 'No, it's mine,' and so the fight will begin." So they put a brick between them, and the first said, "This brick is mine," and the other said, "No, it's mine," and the first responded, "O.K., if it's yours, take it and go." So they gave it up without being able to find an occasion for argument.[11]

One final point should be made concerning the ascetical practices of these early monks and nuns. As mentioned earlier, at times an element of competition crept in, especially in the generations following the first. Some would try to outdo others in the severity of their fasting, the length of their night vigils, or the extent of their abstinence from sleep. The more perceptive monastics recognized the absurdity of such competition and roundly castigated it. The nun Syncletica, for example, said that the way to distinguish between ascetical practice that was in accord with God's will and that which was a sign of "demonic tyranny" was through the criterion of balance: "In truth, lack of proportion always corrupts. While you are young and healthy, fast, for old age with its weakness will come. As long as you can, lay up treasure, so that when you cannot, you will be at peace."[12] Indeed, in the best of cases it was neither competition nor any kind of masochism that led to these practices of self-denial. Sister Benedicta Ward, who has translated much of this desert literature into English, writes in one of her introductions: "The monks went without sleep because they were watching for the Lord; they did not speak because they were listening to God; they fasted because they were fed by the Word of God. It was the end that mattered; the ascetic practices were only a means."[13] One saying illustrates this in a striking way: "[An] elder came to see one of the fathers, who cooked a few lentils and said to him, 'Let us say a few prayers.' So the first completed the entire Psalter, while the other recited the two great prophets by heart. When morning came, the visitor went away, and they had forgotten the food."[14]

That last saying, as well as most of those referred to earlier, concerned monastics who for the most part lived in solitude or in small groups (the latter kind of monk being known as a semi-anchorite). While they were generally very hospitable toward those who visited them, the very life of solitude

11. *Wisdom of the Desert Fathers,* 51.

12. *The Sayings of the Desert Fathers: The Alphabetical Collection*, rev. ed., trans. Benedicta Ward (Kalamazoo, Mich.: Cistercian Publications, 1984), 233-34.

13. Ibid., xvi.

14. Ibid., 5.

meant that there were relatively few opportunities to practice love of others in an obvious, practical way. For many observers of their way of life this did not seem especially problematic, but for one famous monastic legislator, Basil the Great, it definitely was.

BASIL THE GREAT

As regards the circumstances that led Antony and Pachomius to take up the monastic life, we have to rely on what their various biographers tell us. With Basil it is different, for among his many letters that have come down to us there are several in which he himself describes his early attraction to the monastic way. One of the most important was written to Eustathius of Sebaste in the year 375, when Basil was in his mid-forties. He there recounts that in the years immediately following his university studies in Athens, he had for some time pursued worldly honors as a professor of rhetoric in the city of Caesarea in Cappadocia, part of modern-day Turkey. But one day he says he arose as if from a deep sleep, beheld the uselessness of the kind of human wisdom he had been pursuing, and looked instead to the light of the Gospel which had guided him in his younger years. Here are his own words as to what happened next:

> Accordingly, having read the Gospel, and having perceived therein that the greatest incentive to perfection is the selling of one's goods and the sharing of them with the needy . . . I prayed that I might find some one of the brethren who had taken on this way of life, so as to traverse with him this life's brief flood.
>
> [So I began to travel.] And I indeed found many men in Alexandria, and many throughout the rest of Egypt, and others in Palestine, and in Coele-Syria and Mesopotamia, at whose continence in living I marveled . . . I was amazed at their vigor in prayers, at how they gained the mastery over sleep, being bowed down by no necessity of nature, ever preserving exalted and unshackled the purpose of their soul . . . Having marveled at all this and having deemed the lives of these men blessed . . . I prayed that I myself . . . might be an emulator of them.[15]

Upon returning to his native Asia Minor, he chose a location along the Iris River, near a community of ascetic women that his widowed mother and her daughter Macrina had founded some years earlier. In a letter to his best

15. St. Basil the Great, Letter 223, in *The Letters* [of St. Basil], vol. 3, trans. Roy J. DeFerrari, Loeb Classical Library (London: William Heinemann; New York: G. P. Putnam's Sons, 1930), 293-95.

friend, Gregory of Nazianzus, Basil praised the spot for its natural beauty as well as for the tranquillity it afforded. In a slightly earlier letter to Gregory, Basil rhapsodized about the daily round of prayer and work in a way that reveals the deep attraction he felt for this way of life. "What is more blessed," he wrote, "than to imitate on earth the anthems of angels' choirs; to hasten to prayer at the very break of day, and to worship our Creator with hymns and songs; and then, when the sun is shining brightly and we turn to our tasks . . . to season our labors with sacred song as food with salt?"[16]

Since there was no ascetic of Basil's time and place who was more thoroughly versed in the knowledge of Scripture and in human wisdom or who had the same extensive experience of the world and of the church, it is not surprising that his counsel was sought by other ascetics. Basil's responses to their questions were soon collected, gradually revised and expanded upon by Basil himself, and so have come down to us in several editions. The details of the manuscript transmission are complicated, but the important point for our purposes is the fact that at the head of this work, prior to the collection of questions actually posed by monks or nuns of his day, Basil introduced the principles essential to his understanding of the ascetic life lived according to the gospel.

Just as in the case of the Egyptian monastics, Basil placed the greatest emphasis on the two great commandments of love of God and love of neighbor. The love of God is, he says, innate in us, for "We are by nature desirous of the beautiful . . . Now, what is more admirable than Divine Beauty? What reflection is sweeter than the thought of the magnificence of God? What desire of the soul is so poignant and so intolerably keen as that desire implanted by God in a soul purified from all vice and affirming with sincerity, [in the words of the Song of Songs,] 'I languish with love.'"[17] But if this love has been implanted in us by nature, so too has the love of one another. "Who does not know," he asks, "that the human being is a civilized and gregarious animal, neither savage nor a lover of solitude. Nothing, indeed, is so compatible with our nature as living in society and in dependence upon one another and loving our own kind."[18] For this reason, Basil was extremely critical of the eremitical form of monastic life, precisely because in his opinion a life lived utterly in solitude is concerned only with individual needs, not the needs of one's neighbor. In some of the most memorable lines in his treatment of this question, he writes:

---

16. St. Basil the Great, Letter 2, in *The Letters* [of St. Basil], vol. 1, trans. Roy J. DeFerrari, Loeb Classical Library (London: William Heinemann; New York: G. P. Putnam's Sons, 1926), 13.

17. St. Basil the Great, *The Long Rules*, in idem, *Ascetical Works*, trans. Sr. M. Monica Wagner, Fathers of the Church 9 (Washington, D.C.: Catholic University of American Press, 1950), 234.

18. Ibid., 239.

> Consider, further, that the Lord [Jesus], by reason of his great love for us, was not content with merely teaching the word, but, so as to transmit to us clearly and exactly the example of humility in the perfection of charity, girded himself and washed the feet of the disciples. Whom, therefore, will you wash [if you live alone]? To whom will you minister? . . . How, moreover, in a solitude, will that good and pleasant thing be accomplished, the dwelling of brothers together in one habitation, which the Holy Spirit [in the Psalms] likens to ointment emitting its fragrance from the head of the high priest?[19]

Later on in this treatise Basil does indeed turn to all kinds of particular questions about life in a monastic community—questions about garb, food, admission to the community, silence, hospitality, correction of faults, appropriate kinds of work, relations with one's natural family, medical treatment, and the like. Important as these matters are for understanding his spirituality, they are clearly secondary to his emphasis on the fundamental principles governing the entire way of life of his communities: love of God and love of one another. In this he was altogether in accord with Antony, Pachomius, and all the other leading monks of the Egyptian desert, however much Basil might have disagreed with one or another of them on the issue of the eremitical life. There was, in other words, a clear agreement about basic principles among all the leading figures of Christian monasticism in the third and fourth centuries. During this period, the movement flourished primarily in that part of the Christian world where the language of educated persons was Greek. Soon, however, it spread to the Latin-speaking areas as well, largely through the influence of a remarkable monastic traveler, John Cassian.

JOHN CASSIAN

We have just seen how Basil, before embarking on the monastic life himself, traveled to many areas in the eastern Mediterranean in order to gain firsthand knowledge of how monks lived. Cassian, too, traveled widely, but most of his travels came after he had already become a monk. Born around the year 360, either in Gaul or, more likely, in what is present-day Romania, he entered a monastic community in Bethlehem as a young man. Soon, however, he became disenchanted with the level of observance in that monastery and, having heard of the fervor of the monks in Egypt, received his abbot's permission to travel there together with another monk, his long-

19. Basil the Great, *Ascetical Works,* 252.

time friend Germanus. At one point they returned to Bethlehem, only to get permission to return once more to Egypt, where they stayed until the beginning of the fifth century. During these trips Cassian and Germanus became acquainted with some of the best-known monks, who were regularly referred to by the title Abba (Father). Some thirty years later, after sojourns in Constantinople, Rome, and possibly Antioch, Cassian settled in southern Gaul near the city of Marseilles, where he founded two monasteries, one for men, another for women. It was at this time, at the request of some local bishops, that he also wrote his two most important works, one entitled *The Institutes of the Cenobia and the Remedies for the Eight Principal Vices*, the other entitled simply *The Conferences*. Composed in Latin (although Cassian would have spoken Greek in his meetings with the monks of Egypt), these two works exerted immense influence not only on the monastic movement but also on the spirituality of the Western church as a whole.

As is evident from its full title, the *Institutes* focuses primarily on cenobitic monasticism. The first three of its twelve books give detailed information about such things as the garb of the Egyptian monks, the times of day at which they gathered for the canonical prayers, and the fervor with which they conducted their lives (which Cassian often contrasts with what he found to be the mediocre level of observance among the monks of Gaul), the last eight books discuss the principal vices (gluttony, fornication, avarice, anger, sadness, acedia, vainglory, and pride, which in slightly different configuration later became "the seven capital sins"), while the fourth and longest book presents a general account of the spirit of Egyptian monasticism, much of this placed on the lips of Abba Pinufius as he speaks to a young man just beginning the monastic way of life. Even as one of the desert sayings referred to earlier spoke of the need to keep one's eyes fixed on the Crucified, Pinufius's discourse likewise emphasizes that the whole point of monastic renunciation is to conform the monk more closely to Christ. The abba's words so vividly portray the Christocentric nature of monastic spirituality at its best that they deserve to be quoted at some length:

> Renunciation is nothing else than a manifestation of the cross and a dying . . . Consider, then, what the cross implies, within whose mystery it behooves you henceforth to proceed in this world, since you no longer live, but he lives in you who was crucified for you . . .
>
> Our cross is the fear of the Lord. Just as someone who has been crucified, then, no longer has the ability to move or to turn his limbs in any direction by an act of his mind, neither must we exercise our desires and yearnings in accordance with what is easy for us and gives us pleasure at

> the moment but in accordance with the law of the Lord . . . And just as he who is fixed to the gibbet of the cross no longer contemplates present realities or reflects on his own affections; is not distracted by worry or care for the morrow; is not stirred up by the desire for possessions; is not inflamed by pride or wrangling or envy; does not sorrow over present slights and no longer remembers those of the past . . . so also it behooves us who have been crucified by the fear of the Lord to have died to all these things, not only to fleshly vices but to every earthly thing as well, and to have the eyes of our soul set upon the place where we must hope that we shall go at any moment.[20]

Several points in this passage are especially worth noticing in addition to the basic exhortation to live after the example of Christ crucified. For one thing, such sentiments as not caring about the morrow, not sorrowing over present slights, and not remembering slights of the past are all manifestations of *apatheia*. That Cassian does not use this term, so frequent in the works of his own mentor Evagrius Ponticus, is surely because Evagrius was by this time looked at askance by church leaders; among other objections, his understanding of *apatheia* was caricatured by St. Jerome as an audacious claim of sinlessness. Second, even though only some of the eight principal vices are named or alluded to in this passage (avarice, pride, anger, and envy), it does indicate Cassian's conviction that the main work of the cenobitic monk is that of the "active (or practical) life," which at that time referred not primarily to pastoral activity but rather to the cultivation of the virtues and the avoidance of vices. Finally, the last sentence in the passage, with its reference to having "the eyes of our soul set upon the place where we must hope that we shall go at any moment," expresses what is surely the pivotal orientation of Cassian's work, its eschatology. As will be seen in even greater detail in the *Conferences*, for Cassian a monk is someone whose whole being is directed toward what he calls the final aim of monastic life, "the kingdom of heaven." Apart from this orientation, the life would make no sense at all.

Before turning to the *Conferences*, however, one further point should be made about the *Institutes*. One sometimes sees Cassian referred to as an astute psychologist and a keen observer of human nature. Nothing makes him more deserving of this characterization than the way he describes persons caught in the grip of one or another of the principal vices. Probably the best known of all these descriptions is that of a monk who has fallen prey to acedia, a Greek term that has no exact English equivalent but that includes

---

20. Cassian, *Institutes* 4.34-35, trans. Boniface Ramsey, O.P., Ancient Christian Writers 58 (New York: Newman Press, 2000), 97-98.

the notions of spiritual weariness, sloth, and boredom. With a touch of humor, Cassian expounds at great length on the effects of this vice, a small part of his lengthy description reading as follows:

> Once this has seized possession of a wretched mind it makes a person horrified at where he is, disgusted with his cell, and also disdainful and contemptuous of the brothers who live with him or at a slight distance . . . He makes a great deal of far-off and distant monasteries, describing such places as more suited to progress and more conducive to salvation, and also depicting the fellowship of the brothers there as pleasant and of an utterly spiritual cast . . . Next he glances around anxiously here and there and sighs that none of the brothers is coming to see him. Constantly in and out of his cell, he looks at the sun as if it were too slow in setting. So filled is he with a kind of irrational confusion of mind . . . that he thinks that no other remedy for such an attack can be found than the visit of a brother or the solace of sleep alone . . .
>
> And so the unhappy soul . . . is gradually drawn out of his cell and begins to forget the reason for his profession, which is nothing other than the vision and contemplation of that divine purity which is more excellent than anything else and which can be acquired only by silence, by remaining constantly in one's cell, and by meditation. (*Institutes* 10.2-3; Ramsey pp. 219-20)

It was to counteract this temptation to be always moving about, seeking greener pastures in other settings, that many of the sayings of the desert fathers and mothers stressed the importance of remaining in one's cell, "for the cell will teach you everything," even as some later monastic rules made the promise of stability to a particular community part of the profession formula. The final sentence quoted above is also of great significance for the way it singles out the contemplation of God as "more excellent than anything else." Though not foreign to the life of cenobites as described in the *Institutes*, according to Cassian contemplation was the special work of the anchorites or hermits, whose teaching he presented in his much longer and greater work, the *Conferences*.

This latter treatise comprises twenty-four conferences or instructions placed on the lips of some of the Egyptian abbas and presented in the form of dialogues, the principal interlocutor being Germanus. Titles that were given by later writers to the individual conferences often do not convey the variety of topics treated, for like many other conversations these often diverged from the original theme of the dialogue. While it is impossible to determine exactly to what extent Cassian rephrased the original teaching over the thirty or more years between his sojourn in Egypt and the composition of the work, its subsequent influence on Christian spirituality was enormous, ranging far beyond the monastic milieu; for example, St. Dominic, founder of the Order of Preachers in the thirteenth century, regularly had a manuscript of the *Conferences* with him on his travels. For our present purposes, the first conference (on "The Goal and the End of the Monk") and the ninth and tenth conferences, both "On Prayer," are especially important.

Cassian attributes the teaching on the goal and end of the monastic life to a certain Abba Moses, about whom little else is known (although he was almost certainly not the famous reformed robber and murderer Moses the Ethiopian, for the latter embraced monasticism as an adult whereas the Moses of the first conference was a monk from his youth). The conference itself hinges on a distinction between the ultimate *telos* or end of the monastic life, "the kingdom of heaven," and the more immediate *scopos* or goal that leads there. This goal is regularly described as "purity of heart," although it is functionally equivalent to divine contemplation (*theōria*). Cassian leaves no doubt about what he means by contemplation or the central role it plays in a monk's life, for he has Abba Moses say that "this should be pursued as the fixed goal of our heart, so that our mind may always be attached to divine things and to God. Whatever is different from this, however great it may be, is nevertheless to be judged as secondary or even as base, and indeed as harmful."[21] The text goes on to say that this contemplation of God can be arrived at in numerous ways, as by pondering the greatness of the things God has created, the works God has accomplished through the saints over the course of generations, or the gentleness and patience with which God tolerates human failings (1.15.1-2). Using the story of the sisters Martha and Mary in Luke's Gospel (Lk 10:38-42), Cassian's Moses presents Mary as the model contemplative and Martha as the exemplar of the active life (1.8.1-4). The work of hospitality that occupied Martha during Christ's visit to their home is indeed called "a holy service," but one that is nevertheless of secondary importance, not least because such activity is called for only in this life, whereas life in the heavenly kingdom that is our final end will be characterized by the blissful contemplation of God. This was referred to by St. Paul in First Corinthians as seeing "face to face" (1 Cor 13:12), one of the principal scriptural warrants for the later doctrine of the beatific vision.

In a passage crucial for understanding Cassian's view of how monastic life

---

21. Cassian, *Conferences* 1.8.1, trans. Boniface Ramsey, O.P., Ancient Christian Writers 57 (New York: Newman Press, 1997), 46-47. Subsequent parenthetical references to this work indicate the number of the conference, the chapter, and the subdivision within that chapter.

differs from that of other Christians, he writes that while all are called eventually—after death—to "pass over from this multiform or practical activity to the contemplation of divine things in perpetual purity of heart," there are some, the monastics, who have chosen to live in such a way as to anticipate this heavenly way of life even now: "Those whose concern it is to press on to knowledge and to the purification of their minds have chosen, even while living in the present world, to give themselves to this objective with all their power and strength. While they are still dwelling in corruptible flesh they set themselves this charge, in which they will abide once corruption has been laid aside, when they come to that promise of the Lord, the Savior, which says: 'Blessed are the pure of heart, for they shall see God'" (1.10.4).

This eschatological theme runs throughout all twenty-four of the conferences, but is particularly prominent in the two on prayer, both ascribed to Abba Isaac, for prayer is the contemplative activity par excellence. Like Origen, Cassian holds that one's entire life should be a prayer, such that "one's whole way of life and all the yearnings of one's heart become a single and continuous prayer" (10.7.3), but he goes into much more detail than did Origen about specific ways in which this can be brought about. In the ninth conference he provides a commentary on the Lord's Prayer, while in the following conference he discusses still more forms of prayer, including the Psalms, to whose central place in the communal hours of prayer he had already referred in the *Institutes*. In this tenth conference Cassian's emphasis is on the way in which the sentiments expressed in the Psalms should become those of the monk, so that "he will begin to repeat them and to treat them in his profound compunction of heart not as if they were composed by the prophet but as if they were his own utterances and his own prayer" (10.11.4). He also singles out one particular verse, the beginning of Psalm 70, as being of such special importance that it should be in the mind and on the lips at all times throughout the day. Indeed, Cassian has Abba Isaac claim that this way of praying is one that the monks did not readily pass on to just any inquirer, but since he finds Germanus and Cassian serious in their intent he agrees to divulge the method of steadfastly praying the words "O God, come to my assistance; O Lord, make haste to help me" (Ps 70:2). "You should," he tells them, "meditate constantly on this verse in your heart. You should not stop repeating it when you are doing any kind of work or performing some service or are on a journey. Meditate on it while sleeping and eating and attending to the least needs of nature. This heart's reflection . . . will lead you to the theoria of invisible and heavenly realities, and raise you to that ineffably ardent prayer which is experienced by very few" (10.10.14).

This "ineffably ardent [or fiery] prayer" (*oratio ignita*) is discussed in both of these conferences on prayer, where it is presented as the highest point to which human prayer can reach, for it "transcends all human understanding and is distinguished not, I would say, by a sound of the voice . . . Rather, the mind is aware of it when it is illuminated by an infusion of heavenly light . . . and speaks ineffably to God, producing more in that very brief moment than the self-conscious mind is able to articulate easily or to reflect upon" (9.25.1). It is to this kind of prayer that all of the monastic's contemplative activity ideally leads.

Inspiring as the words are, they nevertheless raise a basic question about Cassian's spiritual doctrine that has even led some commentators to question its compatibility with the teaching of the New Testament.[22] Granted that Cassian calls the kind of service that Martha provided the Lord in the Lukan pericope "holy" and that he does have Abba Moses say in the first conference that those who feed the hungry and give drink to the thirsty will receive a heavenly reward for their good works (1.10.1), it is clear that he considers such activity not only distinct from contemplation itself but even in some respects detrimental to it. This is perhaps nowhere so clear in his works as in the next-to-last conference, where Abba Theonas says that "it greatly hinders and holds back holy persons from the contemplation of that sublime good if they are taken up with what are still earthly pursuits, even if they are good works . . . If someone distributes sustenance to the poor or with gracious hospitality receives crowds of visitors, how can he, at the very moment when he is being distracted and is anxious in mind over the needs of his brothers, reflect upon the vastness of heavenly blessedness?" (23.4; 23.5.1). Whereas we have already seen Cassian teaching that God can be contemplated in multiple ways—through the contemplation of the wonders of the created world, of God's patience with human failings, and the like—nowhere does Cassian have any Egyptian abba speak explicitly of being able to see God, or Christ, in one's neighbor. Whereas the twenty-fifth chapter of Matthew's Gospel speaks quite directly of finding Christ in the brother or sister who is in need, Cassian is much more ready to speak of contemplating God in nature than in one's fellow human beings, the latter regularly constituting a certain "distraction" from contemplating the things of God. This way of distinguishing the active from the contemplative life sees the latter as being essentially incompatible with thoughts about "the arrival of a brother, or of visiting the sick, or the work of one's hands, or at least of showing hospitality to travelers or visitors" (1.12), so much so that the mind falling into such thoughts

22. See, e.g., Daniel A. Csányi, S.O.Cist., "Optima Pars: Die Auslegungsgeschichte von Lk 10, 38-42 bei den Kirchenvätern der ersten vier Jahrhunderte," *Studia Monastica* 2 (1960): 59-64.

"should judge as fornication even a moment's separation from the contemplation of Christ" (1.13.1). One way of summarizing the criticism to which Cassian is here liable would be to say that his notion of a monastic's anticipating a heavenly way of life already here on earth is not in itself unviable but that he had so static an understanding of heavenly life that it seemed not consonant with the works of mercy or any other practice of the "active life." Cassian's understanding was altogether different from that of someone like St. Thérèse of Lisieux, whom we shall discuss in chapter 7, for she often spoke of her desire to spend her heaven doing good on earth. This more dynamic, indeed *active*, view of eternal life could go a long way toward helping overcome the sharp dichotomy that Cassian draws between the active and contemplative lives, a dichotomy that has often had the regrettable effect of giving a negative, otherworldly connotation to the term "monastic."

In one other respect, however, Cassian remains a valuable guide for Christian spirituality today. Earlier we referred briefly to extreme forms of asceticism found in some parts of the early monastic world. This was especially the case in Syria, where one of the most idealized saints was the fifth-century monk Simeon, known as the Stylite because he was the first to live for many years atop a succession of pillars (*styloi*), the last of which was more than fifty feet high. A major source of information about this monk is a treatise by one of his contemporaries, Theodoret of Cyrrhus.[23] This author emphasizes the modesty of Simeon, the kindly way in which he would answer anyone who addressed him, and the intensity of his prayer. Theodoret also helps rationalize this strange manner of life by pointing to the unusual activities of some of the prophets of ancient Israel. Still, the overall impression of Simeon's ascetical practices and the harm that it did to his body—Theodoret mentions, for example, the malignant ulcer that developed on the Stylite's foot as a result of his prolonged standing atop the pillar—cannot but appear to us as excessive. This is precisely the kind of practice that had no place in Cassian's understanding of the monastic life. Already in the first conference he has Abba Moses praise the virtue of discretion as being essential if a monk is to act correctly, avoiding excesses of every kind. This is discussed at still greater length in the next conference, where Moses recalls how Antony of Egypt had once told a gathering of monks that discretion was the most necessary virtue of all if one would proceed "with sure steps to the summit of perfection" (2.2.1). Excessive fasts or vigils or any other singular feats of asceticism were foreign to Cassian's teaching. This was among the most important points that he passed on to the author of the most influential monastic rule in the Western church, the *Rule of Benedict*, a consideration of which will conclude this chapter.

23. Theodoret of Cyrrhus, *A History of the Monks of Syria*, trans. R. M. Price (Kalamazoo, Mich.: Cisterican Publications, 1985), 160-76.

BENEDICT OF NURSIA

Until fairly recently it was common for those writing about Benedict to emphasize that most of what we know about his life comes from book 2 of the *Dialogues* of Pope St. Gregory the Great, one of the most influential and respected writers of the early church. Although there are still ardent supporters of Gregory's authorship of this work, the British scholar Francis Clark has cast serious doubt on this, arguing in great detail that the dialogues are in fact a late-seventh-century forgery aimed at promoting the saints of Italy against those of Byzantium but yet containing enough passages inserted from some of Gregory's own unpublished works as to give the whole a certain Gregorian flavor.[24] If Clark is correct, then what we can state with some confidence about Benedict's own life is greatly reduced. Even book 2 of the *Dialogues*, however, claims that the *Rule of Benedict* itself, a document remarkable "for its discretion and its clarity of language," tells us a great deal about its author: "Anyone who wishes to know more about his life and character can discover in his Rule what he was like as an abbot, for his life could not have differed from his teaching."[25]

That author's reference to Benedict's discretion is particularly noteworthy. There are a number of indications in the rule that Benedict was troubled by what he considered a mediocre level of observance by his contemporaries, Italian monks of the early sixth century. In this sense, he was realistically concerned with "holding the line," doing what he could to promote an acceptable degree of adherence to traditional monastic practice while trusting that at least some of the monks would generously go beyond the minimum required of all. In words that have rightly been seen as a preeminent mark of this discretion, Benedict writes that the abbot "should be discerning and moderate, bearing in mind the discretion of holy Jacob, who said: *If I drive my flocks too hard, they will all die in a single day* [Gen 33:13]. Therefore, drawing on this and other examples of discretion, the mother of virtues, he must so arrange everything that the strong have something to yearn for and the weak nothing to run from."[26]

Another personal trait that can be discovered through even the most cursory reading of the *Rule* is Benedict's desire and ability to weave together

24. Francis Clark, *The "Gregorian" Dialogues and the Origins of Benedictine Monasticism* (Leiden: Brill, 2003). See also the review of this work by Terrence Kardong in *American Benedictine Review* 55 (2004): 115-18.

25. *Life and Miracles of St. Benedict* 36, trans. Odo Zimmermann, O.S.B. (Collegeville, Minn.: Liturgical Press, n.d.), 74.

26. *The Rule of St. Benedict* 64.17-19, ed. Timothy Fry, O.S.B., et al. (Collegeville, Minn.: Liturgical Press, 1982), 88.

material from earlier authors who were in some respects quite different from one another. We have seen Basil's suspicion of the eremitical way of life on the grounds that it did not offer adequate scope for practicing the love of one's neighbor, whereas Cassian exalted the contemplative life proper to hermits above the predominantly active life of monks living in community. Benedict recommends the works of both authors, along with the Bible and "the teachings of the holy Fathers," as being sure guides to "the perfection of monastic life" (*Rule* 73.2-5). What allowed him to do this so naturally, and very likely without even realizing that it represented a delicate challenge that could easily have gone awry, was precisely the fact that Basil, Cassian, and the other leading figures of early monasticism were all trying to provide a setting in which one could live out more readily than elsewhere the two great commandments of love of God and love of neighbor (even though, as we have seen, Cassian felt that the love of neighbor was more properly practiced by cenobites than by hermits). These two commandments are the very ones with which Benedict begins chapter 4 of his *Rule,* a chapter entitled "The Tools for Good Works." The love of God is also proposed as the ultimate goal of the twelve steps of humility, which Benedict discusses in the well-known seventh chapter of the *Rule,* whose final section begins with the words: "Now, therefore, after ascending all these steps of humility, the monk will quickly arrive at that 'perfect love of God which casts out fear' [1 Jn 4:18]. Through this love, all that he once performed with dread, he will now begin to observe without effort, as though naturally, from habit, no longer out of fear of hell, but out of love for Christ, good habit, and delight in virtue" (*Rule* 7.67-69). Then, toward the end of the *Rule,* in a section comprising six chapters that Benedict apparently added later to make up for some omissions or oversights in a first edition, he wrote the short seventy-second chapter, perhaps the most beautiful of the entire *Rule* and one that readily conjoins the themes of love of God and love of one another. The chapter is worth reading in its entirety:

> Just as there is a wicked zeal of bitterness which separates from God and leads to hell, so there is a good zeal which separates from evil and leads to God and everlasting life. This, then, is the good zeal which monks must foster with fervent love. *They should each try to be the first to show respect for the other* [Rom 12:10], supporting with the greatest patience one another's weaknesses of body or behavior, and earnestly competing in obedience to one another. No one is to pursue what he judges better for himself, but instead, what he judges better for someone else. To their fellow monks they show the pure love of brothers; to God, loving fear; to their abbot, unfeigned and humble love. Let them prefer nothing whatever to Christ, and may he bring us all together to everlasting life.

Like Basil, and with even more attention to detail, Benedict also considers many other aspects of monastic life. He goes into considerable detail about which Psalms are to be sung at certain hours of the day, spells out precisely the kinds of correction that are to be administered for greater and lesser faults, and regulates the amount of time to be given to manual labor and to that prayerful, meditative reading of the Scriptures that still today is commonly referred to by its Latin name *lectio divina*. He also discusses all the possible avenues by which someone might enter the monastic community, whether as a child offered to the community by its parents, as an adult layperson, as a monk from another monastery (for which the permission of one's former abbot is required), or as a priest seeking admission (something relatively uncommon at that time, since monasticism was originally a strictly lay movement that became clericalized only in the Middle Ages). While avoiding the ludicrous detail of a slightly earlier rule known as *The Rule of the Master* (a document which, almost incredibly, even specifies the direction one should face when blowing one's nose in choir so as not to give offense to the attending angels!), Benedict nevertheless allowed enough of his Roman practicality to characterize his document that within two and a half centuries it was the rule followed by almost all the monasteries of continental Europe, eventually spreading from there to every continent on earth. Although parts of the *Rule* are inevitably quite time-bound, such as its ready acceptance of corporal punishment as a corrective for faults, its genial blend of inspiring doctrine and practical directives continues to make it a primary spiritual resource for laypersons as well as monastics. In fact, books by modern authors such as Esther de Waal, Joan Chittister, and David Robinson have given the *Rule of Benedict* a currency in Christian circles that it has not enjoyed since the Middle Ages.[27]

QUESTIONS FOR REFLECTION

1. What values do you find in the eremitical life such as it was lived for many years by Antony of Egypt at the "Inner Mountain"? Despite the objections of Basil, do you think there is a legitimate role for hermits in Christian spirituality today?
2. What were some of the major qualities of spiritual leadership found in Pachomius? Which of these qualities (or others) do you find most necessary for Christian leaders today?

---

27. See, e.g., Esther de Waal, *Seeking God: The Way of St. Benedict* (Collegeville, Minn.: Liturgical Press, 1984); Joan Chittister, O.S.B., *Wisdom Distilled from the Daily: Living the Rule of St. Benedict Today* (San Francisco: Harper & Row, 1990); and David Robinson, *The Family Cloister: Benedictine Wisdom for the Home* (New York: Crossroad, 2000).

3. How would you describe the contemplative ideal as advocated by Cassian? How might it best be cultivated by persons who do not live as hermits—or should such persons even seek to cultivate it?
4. In what sense was Benedict a synthesizer of earlier monastic currents? Do you share the attraction of many persons today for the kind of spirituality found in the *Rule of Benedict*?

SUGGESTIONS FOR FURTHER READING AND STUDY

On Antony of Egypt

Athanasius, *The Life of Saint Antony*. Translated by Robert T. Meyer. Ancient Christian Writers 10. New York: Newman Press, 1978. The same work is available also in *Athanasius: The Life of Antony and the Letter to Marcellinus*. Translated by Robert C. Gregg. Classics of Western Spirituality. New York: Paulist, 1980; and in *The Life of Antony: The Coptic Life and the Greek Life*. Translated by Tim Vivian and Apostolos N. Athanassakis. Kalamazoo, Mich.: Cistercian Publications, 2003 (see especially sections 1-15, 44-50, and 89-94).

Rubenson, Samuel. *The Letters of St. Antony: Monasticism and the Making of a Saint*. Minneapolis: Fortress, 1995.

On Pachomius

The First Greek Life of Pachomius. In *Pachomian Koinonia*, vol. 1, *The Life of Saint Pachomius and His Disciples*. Translated by Armand Veilleux, 297-423. Kalamazoo, Mich.: Cistercian Publications, 1980. See especially sections 1-30, 110-16, and 136.

Rousseau, Philip. *Pachomius: The Making of a Community in Fourth-Century Egypt*. Berkeley and Los Angeles: University of California Press, 1985.

On the Sayings of the Desert Fathers and Mothers

Burton-Christie, Douglas. *The Word in the Desert: Scripture and the Quest for Holiness in Early Christian Monasticism*. New York/Oxford: Oxford University Press, 1993. See especially chapter 5, "*The Sayings of the Desert Fathers*" (pp. 76-103), and chapter 9, "The Commandment of Love" (pp. 261-95).

Regnault, Lucien. *The Day-to-Day Life of the Desert Fathers in Fourth-Century Egypt*. Translated by Etienne Poirier, Jr. Petersham, Mass.: St. Bede's Publications, 1999. See especially chapter 8, "A Day in the Life of the Anchorite" (pp. 96-111), and chapter 9, "The Hidden Activity" (pp. 112-25).

Swan, Laura. *The Forgotten Desert Mothers: Sayings, Lives, and Stories of Early Christian Women*. New York: Paulist, 2001. See especially chapter 1, "The World of the Desert Mothers" (pp. 5-19), and chapter 2, "Desert Spirituality" (pp. 20-31).

The Sayings of the Desert Fathers: The Alphabetical Collection. Translated by Benedicta Ward, SLG. Rev. ed. Kalamazoo, Mich.: Cistercian Publications, 1984.

The Wisdom of the Desert Fathers: Apophthegmata Patrum *from the Anonymous Series*. Translated by Sister Benedict Ward, SLG. Oxford: SLG Press, 1975.

On Basil

Basil. *The Long Rules*. In idem, *Ascetical Works*. Translated by Sister M. Monica Wagner, C.S.C., 223-57. Fathers of the Church 9. Washington, D.C.: Catholic University of America Press, 1950. See especially Basil's preface and questions 1-8 (pp. 223-57).

Rousseau, Philip. *Basil of Caesarea*. Berkeley: University of California Press, 1994.

On John Cassian

John Cassian. *The Conferences*. Translated by Boniface Ramsey, O.P. Ancient Christian Writers 57. New York: Newman Press, 1997. See especially conference 1, "On the Goal and the End of the Monk" (pp. 35-75), and conferences 9 and 10, both "On Prayer" (pp. 323-93).

———. *The Institutes*. Translated by Boniface Ramsey, O.P. Ancient Christian Writers 58. New York: Newman Press, 2000. See especially book 4, "The Institutes of the Renunciants" (pp. 75-112).

Stewart, Columba. *Cassian the Monk*. New York/Oxford: Oxford University Press, 1998. See especially chapter 3, "Cassian the Theologian" (pp. 40-61), and chapter 6, "Unceasing Prayer" (pp. 100-113).

On Benedict of Nursia

RB 1980: The Rule of St. Benedict in Latin and English with Notes. Edited by Timothy Fry, O.S.B. Collegeville, Minn.: Liturgical Press, 1982.

Chittister, Joan, O.S.B. *Wisdom Distilled from the Daily: Living the Rule of St. Benedict Today*. San Francisco: Harper & Row, 1990. See especially chapter 1, "The Rule: A Book of Wisdom" (pp. 1-13), and chapter 15, "The Monastic Vision: Gift for a Needy World" (pp. 194-207).

Kardong, Terrence, O.S.B. *The Benedictines*. Wilmington, Del.: Michael Glazier, 1988. See especially chapter 1, "An Overview of the Rule of Benedict" (pp. 11-29) and chapter 4, "Benedictine Spirituality" (pp. 70-98).

5

The Patristic Era

ALREADY IN THE MIDDLE of the fourth century the term "Fathers" was used by writers like Basil and his close friend Gregory of Nazianzus to refer to earlier churchmen whose teachings were considered authoritative, such as those bishops who had assembled at the Council of Nicaea in 325. Nowadays much later figures, even the twelfth-century monk Bernard of Clairvaux, are sometimes numbered among the fathers of the church, although it is more common to close the patristic era with Gregory the Great (d. 604) in the West and John of Damascus (d. 749) in the East. Not only is there this diversity of opinion about when the era of the fathers ended; there is also no universally agreed-upon list of just who should be so designated. The very term "fathers of the church" likewise raises the question of whether we might also speak of "mothers of the church." This is not regularly done, if only because we have so few writings from women in the first millennium of the church's history, but women unquestionably played a very important role in the shaping of Christian spirituality during its formative period. We will therefore be looking at the contributions of a couple of these women in this chapter, even though in one case we know of her life and teaching only secondhand.

In addition to the inclusion of women, there is a second way in which the range of persons to be considered in this chapter will be broadened. It has been all too common to limit studies of the patristic era to the Greek (or Eastern) fathers and the Latin (or Western) fathers, thereby overlooking the Syriac, Coptic, and Ethiopian traditions. We have earlier alluded to the Syriac *Odes of Solomon* of the late second century and to the Coptic monks Antony and Pachomius. In this present chapter we will begin with two later Syriac works, the poems of Ephrem the Syrian and the anonymously written *Book of Steps*, both dating from the fourth century, that is, prior to the time when Greek influence on Syriac authors became prominent. This point is especially pertinent to the present work's emphasis on global perspectives, for as one prominent scholar of this tradition has said,

> early Syriac Christianity takes on a new relevance in the modern world where the churches of Asia, Africa, and South America are rightly seeking to shake off the European cultural baggage from Christianity which they have usually received through the mediary of European or North American missionaries: here, in the early Syriac tradition, we encounter a form of Christianity whose theological expression is as yet uninfluenced by the Greek philosophical tradition, but which employs thought forms that are far more conducive to these churches' own cultural backgrounds.[1]

Later in this chapter, and under the constraint of having to be very selective, we will look at several of the most important representatives of Greek spirituality in this era—Gregory of Nyssa, his sister Macrina, and John Chrysostom—and then at two from the Latin West: Augustine of Hippo and the Frankish noblewoman Dhuoda. The chapter will conclude by moving south into Africa, into the ancient kingdoms of Nubia and Ethiopia.

EPHREM THE SYRIAN

Ephrem was born in Nisibis in northeastern Mesopotamia around the year 306, a time when the city was within the Roman empire but threatened by the Persians. It eventually fell to the Persian army under Shapur II when Ephrem was in his fifties, whereupon he and the entire Christian population of Nisibis were allowed to migrate to adjacent cities under the control of Rome. Ephrem himself settled in Edessa in 363, where he served the church as a deacon and teacher until his death ten years later.

One of the points emphasized in our opening chapter was that the data for the study of spirituality should not be limited to Scripture and doctrinal treatises. Ephrem did write some meditations and biblical commentaries in prose, but he is far more renowned for his poetry, which he regularly intended to be sung as hymns. His poetic output was both enormous and intensely symbolic. In the words of one of his modern translators, his poetry "is based upon a vision of the world as a vast system of symbols or mysteries. No person, thing or event in the world exists without a mysterious relation to the whole."[2] Like some of the authors we have already studied, notably Origen

---

1. Sebastian Brock, introduction to *The Syriac Fathers on Prayer and the Spiritual Life* (Kalamazoo, Mich.: Cistercian Publications, 1987), xi.
2. Kathleen E. McVey, introduction to *Ephrem the Syrian: Hymns*, Classics of Western Spirituality (New York: Paulist, 1989), 41.

and Cassian, he emphasizes the contemplation of God in Scripture and in the world of nature, as when he writes at the end of one of his hymns:

> In every place, if you look, His symbol is there,
> and when you read, you will find His types.
> For by Him were created all creatures,
> and He engraved His symbols upon His possessions.
> When He created the world,
> He gazed at it and adorned it with His images.
> Streams of His symbols were opened, flowed and poured forth
> His symbols on His members.[3]

Among the symbols is that of Christ as a "Skilled Sailor Who has conquered the raging sea" and whose cross "has become the rudder of life" (20.15), but immediately after this reference to the cross, the most common of all Christian symbols, Ephrem turns to far less momentous signs of God's love, ones that might easily be overlooked but for which he urges his readers to be always mindful and thankful:

> But remaining are all those things the Gracious One made in His mercy.
> Let us see those things that He does for us every day!
> How many tastes for the mouth! How many beauties for the eye!
> How many melodies for the ear! How many scents for the nostrils!
> Who is sufficient in comparison to the goodness of these little things?
> Who is able to make thousands of remunerations in a day? (20.16-17)

Again like Cassian, Ephrem sees Mary of Bethany as the model for those who would lead a contemplative way of life, for she "turned her face from everything / to gaze on one beauty alone . . . Let you also portray the Messiah in your heart / and love Him in your mind" (24.7). There is, however, one major difference from Cassian in Ephrem's teaching on contemplation. Whereas Cassian does not discuss the possibility of seeing Christ in other human beings and even speaks of the performance of the works of mercy as

3. Ephrem, *The Hymns on Virginity and on the Symbols of the Lord* 20.12; McVey, *Ephrem,* 348-49. Subsequent parenthetical references to these hymns indicate the number of the hymn and the strophe.

something of a distraction from divine contemplation, one of Ephrem's finest hymns emphasizes the presence of Christ in all of his followers. Referring to the scene in the Fourth Gospel where the crucified Jesus gives the beloved disciple to Mary to be her son and Mary to the disciple to be his mother (Jn 19:26-27), Ephrem writes:

> Your mother saw You in Your disciple;
> And he saw You in Your mother.
> Oh, the seers who at every moment
> see you, Lord, in a mirror
> manifest a type so that we, too, in one another
> may see You, our Savior. (25.9)

Because Ephrem was so aware of our being able to see and find Christ in our neighbor, there is in his work nothing of the divorce between action and contemplation that crops up in Cassian and in later authors who adopted that schema. One of Ephrem's hymns is addressed specifically to women consecrated to a life of virginity, but there is no reason to think that the advice with which he concludes that hymn would not apply to all Christians: giving alms and visiting the sick are presented as altogether compatible with honoring the image of the Lord portrayed on one's heart:

> Imprint your tongue with the word of life and upon your
> hands [imprint] all alms.
> Stamp your footsteps with visiting the sick,
> and let the image of your Lord be portrayed in your heart.
> (2.15)

As impressive as are such words, even more impressive is the fact that this saint, genuinely contemplative in spirit, died while ministering to the sick during an outbreak of the plague in Edessa in 373. By both word and example, Ephrem is a vibrant model of Christian spirituality at its best.

THE BOOK OF STEPS

Around the time of Ephrem's death an anonymous Syriac writer, probably living in the Persian empire, was composing a remarkable treatise whose title is normally rendered in English as *The Book of Steps*. The notion of steps or degrees by which one may advance along the way of Christian holiness finds one of its major scriptural warrants in St. Paul's speaking of those who are still "infants in Christ," able to ingest only milk and not the solid food of those more advanced in the Christian way of life (1 Cor 3:1-3; see also Heb 5:11-14). *The Book of Steps* has still more distinctions than these two, for it refers to some as "the sick," to others as "children," and to still others as those who pursue either "the commandments of faith" or "the commandments of love." The book's major distinction, however, is between "the Upright" (*kēnē*) and "the Perfect" (*gmīrē*). The work of the former consists primarily in caring for the social needs of the world, while the Perfect strive to carry out the fullness of Christ's teaching as given in the Sermon on the Mount: turning the other cheek, praying for their enemies, and not judging others. In the twenty-fifth of the book's thirty discourses (*mēmrē*) the author gives a concise summary of the life of one who is among the Perfect: "He has abandoned the earth according to what our Lord has commanded him and has taken up the cross, has emptied and lowered himself and become celibate; and has become like a servant in his obedience, and not like a lord in his supervision."[4]

Whereas Ephrem writes much about how Christ's grace repairs the harm done by our wrongful use of free will but does not emphasize the Christian's calling to imitate the Savior's way of life, the imitation of Christ is one of the central themes of *The Book of Steps*. This is especially true of the seventeenth *mēmrā*, entitled "On the Sufferings of Our Lord, Who Became through Them an Example for Us." Here the author makes much of the fact that when Jesus washed the feet of his disciples at the Last Supper he first washed those of Judas, the one he knew would hand him over, and only afterwards washed the feet of the others, "his friends." Alluding to unnamed difficulties either within the Christian community itself or within a society many of whose members were hostile to Christians, he goes on to say: "If you know who are your betrayers and your sellers and the companions of your murderers, control your tendency [to strike out] and make them sit down and wipe their feet . . . and do not make [it] known that they are your enemies" (17.3). In this way, "you will become perfect, submitting yourself to whoever seeks to kill and harm you. You will become all [things] with all [people], making disciples of sinners and harlots" (17.7; see also 29.1).

Like the work of Jesus and his closest disciples, much of the activity of the Perfect consists in proclaiming the word, so that even though they strive to have no cares about the morrow and rely on the goodness of the Upright and of others to provide for their material needs, they live very much in the midst of society and are called to be intent on correcting faults and resolving tensions within the church. Indeed, the work seems to have been written because

4. *The Book of Steps* 25.7, trans. Robert A. Kitchen and Martien F. G. Parmentier (Kalamazoo, Mich.: Cistercian Publications, 2004), 297. Subsequent parenthetical references to this work indicate the number and section of the *mēmrā*.

the author was aware of how "the vision of the Church as the road to Perfection and the heavenly city was unraveling."[5] At one point he says forthrightly that even though members of his flock quote Psalm 101 to the effect that "An evil heart has left us and we do not know evil," in fact "we hate one another so that not even a word of mouth or a greeting of lips do we exchange with one another. And on occasions we even throw evil pestilences against one another and repay evil things to one another" (29.3).

The author of *The Book of Steps* was, in sum, primarily the pastor of a flock, using all of his rhetorical powers to bring about a conversion of heart and a desire for perfection in each of his hearers or readers. Since such conversion is a constant of Christian spirituality at all times and places, his English translator is surely correct in claiming that the author of this work is "one of the great, though unsung, spiritual masters of the early Church,"[6] with three features of his teaching being of special importance: First, he does not gloss over the challenges of the way of perfection but describes the obstacles and pitfalls with undisguised candor, as seen in the passage quoted above about the way some members of his church actually hated one another. Such frankness, however, actually makes progress toward spiritual perfection "more attainable, for it is a road traveled by authentic and finite human beings, not floated over by angels."[7] Second, there is the call to imitate Christ, especially in his self-emptying. This point has also been singled out by Sebastian Brock, perhaps the most highly respected scholar of Syriac Christianity in recent times. In his words, the term self-emptying (*msarrqūtā*) "has a long ancestry in Syriac tradition. The noun, which is first encountered in the *Book of Steps*, is based on Phil 2:7, 'Christ . . . emptied himself, taking the form of a servant,' and so conveys with it the idea of self-emptying in imitation of Christ's own self-emptying: divine *kenōsis* needs to be met by human *kenōsis*."[8] Third and last, for all of the author's praise of those who generously follow the way of the Perfect, there are many indications toward the end of the work that he had gradually become disenchanted with most of them and therefore concludes the final *mēmrā* with a strong affirmation of the ministry of the Upright, based on the model of the publican Zacchaeus in Luke's Gospel:

> See, while he [Zacchaeus] did not say to our Lord, "I will abandon everything I have," our Lord did say the following to him, "Today salvation has come into this house." Zacchaeus shall be called a son of Abraham . . .

5. Robert A. Kitchen, introduction to *The Book of Steps*, lxii.
6. Ibid., lxxx.
7. Ibid., lxxxi.
8. Brock, introduction to *The Syriac Fathers*, xxxi.

> Therefore, let no one say that whoever does not empty everything he has and follow our Lord is not saved. If people then desire to become sons of Abraham while being wealthy, as Zacchaeus has become, they will grow in abundance and receive whatever is better in the kingdom. (30.27-28)

While much of early Syriac spiritual literature extols the values of celibacy and renunciation of possessions, passages like the one just quoted show that "the persistent faithfulness of the Upright—'worldly Christians'—is to be preferred over a false Perfection and is to be celebrated, not denigrated as inadequate."[9] Although it would be an exaggeration to say that this is a direct anticipation of the Second Vatican Council's emphasis on the universal call to holiness, the concluding sections of *The Book of Steps* do mitigate the picture that one might otherwise gain of early Syriac spirituality as being overly focused on severe forms of renunciation.

GREGORY OF NYSSA AND MACRINA

That same fourth century during which Ephrem and the author of *The Book of Steps* were composing their works in Syriac was the period when the greatest Greek fathers were flourishing. We have earlier mentioned Athanasius and Basil and will now turn to Basil's brother, Gregory of Nyssa, and their sister, Macrina (sometimes called Macrina the Younger to distinguish her from the saintly grandmother after whom she was named). During Basil's lifetime Gregory lived very much in the shadow of his renowned brother, but upon the latter's death in 379 the younger brother came very much into his own, both as a theologian arguing the case for the divinity of the Holy Spirit at the Council of Constantinople in 381 and, more to our present purposes, writing treatises that have led some to call him the father of Christian mysticism. Although positively influenced by Origen in many respects, there was one significant point on which he differed from the Alexandrian, a point that made all the difference in his spiritual doctrine. As we have seen, Origen held that humans are essentially rational beings or minds (*noēs*) which, in a state preexisting their fall into bodies, enjoyed the direct vision of the Godhead. Because of this basic affinity with the heavenly or divine realm, it was relatively easy for Origen to speak of our contemplation of God, even in our earthly state, as something for which we are suited. True, he does at times say that the richness of what there is in God is incomprehensible and that God

9. Kitchen, introduction to *The Book of Steps*, lxxxii.

is enveloped in darkness, but he can also add at once that the darkness "hastens towards light, seizing it and becoming light because, not being known, darkness changes its value for him who now does not see, in such a way that, after instruction, he declares that the darkness which was in him has become light once it has become known."[10] It is such passages that have led historians of Christian spirituality to speak of Origen as a "mystic of the light."

One would never say this of Gregory. Having a clearly articulated doctrine of creation out of nothing (*creatio ex nihilo*) that has no place for preexistent souls, Gregory places the entire human being, body and soul, on the lower side of a basic ontological divide between God and the created order.[11] From our side, God dwells in the deepest darkness, a point that Gregory makes most emphatically in his *Life of Moses*. In this two-part work, after giving in book 1 a narrative account of Moses' life as found especially in the Book of Exodus, Gregory returns to the same events in book 2 so as to give them a spiritual interpretation, similar to the way in which Origen regularly sought to give a spiritual sense to scriptural texts. When Gregory comes to the passage that describes Moses' ascent into the dark cloud atop Mount Sinai (Ex 24:15-16), he writes:

> What does it mean that Moses entered the darkness and then saw God in it? . . . As the mind progresses and, through an ever greater and more perfect diligence, comes to apprehend reality, as it approaches more nearly to contemplation, it sees more clearly what of the divine nature is uncontemplated.
>
> For leaving behind everything that is observed, not only what sense comprehends but also what the intelligence thinks it sees, it keeps on penetrating deeper until by the intelligence's yearning for understanding it gains access to the invisible and the incomprehensible, and there it sees God. This is the true knowledge of what is sought; this is the seeing that consists in not seeing, because that which is sought transcends all knowledge, being separated on all sides by incomprehensibility as by a kind of darkness.[12]

This is a classic expression of what has come to be called apophatic mysticism or negative theology. The word "apophatic" comes from a Greek verb

10. Origen, *Commentary on John* 2.28, quoted by Andrew Louth, *The Origins of the Christian Mystical Tradition: From Plato to Denys* (Oxford: Clarendon, 1981), 72.

11. For a fine treatment of this point, see Louth's chapter on Nicene orthodoxy in *Origins of the Christian Mystical Tradition*, 75-97.

12. Gregory of Nyssa, *The Life of Moses* 162-63, trans. Abraham J. Malherbe and Everett Ferguson, Classics of Western Spirituality (New York: Paulist, 1978), 94-95.

meaning "to say no; to deny." In this case, what is being denied is the ability of human words or concepts to grasp the divine reality. It is sometimes thought that the main characteristic of apophatic mysticism is the use of negative images of the divine (such as "darkness"), but the essential point is that *all* words and images, whether positive or negative, fail. This is why theologians like Gregory regularly resort to paradoxical language, as in the passage above where he speaks of "the seeing that consists in not seeing." Expressions of this sort may provoke sighs of frustration from linguistic analysts, but Gregory is doing violence to the language only to drive home the point that our words must ultimately fall short when we are attempting to speak of God. For all their verbiage, apophatic mystics frequently and understandably counsel silence when it comes to "God talk," as Gregory does several times in another of his works: "Thus in speaking of God, when there is question of His essence, then is the *time to keep silence* (Eccl 3:7)."[13]

All this does, of course, raise the question of whether Gregory sees any possibility of direct access to God. Indeed he does, but it is not by sight. Like Origen before him and many spiritual writers in later centuries, Gregory wrote and preached extensively on the Song of Songs. In his eleventh sermon on this book of Scripture, he asks how God, who is invisible, can possibly be revealed to us, and he gives this reply: "He gives the soul some sense of His presence [*aisthēsin tina . . . tēs parousias*], even while He eludes her clear apprehension, concealed as He is by the invisibility of His nature."[14] The sense or perception of which Gregory speaks is that of love, as when he places these words on the lips of the bride in the Song of Songs: "I am suddenly introduced into the realm of the invisible, surrounded by the divine darkness, searching for Him Who is hidden in the *dark cloud*. Then it was that I felt that love for Him Whom I desired—though the Beloved Himself resists the grasp of our thoughts."[15]

This raises one final point to be made about Gregory's spiritual doctrine. It is a commonplace that lovers are seldom if ever completely satisfied with the degree of union that they have reached. For all the bliss, there is usually a sense of unfulfillment as well, leading to expressions like "the wound of love" (as we have seen in Origen) or "sweet pain." Gregory regularly sounds this note of incompleteness, of always being able to enter more deeply into the mystery of God. He here takes his cue from what St. Paul wrote to the

13. Gregory of Nyssa, *Commentary on Ecclesiastes*, sermon 7, in *From Glory to Glory: Texts from Gregory of Nyssa's Mystical Writings*, trans. Herbert Musurillo, S.J. (New York: Charles Scribner's Sons, 1961; repr., Crestwood, N.Y.: St. Vladimir's Seminary Press, 1979), 129.

14. Gregory of Nyssa, *On the Song of Songs*, sermon 11, in *From Glory to Glory*, 248.

15. Ibid., sermon 6, in *From Glory to Glory*, 201.

Philippians: "Forgetting what lies behind and straining forward to what lies ahead, I press on toward the goal for the prize of the heavenly call of God in Christ Jesus" (Phil 3:13-14). This notion of ever straining or stretching forward (*epektasis*) figures prominently in Gregory's thought. He readily admits that there is a tendency in us to incline toward evil, but this is counterbalanced by an inclination toward the good, leading him to affirm that "the finest aspect of our mutability is the possibility of growth in good," such that we can be "always improving and ever becoming more perfect by daily growth, and never arriving at any limit of perfection. For that perfection consists in our never stopping in our growth in good."[16]

This same sense of ongoing progress is also true as regards our knowledge of God. Precisely because the divine essence can never be fully known, never comprehended, it is possible to rise ever higher: "For the desire of those who thus rise never rests in what they can already understand; but by an ever greater and greater desire, the soul keeps rising constantly to another which lies ahead, and thus it makes its way through ever higher regions towards the Transcendent."[17] There is no reason to think that Gregory limited this understanding of progress to one's life on earth. Whereas Origen's notion of divine contemplation is rather static, leading some to surmise that the reason his preexistent souls fell from heavenly bliss was from a sense of boredom, Gregory's teaching about contemplation is much more dynamic. The blessed will never tire of the face-to-face vision promised them in the life to come (1 Cor 13:12), for the riches of the Godhead are inexhaustible.

Among those whom Gregory definitely considered to be among the blessed in heaven was his sister Macrina, whose life he described in the form of a lengthy letter to a monk named Olympus. The *Life of Macrina*, just like the *Life of Antony* discussed in the preceding chapter, was by no means a biography in our contemporary sense of the word.[18] Gregory is writing hagiography, emphasizing the saintly qualities of his sister and accordingly describing other details only in passing. Although a hagiographer's aim is quite different from that of a modern historian, the *Life of Macrina* nevertheless furnishes us with valuable information about women's spirituality in the patristic era. Gregory writes that Macrina was the firstborn of the ten children in the family and that her mother decided to educate her in knowledge not of pagan literature but of the Scriptures, especially the Book of Wisdom and the

16. Gregory of Nyssa, *On Perfection*, in *From Glory to Glory*, 84.

17. Gregory of Nyssa, *On the Song of Songs*, sermon 8, in *From Glory to Glory*, 213.

18. We use the English translation contained in *Handmaids of the Lord: Contemporary Descriptions of Feminine Asceticism in the First Six Christian Centuries*, trans. Joan M. Petersen, 51-86 (Kalmazoo, Mich.: Cistercian Publications, 1996). Parenthetical references to this work indicate the page number in this collection.

Psalms. According to the custom of the time, as a young girl Macrina was promised in marriage to a respectable young man, but when he died unexpectedly, she came to regard the marriage arranged for her as though it had actually taken place and firmly refused her parents' request that she marry someone else. Thus committed to a life of virginity, Macrina remained living in the family home, helping out even in the menial chores that were normally considered tasks for slaves. When Basil returned home from his studies in Athens in 355, Macrina found him puffed up with pride and soon persuaded him to abandon all desire for secular advancement and devote himself to "philosophy," that is, to a monastic way of life. After her father's death, Macrina turned the household into a kind of domestic monastery, even persuading her mother to give up the services of her maids and to regard herself as being of the same rank as all the other women, whether slave or free. Even if Gregory painted an overly rosy picture of the life lived by these women, his description nevertheless does portray the spiritual ideal of many women at that time, whether in Cappadocia, Palestine, Egypt, or elsewhere:

> Their delight was in self-control; their glory was to be unknown; their wealth was to possess nothing, having shaken off all material superfluity from their bodies as though it were dust. Their work, except incidentally, was unconnected with the tasks about which people busy themselves in this life. It consisted only of attention to the things of God, prayer without ceasing, and the uninterrupted chanting of the Psalms, which was extended equally in time through night and day, so that for the virgins it was both work and rest from work. (60)

On his way back to Cappadocia from a church council in Antioch, Gregory was informed that his sister was sick, so he hurried home and found her seriously ill with fever, yet resting not on a bed but simply on the floor, on a board covered with a sack. He writes that their conversations over the next few days showed that she was already looking toward death: "It seemed to me that she revealed to those around her that pure love for the unseen Bridegroom which she cherished, hidden in the secret places of her soul, and made public the inclination of her heart to hasten to him for whom she longed, so that, once freed from the fetters of her body, she might be with him as soon as possible" (69-70). Gregory also places on Macrina's lips a beautiful prayer, a mosaic of passages from the Bible that he himself may have woven together from individual sentiments voiced by his sister as she lay dying. A few lines from that prayer offer a fine example of the attitude that Gregory believed should be those of any Christian at the time of death:

> It is you, O lord, who have freed us from the fear of death. You have made our life here the beginning of our true life. You grant our bodies to rest in sleep for a season and you rouse our bodies again at the last trumpet . . .
>
> Eternal God, for whom I was snatched from my mother's womb, whom my soul loved with all its strength, to whom I consecrated my flesh from my youth until now, entrust to me an angel of light, who will lead me by the hand to the place of refreshment, where the "water of repose" is, in the bosom of the holy patriarchs. (70-71)

JOHN CHRYSOSTOM

Readers already familiar with Christian spirituality may be surprised to see John Chrysostom ("John the golden mouthed") included among the few figures considered in this chapter on the patristic era. After all, there are some anti-Judaic passages in his sermons that make one cringe (although he was by no means the only one among fathers of the church who had disparaging things to say about the Jewish people), and even apart from that, some might categorize him more as a moralist than as a spiritual master. There are, however, several reasons why he deserves a place here. It is too often the case that considerations of Christian spirituality become overly ethereal, too divorced from the lives of ordinary Christians, the proverbial "butcher, baker, and candlestick maker." It was largely before such persons that John Chrysostom preached, whether as a priest in Antioch of Syria or, later in life, as patriarch of Constantinople, and much of what he said to them is of lasting importance for Christian spirituality.

Born in Antioch around the middle of the fourth century, John spent some years in his youth as a cenobitic monk and then as a hermit not far from the city. Having been persuaded by friends to return to Antioch because of ill health, he was ordained a deacon in 381 and a priest five years later. Both in his native city and later in the imperial capital at Constantinople, John became one of the most influential preachers of his or any age. This was not due to an imposing physique or powerful voice, for he had a thin, sickly face and a comparatively weak voice, but his words with their forceful images and striking comparisons would often bring the congregation to break out in enthusiastic, admiring applause. One of his best modern biographers gives a vivid picture of the cross-section of humanity who would come to hear him preach: "weary, worn-out male and female slaves, workmen, and servants . . . theatrical and circus people, small tradesmen and hand workers, soldiers, sailors and officers, officials of all grades, rhetoricians and professors; but also wealthy merchants, owners of splendid villas and palaces, and . . . his own spiritual brothers, even sometimes the Patriarch [of Antioch]."[19] It was especially the wealthy and powerful whom John would often upset with his sermons, for he relentlessly preached the need for Christians to give heed to the plight of the poor and to recognize that possessions that they did not really need belonged not to themselves but to those who could use them. The directness with which he broached such themes had much to do with his eventually losing the support of the empress after he had become patriarch of Constantinople, so he died a physically broken man in exile, but his unflagging insistence on the importance of the New Testament's call to care for the least of Christ's brothers and sisters has earned John Chrysostom an honored place in the history of Christian spirituality.

The same could be said of another aspect of his preaching, namely, his understanding of how Christians form one body, especially when they gather to celebrate the eucharist. A common complaint of some persons about many spiritual books is that they are too individualistic, too focused on a "me and God" relationship without any reference to the communal nature of Christian life. Such a criticism could never be made of John Chrysostom's sermons. He had a keen awareness that when the Christian people come together at the eucharist they do so as one body. He did not, of course, ignore the reality of a distinction between the ordained minister presiding at the service and the laity gathered around him, but he went out of his way to emphasize what they all had in common. In words that could just as well have been voiced by leading liturgists in the aftermath of the Second Vatican Council's Constitution on the Sacred Liturgy, Chrysostom said in one of his sermons:

> There are occasions in which there is no difference at all between the priest and those under him. For instance, when we are to partake of the awesome mysteries we are all alike counted worthy of the same things. It is not as under the Old Testament, when . . . it was not lawful for the people to partake of those things of which the priest partook. Not so now, but before all is set one body and one cup. In the prayers also, one may observe the people contributing much, for the prayers made on behalf of the possessed or the penitents are made in common by both the priest and the people . . . The offering of thanksgiving again is common, for the priest does not give thanks alone, but all the people [do so with him] . . .
>
> I have said all this in order that each one of the laity may be aware that we are all one body . . . and may not place the whole responsibility upon

19. Chrysostomus Baur, O.S.B., *John Chrysostom and His Time*, vol. 1, trans. Sr. M. Gonzaga, R.S.M. (Westminster, Md.: Newman Press, 1959), 207.

the priests, but may so care for the whole church as for a body common to us all . . . In this way the church ought to dwell as one house, as one body.[20]

AUGUSTINE OF HIPPO

The two saints just considered—Macrina and John Chrysostom—are depicted by their biographers as having led holy lives from their youth. It is an altogether different story with the man who became the most celebrated of all the fathers of the Western church and whose writings, after those of Scripture, have arguably become the most influential in Christian history. Of the many ways in which one might approach the spirituality of Augustine, perhaps the most helpful is from the perspective of conversion. Already at the very beginning of Mark's Gospel, conversion is sounded as the keynote of Jesus' preaching: "The time is fulfilled, and the kingdom of God has come near; repent [*metanoeite*, literally, "have a change of mind"] and believe in the good news" (Mk 1:15), while the twentieth-century theologian Bernard Lonergan, already discussed in our opening chapter, wrote at considerable length about the crucial importance of various kinds of conversion—religious, intellectual, and moral—in his influential work on theological method.[21] Apart from that of St. Paul, no conversion in the history of the church has had as momentous an impact as Augustine's, recounted by him in his best-known work, the *Confessions*, much of which is in the form of a prayer addressed to God.[22]

Written after Augustine had become bishop of Hippo in North Africa in 396, the *Confessions* may have been motivated in part by his need to address the concerns of those who doubted the sincerity of his conversion from the Manichean religion. In any case, with a brutal honesty that seemed inappropriate to some members of his flock at Hippo, Augustine traced the course of his gradual turning to the Lord over the first half of his life. In doing so, he inevitably drew a sharp contrast with the more sudden conversion of Paul on the road to Damascus, for Augustine's took many years and was marked by various turnings. For students of Christian spirituality, the *Confessions* are

20. John Chrysostom, *Eighteenth Homily on Second Corinthians*, in *The Nicene and Post-Nicene Fathers*, vol. 12, ed. Philip Schaff (Buffalo: Christian Literature Co., 1889; repr., Peabody, Mass.: Hendrickson, 1994), 365-66. Translation slightly revised.

21. Bernard J. F. Lonergan, *Method in Theology* (New York: Herder & Herder, Seabury paperback, 1972), 237-44.

22. Augustine's *Confessions* may be found in numerous modern English translations. We use that of Maria Boulding, O.S.B. (Hyde Park, N.Y.: New City, 1997). Parenthetical references to this work indicate the number of the book, the chapter (as marked in printed editions since the fifteenth century), and the paragraph (as given in the Maurist edition of 1679).

notable for showing how crucial even non-Christian writings can be in the process of ongoing conversion. While it would be pointless to try to summarize the work in a few pages, at least some of the milestones of Augustine's spiritual journey may usefully be pointed out.

Augustine was born in 354 in Thagaste, Numidia, located in modern-day Algeria, of a Christian mother, Monica, and a pagan father, Patricius. Augustine was a Christian catechumen from birth but, in accord with common practice at that time, was not baptized, it being thought better to delay the saving waters of this sacrament until one had left behind the sins of one's youth. After receiving his early schooling in Thagaste and in nearby Madaura, Augustine went in his mid-teens to Carthage for more advanced training in rhetoric. He opens the third book of the *Confessions* with the well-known line, "So I arrived in Carthage, where the din of scandalous love-affairs raged cauldron-like around me" and where he fell prey to "the iron rods and burning scourges of jealousy and suspicion, of fear, anger and quarrels" (3.1.1). His career goal at this time was to serve in the courts of law, "where I would earn a reputation all the higher in the measure that my performance was the more unscrupulous" (3.3.6). Then, quite unexpectedly, came the first step on the way back to God, for in the course of his studies he happened upon Cicero's *Hortensius*, whose exhortation to philosophy (literally, "love of wisdom") "changed my way of feeling and the character of my prayers to you, O Lord, for under its influence my petitions and desires altered. All my hollow hopes suddenly seemed worthless, and with unbelievable intensity my heart burned with longing for the immortality that wisdom seemed to promise" (3.4.7). This was the first of a number of pagan writings that would have immense influence on Augustine and is an excellent example of the way in which the reading of such texts can find a rightful place in Christian spirituality. Augustine was, however, still far from full acceptance of Christianity, for in Carthage he joined the Manichees, a Gnostic religious group founded more than a century earlier in Babylonia. Among the attractions of this sect was its teaching that when we do wrong, it is not we who sin but some alien force within us, absolving us for any need to feel personally guilty. As he explains later in his work, "when I had done something wrong it was pleasant to avoid having to confess that I had done it . . . I liked to excuse myself and lay the blame on some other force that was with me but was not myself" (5.10.18).

After finishing his studies and teaching rhetoric for a year in his hometown, Augustine returned to Carthage for a period of seven years. All this time he was living with a concubine whom he never names but by whom he had a son Adeodatus ("given by God"). In 383 the three of them sailed to Rome, where he had heard the students were better disciplined, and a year later he obtained the position of public rhetor in the imperial city of Milan. Having by now broken with the Manichees because he had found their teachings to be lacking in credibility, he adopted the skeptical position of those whose school was called the New Academy. Still intent on furthering himself as a teacher of rhetoric, Augustine began attending the sermons of Ambrose, the Catholic bishop of the city, not out of any desire to assimilate the content of his preaching but only to appreciate and learn from his vaunted eloquence. He was, however, unavoidably impressed by what Ambrose was saying: "As I opened my heart to appreciate how skillfully he spoke, the recognition that he was speaking the truth crept in at the same time . . . This realization was particularly keen when once, and again, and indeed frequently, I heard some difficult passage of the Old Testament explained figuratively; such passages had been death to me because I was taking them literally" (5.14.24). Augustine was in fact experiencing the same kind of "mystical interpretation" of Scripture that had been advocated by Origen in the previous century, for Ambrose had gleaned much from the Alexandrian's exegesis. Hereupon Augustine resolved "to live as a catechumen in the Catholic Church, which was what my parents had wished for me, until some kind of certainty dawned by which I might direct my steps aright" (5.14.25).

That certainty was still rather far off, not least because Augustine, like many of the ancients, was a strict materialist, believing that even God was corporeal in nature, though of a very refined sort of corporeality. Just as the reading of Cicero's *Hortensius* had once enkindled in him a love of wisdom, works of other pagan philosophers now led him beyond the mind-set of materialism. These were the philosophers later named Neoplatonists, some of whose works translated from Greek into Latin had been lent to Augustine by an acquaintance. These proved to be a further pivotal step in his conversion, for "after reading the books of the Platonists and following their advice to seek for truth beyond corporeal forms, I turned my gaze toward your invisible reality, trying to understand it through created things, and though I was rebuffed I did perceive what the reality was which the darkness of my soul would not permit me to contemplate" (7.20.26). At the same time, Augustine recognized that there was something incomplete in these writings: "Where was that charity which builds on the foundation of humility that is Christ Jesus? And when would those books have taught it to me? I believe that you willed me to stumble upon them before I gave my mind to your scriptures, so that the memory of how I had been affected by them might be impressed upon me when later I had been brought to a new gentleness through the study of your books" (ibid.).

Augustine did, then, turn next to the Christian Scriptures, above all to the writings of St. Paul: "So I began to read, and discovered that every truth I had read in those other books was taught here also, but now inseparably from your gift of grace . . . In awe-inspiring ways these truths were striking deep roots within me as I read the least of your apostles" (7.21.27). The full power of that grace would become manifest within a few months upon his reading of a few verses from Paul's Letter to the Romans, but one more written work—again one translated from Greek into Latin—would first have to intervene. Augustine recounts how one day in August 386 he and his friend Alypius were visited by a government official and fellow African named Ponticianus, who told them of two young men who had suddenly left their lucrative positions in the imperial bureaucracy in Trier and had become monks after reading the *Life of Antony*. On hearing this, Augustine was cut to the quick, envious of their bold decision and disgusted with himself: "By contrast with them I felt myself loathsome, remembering how many of my years—twelve, perhaps—had gone to waste, and I with them, since my nineteenth year when I was aroused to pursue wisdom by the reading of Cicero's *Hortensius*" (8.7.17).

After Ponticianus had left, Augustine and Alypius retreated to a garden adjacent to the house in which they were staying in Milan. Pondering his years of futile pursuits and weeping copiously, Augustine withdrew to the back of the garden, asking himself in great agitation: "Why must I go on saying, 'Tomorrow . . . tomorrow'? Why not now? Why not put an end to my depravity this very hour?" (8.12.28). Hearing a voice from a nearby house singing over and over the words "Pick it up and read," he took this as a divine command to open the book of St. Paul's letters that he had left lying on a table in the garden. Returning to the place where Alypius was sitting, he opened the book and read in silence the first passage he saw, from the Letter to the Romans: "Not in dissipation and drunkenness, nor in debauchery and lewdness, nor in arguing and jealousy; but put on the Lord Jesus Christ, and make no provision for the flesh or the gratification of your desires" (Rom 13:13-14). Feeling at once the light of certainty, he resolved to seek baptism, which Ambrose administered the following Easter.

Although this scene from the garden at Milan was in some respects the culmination of Augustine's years-long process of conversion, crucially aided as we have seen by his familiarity with the writings of many authors, some of whom were not even Christian, it would be more accurate to say that his ongoing conversion now entered a different stage. Abandoning all desire to make his mark in the world through fame or wealth, Augustine soon returned to his native town of Thagaste with the intention to live a monastic way of life with some like-minded friends. This venture lasted only about three years, for during a visit to Hippo in 391 to see a candidate for the monastery, he was persuaded one Sunday by the congregation in the basilica to allow himself to be ordained a priest. Five years later, upon the death of Bishop Valerius, Augustine was consecrated his successor and so spent the rest of his life as bishop of this coastal city.

Of the many aspects of Augustine's spirituality as he lived and taught it for the remaining thirty-four years of his life, two may be singled out as especially significant: his preaching and his loving service to the people of his diocese. Upon being ordained a priest and asked by Valerius to preach regularly in the city's basilica—a task usually reserved for bishops at that time but one that was difficult for this particular bishop—Augustine requested and received permission to spend six months immersing himself more thoroughly in the Bible, since it would be the foundation of all his sermons. Thanks to *notarii* (stenographers), hundreds of these scripturally based sermons have come down to us, some of them showing through their quasi-dialogue form the easy rapport that Augustine had with his congregation. Even more significantly, they also reveal the profoundly ecclesial character of his spirituality, his keen appreciation of the Pauline teaching that all members of the church are part of the one body of Christ, with Christ as their head. As he said in one of numerous sermons on the Lord's Prayer, "The Eucharist is our daily bread. But let us receive it in such a way that we are refreshed not only in our bodies but in our souls. For the virtue that is apprehended there is unity, so that gathered together into His body and made His members, we may be what we receive."[23] Even more emphatically, insisting that the eucharist is not only a memorial of the one sacrifice of Christ but also an occasion for each of the faithful to be mindful of their oneness with Christ and one another, Augustine said on another occasion, "Behold what you have received! Therefore, just as you see that the bread which was made is one mass, so may you also be one Body by loving one another . . . There you are on the table, and there you are in the chalice, for you are one with us."[24]

Augustine's service to his people was by no means limited to the care with which he prepared such sermons. As already noted, by temperament he would have preferred the relatively cloistered life of a monk as he had enjoyed it for a few years in Thagaste before his ordination. In a sermon he gave on one of the annual celebrations of the anniversary of his consecration as bishop, he enumerated all the things that were demanded of him: "To rebuke those who stir up strife, to comfort those of little courage, to take the part of

---

23. Augustine, Sermon 7 on the Gospels (Sermon 57 in the Maurist ed.), in *The Nicene and Post-Nicene Fathers*, first series, vol. 6, ed. Philip Schaff (Buffalo: Christian Literature Co., 1888; repr., Peabody, Mass.: Hendrickson, 1994), 282. Translation slightly revised.

24. Augustine, Sermon 229, in idem, *Sermons on the Liturgical Seasons*, trans. Sr. Mary Sarah Muldowney, R.S.M. (New York: Fathers of the Church, 1959), 202.

the weak, to refute opponents, to be on guard against traps, to teach the ignorant, to shake the indolent awake, to put the presumptuous in their place, to mollify the quarrelsome, to help the poor, to liberate the oppressed, to encourage the good, to suffer the evil, and to love all."[25] Much of this work required trips to church councils in Carthage and countless hours in his study composing treatises to deal with such issues as the Donatist schism, the Pelagian heresy, and the charge made by some pagans that Christianity was to blame for the sack of Rome by Alaric the Goth in 410. Even as he entered old age, Augustine was unable to find much leisure. Only in the fall of 426, less than four years before his death, was he able to hand over to the young priest Eraclius the bulk of his administrative duties. We have a record of what happened when Augustine made the announcement of this appointment and expressed in a touching and somewhat amusing way how heavy had been the burden of devoting himself to the people of his diocese. After noting that Eraclius would immediately take over many of his responsibilities and eventually succeed him as bishop, Augustine went on as follows:

> You know what it was that I was anxious to do some years ago, though at that time you would not let me do it. We had agreed with one another that in view of the scriptural studies which my fathers and fellow-bishops had enjoined me to undertake, no one was to disturb me for five days in the week. This was entered into the record and approved by acclamation . . . For a short while you kept to your bargain, but you have ever since most outrageously failed to keep it, for you leave me no time to do what I want to do. Both morning and afternoon, you take all my time. I beseech you most earnestly, in the name of Christ, that you will agree to my handing over all my more time-consuming tasks to this young man whom I have this day designated as my successor, namely the priest Eraclius.[26]

This was agreed to by the congregation, whom the *notarii* record as having shouted their approval and their thanks for several minutes. When all was quiet again, Augustine concluded his sermon with these heartfelt words: "Now the time has come for us to concern ourselves with the things of God at the altar. During the common prayer, my beloved, I shall take you all to my heart, and that most earnestly, having in mind all your cares and needs, and I shall pray to the Lord for this our church and for myself and for the priest Eraclius."

---

25. Augustine, Sermon 340, 1, quoted by F. van der Meer, *Augustine the Bishop: The Life and Work of a Father of the Church*, trans. Brian Battershaw and G. R. Lamb (London/New York: Sheed & Ward, 1961), 268.

26. Augustine, *Acta ecclesiastica*, Letter 213, quoted in van der Meer, *Augustine,* 272.

It is obvious that by temperament Augustine was not attracted to the busy life of a leader of the church. In a letter he once wrote to the abbot of a monastery situated on an island in the Mediterranean, Augustine confessed that he often envied the abbot his quiet, adding that one could live more serenely in the midst of the waves of the sea than in his audience chamber. The fact that Augustine, despite this inclination, did not excuse himself from the demands of that audience chamber and of the church at large teaches more powerfully than words alone his recognition that the heart of Christian spirituality is to be found in love—a love of God that in large measure becomes manifest in the love and service that one offers to one's fellow human beings. As he said in concluding the above-mentioned sermon preached on one of the anniversaries of his episcopal consecration:

> No one can long more than I to be free from troubles and cares, for nothing is better, nothing is more sweet, than to browse among the heavenly treasures, away from all distraction and noise . . . Yet it is the Gospel itself that makes me fear that way of life. I might well say, "What do I get by boring people, by reproving the evil, by telling them, Don't do this. Stop doing that? Why should I feel myself responsible for others?" It is there that the Gospel holds me back.[27]

Whatever criticisms might legitimately be directed against some aspects of Augustine's thought, such as his less-than-positive appreciation of marital relations, we remain indebted to him for his willingness to look deep within himself and to confront with relentless honesty the ways in which the human heart can, even over a prolonged period of time, resist the ever-present call of God and then, finally and through God's grace, yield.

DHUODA

Compared to such immensely influential authors as Augustine and John Chrysostom, the early medieval Frankish laywoman Dhuoda may seem out of place in this chapter, but there are good reasons for including her. For one thing, she is one of the very few women in the first millennium of the church's history from whom we have something written by herself. Second, if we accept Walter Principe's description of spirituality as a striving to live according to the highest ideals of one's faith tradition, it must be recognized that even within a single tradition this ideal will have different modalities

27. Augustine, Sermon 340, 7, quoted in van der Meer, *Augustine,* 268.

according to one's state in life. The celibate bishop Augustine would inevitably express this ideal in different terms from those of a wife and mother like Dhuoda. She may, in fact, stand in for the countless, anonymous Christian women of the first millennium who strove to bring up their children in accord with the teaching of Scripture and of the church. In the words of one scholar of her work, Dhuoda's writings "are precious for us in that they offer a view of the intellectual and spiritual life of her age, but they are more precious in that they also offer an insight into the mind and heart of what must have been a remarkable woman."[28]

All that we know of Dhuoda must be gleaned from the *Manual* that she wrote as a guidebook for her son William. She was married in 824 in the imperial palace at Aachen to Bernhard of Septimania, who several years later rose to the position of *camerarius*, second in command to the emperor, Louis the Pious. Bernhard, entrusted with the defense of the Spanish marches, was often away with the army, leaving Dhuoda in semi-abandonment at his castle at Uzès in southern France. He also arranged to have their firstborn son, William, sent far away to serve at the court of one of Louis' sons, Charles the Bald, and had their second son taken from her before his baptism, so that two years later she still did not even know his name. William was in his mid-teens when Dhuoda composed her *Manual*, begun in Advent of 841 and completed in February 843. The next year her husband was captured in battle and beheaded, while William, perhaps ignoring the advice of his mother about how one ought to live, suffered the same fate in 850. We do not know when Dhuoda herself died.

Although Dhuoda's *Manual* does not have a highly organized structure and the various manuscripts differ among themselves in defining chapters and chapter headings, some themes are prominent and will be briefly considered: God's sovereignty, reverence in prayer, conduct toward one's parents and earthly superiors, and kindness to the lowly no less than to those in high station. Although Dhuoda several times mentions her ignorance and "the poverty of my intelligence,"[29] it is clear that she was familiar not only with the Bible but also with authors such as Vergil, the Christian poet Prudentius, Augustine, Benedict, and Gregory the Great. In writing of God and admonishing her son to love God dearly, Dhuoda uses a rhetorical device common in the Carolingian period, the recitation of something clearly impossible: If the heavens and earth were spread through the air like a parchment, if all the water in the sea

28. James Marchand, "The Frankish Mother: Dhuoda," in *Medieval Women Writers*, ed. Katharina M. Wilson (Athens, Ga.: University of Georgia Press, 1984), 1.

29. Dhuoda, *Manual*, in *Medieval Women Writers*, 14. Subsequent parenthetical references to this work indicate the page number in this collection.

were changed into ink, and if all the persons who ever lived were scribes, they would still not be able to comprehend in their writings the sublimity, profundity, and clemency of God: "Since He is thus and so great that no one can comprehend His essence, I beg you to fear Him and to love Him with all your heart, all your mind, all your understanding, to bless Him in all your ways and deeds, and to sing, 'For He is good, for His mercy endures forever!'" (15).

At several places in her *Manual* Dhuoda urges her son to pray frequently, sometimes by reciting the Psalms, since they "possess so many and such virtues" (24), but at other times praying more extemporaneously in "short, firm, and pure speech," using such words as these: "Mercy-giving and Merciful, Just and Pious, Clement and True, have pity on Your creation, whom You created and redeemed with Your blood; have pity on me, and grant that I may walk in Your paths and Your justice; give me memory and sense that I may understand, believe, love, fear, praise, and thank You and be perfect in every good work through proper faith and goodwill, O Lord, my God. Amen" (16).

Even though Dhuoda herself had been treated harshly by her husband Bernhard, she asks her son to show him all respect and love: "I admonish you, most beloved son William, that you first love God as you have it written down above; after that, love, fear, and cherish your father; know that your status in life comes from him" (17). She likewise admonishes William to be faithful to his earthly lord, Charles, at whose court he was serving. Then, referring to the hymn quoted by St. Paul in the second chapter of his Letter to the Philippians, she tells him that just as Christ, although the Creator of all, was willing to take on the form of a slave for the sake of those below him, William should be equally ready to come to the aid of his inferiors: "If He, great as He is, comports Himself thus toward the lesser ones, what should we, small as we are, do toward those who are worse off? Those who are able ought to help them and, according to the urgings and words of the Apostle Paul, bear one another's burdens" (19). Dhuoda then concludes her guidebook with a request that William have inscribed on her gravestone a twenty-four-line verse that she composed and that he and all who would one day read her *Manual* pray for her after her death.

NUBIA AND ETHIOPIA

Having just seen something of the spirituality of a woman who lived in the southern part of what is today France, we turn next to the area south of Egypt. Here lay the three ancient kingdoms of Nubia, and still farther to the south and east was Ethiopia. There were Christians in Nubia as early as the fifth century, and a missionary sent from Constantinople by the empress Theodora converted the ruling family of the north Nubian kingdom of

Nobatia in the sixth. In the following century Nobatia had absorbed the two southern kingdoms of Makouria and Alwa, resulting in a single Nubian realm with strong ties to the non-Chalcedonian patriarchs of Alexandria.

Christianity reached Ethiopia, with its capital at Axum, even earlier. Although an apocryphal scripture recounting missionary activity by the apostle Matthew cannot be relied upon, we are on firmer ground in holding that Athanasius, while patriarch of Alexandria in the middle of the fourth century, sent a young Syrian named Frumentius to Axum as its bishop, with authority to ordain priests and instruct the people in the Christian faith. Ethiopian tradition also credits him with having translated parts of the Bible into the ancient Ethiopian language, Ge'ez. In the following century, other missionaries introduced monasteries to Ethiopia following the rule of Pachomius. Monastic life in that country even today reflects that early Pachomian influence, while the Ethiopian church, like the early church in Nubia, followed the lead of the Alexandrian patriarchs.

Although we have few writings of individuals from the early days of Christianity in Nubia and Ethiopia, the ancient Ethiopian liturgy provides valuable insight into the spirituality of that part of the Christian world. One of the fourteen Ethiopian anaphoras (eucharistic prayers) is called the "Anaphora of Jesus Christ," with prayers addressed directly to him rather than to the Father. The following prayer, which comes just before the end of the liturgy, expresses the believers' intention to focus on Christ as their ever-present guide and protector:

> Pilot of the soul,
> Guide of the righteous,
> and Glory of the saints:
> grant us, O Lord, eyes of knowledge ever to see you
> and ears also to hearken to your word alone.
> When our souls have been filled with your grace,
> create in us pure hearts, O Lord,
> that we may ever understand your greatness,
> who are good and a lover of men.
> O our God, be gracious to our souls,
> and grant to us your humble servants
> who have received your body and blood,
> a pure and steadfast mind,
> for yours is the Kingdom, O Lord,
> blessed and glorious, Father, Son, and Holy Spirit.[30]

30. "Ethiopian Prayer: Pilot of the Soul," in *Prayers from the East: Traditions of Eastern Christianity*, ed. Richard Marsh (Minneapolis: Fortress, 2004), 93. Translation slightly modernized.

Although Ethiopian Christianity is not well known in many other parts of the world, it continues to flourish and still serves today, as it did centuries ago, "as an important symbol of African independent Christianity's connection to the earliest churches of the apostles by way of Alexandria. With the churches of Egypt, Ethiopia, and later Nubia we find a continuous historical tradition of Christian faith that is very much at home in this continent."[31] We will see something of the spirituality of still further parts of the vast African continent in a later chapter of this book.

QUESTIONS FOR REFLECTION

1. Ephrem is the first person studied in this book who is renowned for his poetry rather than for his prose writings. What do you consider the strengths and/or weaknesses of presenting one's spiritual teaching in poetry? Do you accept Ephrem's claim that God's symbols are everywhere if only one looks properly?
2. Do you agree with Gregory of Nyssa's teaching that God "transcends all knowledge, being separated on all sides by incomprehensibility as by a kind of darkness"? How would you put into your own words what human beings can or cannot know about God? What effect might an emphasis on God's incomprehensibility have on one's spirituality?
3. Both John Chrysostom and Augustine emphasized the unity of the congregation—both clerics and laity—when they gathered for the eucharist. To what extent do you sense this kind of unity in liturgical services today? How do you think it can best be fostered?
4. As noted in this chapter, one scholar of Dhuoda's writings said that they "offer an insight into the mind and heart of what must have been a remarkable woman." If you agree with this assessment, what insights did you glean from the passages quoted or summarized from Dhuoda's *Manual*? Do you consider her *Manual* especially exemplary for Christian mothers today?

SUGGESTIONS FOR FURTHER READING AND STUDY

On Early Syriac Spirituality

Brock, Sebastian. Introduction to *The Syriac Fathers on Prayer and the Spiritual Life*, x-xli. Kalamazoo, Mich.: Cistercian Publications, 1987.

———. "The Poet as Theologian." *Sobornost* 7 (1977): 243-50.

Kitchen, Robert A. Introduction to *The Book of Steps: The Syriac* Liber Graduum, xiii-lxxxiii. Kalamazoo, Mich.: Cistercian Publications, 2004.

31. Dale T. Irvin and Scott W. Sunquist, *History of the World Christian Movement*, vol. 1, *Earliest Christianity to 1453* (Maryknoll, N.Y.: Orbis Books, 2001), 219.

McVey, Kathleen E. Introduction to *Ephrem the Syrian: Hymns*, 3-48. Classics of Western Spirituality. New York: Paulist, 1989.

On Gregory of Nyssa and Macrina

Daniélou, Jean. Introduction to *From Glory to Glory: Texts from Gregory of Nyssa's Mystical Writings*, ed. Herbert Musurillo, S.J., 3-78. Crestwood, N.Y.: St. Vladimir's Seminary Press, 1979. This work contains eighty-three selections from Gregory's writings, many drawn from his *Life of Moses* and his *Commentary on the Song of Songs*.

"Macrina: A Domestic Monastery in Cappadocia." In *Handmaids of the Lord: Contemporary Descriptions of Feminine Asceticism in the First Six Christian Centuries*, translated by Joan M. Peterson, 39-86. Kalamazoo, Mich.: Cistercian Publications, 1996. Gregory's *Life of Macrina* is on pp. 51-86.

On John Chrysostom

Baur, Chrysostomus, O.S.B. *John Chrysostom and His Time*. Translated by Sr. M. Gonzaga, R.S.M. 2 vols. Westminster, Md.: Newman Press, 1959. See especially vol. 1, chap. 20, "Chrysostom as a Pulpit Orator."

On Augustine

Boulding, Maria, O.S.B. Introduction to her translation of *The Confessions*, 9-33. Hyde Park, N.Y.: New City, 1997.

Brown, Peter. *Augustine of Hippo: A Biography*. Berkeley/London: University of California Press, 1967. See especially chap. 16, "The 'Confessions,'" and chap. 22, "Populus Dei."

van der Meer, F. *Augustine the Bishop: The Life and Work of a Father of the Church*. Translated by Brian Battershaw and G. R. Lamb. London/New York: Sheed & Ward, 1961. See especially chap. 7, "Day-to-Day Pastoral Work," and chap. 15, "The Servant of the Word."

On Dhuoda

Marchand, James. "The Frankish Mother: Dhuoda." In *Medieval Women Writers*, edited by Katharina M. Wilson, 1-29. Athens, Ga.: University of Georgia Press, 1984. Marchand's translation of Dhuoda's *Manual* is on pp. 12-28.

6

Spiritual Renewal in the Medieval West and East

IN THE PREVIOUS CHAPTER we noted that Dhuoda was married in the city of Aachen in 824. Seven years earlier an event of much greater significance took place in the same imperial city. The Holy Roman Emperor Louis the Pious, following the same goal of ecclesiastical uniformity that had inspired his father, Charlemagne, convened an assembly of abbots and monks from throughout his realm for the purpose of implementing a common system of monastic legislation, together with carefully selected visitators to ensure their observance. The scheme as such fell through, largely because within twenty years civil war had left the empire in disarray, but the assembly did have lasting results. The *Rule of Benedict* was henceforth regarded as the sole code for monastic communities within the empire, while the patronage of literature, science, and the arts that had begun under Charlemagne and had led to what we call the Carolingian Renaissance influenced the kind of work done by the monks. Many of them became members of the educated class, able to write elegant Latin prose and verse and to see to the preservation of important works of ancient literature and science.

Although this renaissance did not survive the wars of the mid-ninth century that brought the empire into a state of chaos, an institutional and spiritual renewal had taken hold by the middle of the tenth century, largely under the influence of the newly founded reform abbey of Cluny in Burgundy. In a departure from the Benedictine tradition of leaving each monastery quite independent of others, four gifted and long-lived Cluniac abbots who ruled from 927 to 1109 became the heads of a continent-wide body of monasteries whose superiors were appointed by the abbot of Cluny and whose monks took their vow of obedience to him. Cluny itself, along with many of its larger daughter houses, became a place of liturgical splendor, with the monks regularly spending more than eight hours each day in church or in chapter meetings.

THE CISTERCIANS: BERNARD OF CLAIRVAUX

Although there is evidence that the vast majority of the monks relished the amount of time given to liturgical services and the increasing splendor of their churches, this departure from the more balanced horarium of the Benedictine Rule with its prescribed periods of manual labor and *lectio divina* almost inevitably gave rise to still another reform movement. This new reform, inspired by a desire to return to a stricter observance of the *Rule of Benedict*, began at Cîteaux, located only about fifty miles to the northeast of Cluny. Scholars debate whether or not the documents that are ascribed to the earliest Cistercian reformers were subsequently modified for polemical purposes, but the general tenor of the literature is certainly accurate. One of the basic documents relates how in 1098 a group of twenty-one monks had left their own monastery of Molesme, whose level of observance they had found too lax, for the almost inaccessible wilderness of Cîteaux: "For these men while at Molesme had often spoken among themselves with bitterness and sorrow . . . of their transgression of the rule of St Benedict. They saw that they and other monks had promised at solemn profession to keep this rule and had in fact not kept it at all . . . And so, as has been related, by authority of the legate of the apostolic see they had come to this solitude, that they might keep the rule and their vows."[1]

The way of life at Cîteaux was so rigorous that for some time it was not clear whether or not the venture would succeed, but things changed dramatically in 1112 when a young man named Bernard (1090-1153) arrived with some thirty of his relatives and friends. This injected new life into the fledgling community. Within three years Bernard was delegated to found and serve as abbot of a daughter house at Clairvaux, which itself was responsible for many subsequent foundations. By the time Bernard died less than four decades later there were nearly 350 Cistercian monasteries throughout the European continent and the British Isles, while he himself had become the most influential person in the Western church during the twelfth century.

From Bernard of Clairvaux's numerous writings we will look only at a few aspects of his teaching, ones that either sound a new note in Christian spirituality or at least diverge from some earlier emphases. Given Bernard's emphasis on the role of love in Christian spirituality, it is not surprising that his longest and best-known work is a series of eighty-six sermons on the Song of Songs, in which he followed the lead of Origen in seeing the Song

---

1. *Exordium Parvum*, quoted by David Knowles, *Christian Monasticism* (New York: McGraw-Hill, 1969), 68.

as primarily a loving dialogue between Christ and the soul. Bernard was convinced that all the disorder and sinfulness of human life are ultimately due to the turning of the will from God to self (*voluntas propria*) and that love alone engages a person at a deep enough level to bring about true conversion to God. He believed that such love will be elicited not simply by hearing the two great scriptural commandments of love of God and love of neighbor but by reflecting on God's love for us, above all on the surpassing love for us revealed in Jesus Christ. Bernard accordingly wrote in his treatise *On Loving God*: "The faithful know how utterly they stand in need of Jesus and him crucified. They wonder at and reach out to that supreme love of his which passes all knowledge . . . The more surely you know yourself loved, the easier you will find it to love in return."[2] Knowing himself thus loved, Bernard responded with lyrical expressions of his own love for Christ, as in the following lines from his fifteenth sermon on the Song of Songs: "Write what you will, I shall not relish it unless it tells of Jesus. Talk or argue about what you will, I shall not relish it if you exclude the name of Jesus. Jesus to me is honey in the mouth, music in the ear, a song in the heart."[3] Here is that note of affectionate love for Jesus that has led many commentators to speak of Bernard's "affective mysticism."

The experience of Christ's presence that elicited such love from Bernard is described by him in a famous passage from the seventy-fourth sermon on the Song of Songs, where he writes that it was not by any of the five senses that he perceived the presence of the divine Bridegroom. Rather, "only by the warmth of my heart . . . did I know he was there, and I knew the power of his might because my faults were purged . . . I tell you, children, nothing else gives me joy when he is not with me, who alone is the source of my joy."[4] Although this affective note in Bernard's spirituality certainly does not reflect the sharp dichotomy between thought and feeling, theology and devotion, that eventually came to characterize some works of the late Middle Ages, we can definitely sense in him something of the shape of things to come.

One further point, less problematic from our contemporary perspective, can be illustrated by contrasting Bernard with one of the early fathers of the church, Cyprian of Carthage, who was martyred in the year 258. In his treatise *On Death*, Cyprian urged his readers not to weep for those members of the church who had died

---

2. Bernard of Clairvaux, *On Loving God* 3.7, in *Bernard of Clairvaux: Selected Works*, trans. G. R. Evans, Classics of Western Spirituality (New York: Paulist, 1987), 179.

3. Bernard of Clairvaux, Sermon 15 on the Song of Songs, 3.6, in idem, *On the Song of Songs I*, trans. Kilian Walsh, O.C.S.O. (Spencer, Mass.: Cistercian Publications, 1971), 110.

4. Bernard of Clairvaux, Sermon 74 on the Song of Songs, 2.6 and 3.7, in *Bernard of Clairvaux: Selected Writings*, 255-56.

> since we know that they are not lost but have gone on ahead of us . . . in order to lead the way. We must therefore envy them rather than lament them, and not put on somber garments down here, while up there they are clothed in white robes. Let us not give the heathen the opportunity to reproach us, and with reason, that we bewail those whom we declare to be living close to God, as though they were destroyed or lost.[5]

In certain obvious respects Cyprian's urging is in accord with Christian faith in eternal life, but taken literally his words betray a suspicion that human expressions of grief at the death of a loved one are somehow inappropriate for a Christian. In fact, the repression of such feelings is today considered unhealthy, even quite possibly the cause of serious psychological problems later on in one's life. In this respect, Bernard's attitude toward grieving is much more in accord with our contemporary understanding of a healthy spirituality. This is evident above all in his twenty-sixth sermon on the Song of Songs, preached shortly after the death of his brother Gerard, who had himself been a monk at Clairvaux. The entire sermon can be read with profit, but the following lines are especially telling:

> At the tomb of Lazarus Christ neither rebuked those who wept nor forbade them to weep, rather he wept with those who wept . . . These tears were witnesses to his human kindness, not signs that he lacked trust . . .
>
> In the same way, our weeping is not a sign of lack of faith; it indicates the human condition . . . You hear the heavy note of sorrow in my words, but I am far from murmuring . . . I still aver that the sweet and just Lord acted fairly to us both. "My song, O Lord, shall be of mercy and judgment" [Ps 100:1]. Let that mercy poured out by you on your servant Gerard sing to you; and let that judgment that I endure sing to you as well . . .
>
> . . . You entrusted Gerard to us, you have claimed him back; you have but taken what was yours. These tears prevent me speaking further; impose a limit on them, O Lord, bring them to an end.[6]

THE MENDICANTS: DOMINIC, THOMAS AQUINAS, AND FRANCIS AND CLARE OF ASSISI

Bernard of Clairvaux was but one of the major figures in a movement of remarkable spiritual renewal that took place in the Western church in the

---

5. Cyprian of Carthage, *De morte* 20, in *Patrologiae cursus completus: Series Latina,* ed. J.-P. Migne, 221 vols. (Paris: J.-P. Migne, 1844-55), 4:596.

6. Bernard of Clairvaux, Sermon 26 on the Song of Songs, in idem, *On the Song of Songs II,* trans. Kilian Walsh, O.C.S.O. (Kalamazoo, Mich.: Cistercian Publications, 1976), 72-73.

twelfth and thirteenth centuries. Even as Bernard had criticized what he considered the needless opulence of Cluniac churches, others saw the wealth and pompous lifestyle of some ecclesiastical leaders as contributing to the success of heretical movements like that of the Albigensians in the southern part of France.[7] Two such men were a Spanish bishop, Diego of Osma, and a member of his cathedral clergy named Dominic Guzmán (ca. 1170-1221). While traveling through Albigensian territory early in the thirteenth century, they learned by experience that the most effective way to combat that heresy was not through disputation but by leading an evangelical way of life that surpassed the one practiced by those Albigensians who were regarded as "the perfected." After Diego died, Dominic adopted a lifestyle of radical poverty and soon attracted a number of followers. Although he was unable to obtain papal permission to found a new religious order with its own rule, he was permitted to continue his work by agreeing to accept the centuries-old *Rule of Augustine*, supplemented by constitutions that prescribed in some detail the kind of life that he and his followers desired, with a pronounced emphasis on preaching, study, and mendicancy, that is, begging for their daily needs as they traveled throughout much of Europe preaching in public places.

The connection between preaching and study in the incipient Order of Preachers (who came to be popularly known as Dominicans) was not coincidental, for Dominic was insistent that members of his community be well trained in theology. To this end he arranged for theologians to come and teach his friars in Toulouse, and soon thereafter, in 1217, he sent some of them to the University of Paris for their studies. The most gifted of these friars eventually became teachers themselves, so that by the third decade of the century Dominicans held two professorial chairs of theology in Paris. One of these was eventually occupied by Thomas Aquinas (ca. 1225-1274), whose thought was controversial in his own day but is now regarded as one of the most reliable fonts of Christian theology.

Even though most of Thomas's works do not deal with topics that are normally classified as "spiritual writing," his overall influence on Christian spirituality has been profound—and precisely for the reason that he boldly distanced himself from what had been the most common philosophical underpinning of theology up to his day. We have already seen the strong influence that Platonic and Neoplatonic thought had on many thinkers in the early church. While not ignoring or deprecating Plato's philosophy, Thomas made even greater use of the thought of Aristotle, on whose treatises he wrote numerous commentaries. Whereas Plato, at least in his early work, wrote of

7. The Albigensians were very dualistic in outlook, with an extremely negative view of matter, marriage, etc.

the human body as a hindrance in the soul's pursuit of truth, so that "we shall continue closest to knowledge if we avoid as much as we can all contact and association with the body,"[8] Aristotle held to a much more integrated understanding of the human person. According to him, the soul is the very form of the body, and the starting point of human knowledge is the five senses. Although Thomas did not hesitate to reject aspects of Aristotle's thought that he found incompatible with Christian doctrine, he did accept Aristotle's positive understanding of the human body and his interest in the material world. Thomas accordingly avoided the sharply dualistic kind of spirituality that we saw in someone like Origen, and this in turn has helped some later spiritual writers avoid advocating practices that showed an unhealthy contempt for the body.

Around the year Thomas was born, there died the other great founder of a mendicant order, Francis of Assisi (ca. 1181-1226). Like Dominic, he was inspired by the description of the life of Jesus' first disciples as found in the Gospels, especially the account of Jesus' sending of his disciples "to every town and place where he himself intended to go," without purse, bag, or sandals, relying simply on God's providence and the hospitality of those who would provide them with food and drink (Lk 10:1-9; cf. Mt 10:5-9). There was, however, a significant difference between Dominic's and Francis's understandings of this apostolic way of life (*vita apostolica*). A passage from the prologue to the early Dominican constitutions clearly and succinctly states the fundamental aim of the Order of Preachers: Dominic gave any local superior the right to dispense the friars from various common observances "whenever it seems useful to him, particularly in things which seem likely to obstruct study or preaching or the good of souls, since our Order is known to have been founded initially precisely for the sake of preaching and the salvation of souls, and all our concern should be primarily and passionately directed to this all-important goal."[9] The Dominicans thus understood the apostolic life primarily in pragmatic terms; ascetic practices, including the strict practice of poverty, were directed to the goal of effective preaching. Francis, on the other hand, was more inspired by the overall vision of the apostolic life as described in the Gospel. Preaching was indeed part of this and, as such, was enthusiastically taken up as part of the evangelical way of life, but it did not function as what the Dominican constitutions called an "all-important goal."[10]

---

8. Plato, *Phaedo* 67a, trans. Hugh Tredennick, in *The Collected Dialogues of Plato*, ed. Edith Hamilton and Huntington Cairns (New York: Random House, 1961), 49.

9. In *Early Dominicans: Selected Writings*, ed. Simon Tugwell, O.P., Classics of Western Spirituality (New York: Paulist, 1982), 457.

10. For a more detailed description of this contrast, see Simon Tugwell's introduction to *Early Dominicans*, 16-19.

Shortly after Francis's conversion from a worldly way of life in which he had sought fame in the military service of his native city of Assisi and had looked forward to a lucrative business career in the footsteps of his wealthy father, he embarked on the life of a poor, itinerant preacher. Like Dominic, Francis soon attracted a number of like-minded followers. Unlike Dominic—and largely because he asked prior to the Fourth Lateran Council's prohibition of any new religious orders—he was also able to attain permission from Pope Innocent III in 1209 or 1210 to adopt a simple rule of life. This rule, made up mostly of Gospel texts, was later judged to be too difficult for members of his burgeoning religious order to follow, so in 1221 a modified rule was adopted instead, a document that came to be recognized as one of the richest spiritual documents of the Franciscan tradition.[11]

In certain respects this rule reflects the kind of provisions contained in earlier monastic rules such as that of St. Benedict. Both documents, for example, have chapters on the correction of brothers who are at fault and on the care of the sick members of the community, but in other respects, there are major differences. One of the central promises that Benedict required of his monks was that of stability. Most fundamentally this entailed a permanent commitment to the community that the monk had entered, but it also implied that one would normally live, work, and pray within the monastic enclosure. If a monk had to leave the precincts on some business, he was enjoined not to speak subsequently about what he had seen or heard while outside the monastery. On the contrary, both Franciscans and Dominicans—along with the other mendicant orders that arose at this time, the Carmelites and Augustinians—were expected to be out among the people, traveling from one town or city to the next on their preaching journeys and not even limiting themselves to regions where the majority of the population was Christian. Francis even inserted into his rule a chapter entitled "Those Who Are Going among the Saracens and Other Nonbelievers," which begins with the words: "The Lord says, *Behold, I am sending you as lambs in the midst of wolves.* Therefore, be *prudent as serpents and simple as doves* [Mt 10:16]. Therefore, any brother who, by divine inspiration, desires to go among the Saracens and other nonbelievers should go with the permission of his minister and servant."[12] Francis himself traveled much, once even going to Egypt in what

11. This rule of 1221 never received formal approval by a papal decree and so was followed two years later by a much shorter version commonly known as the Later Rule. It is the latter that still today is the fundamental charter for the three main families of Franciscans: the Friars Minor, the Friars Minor Conventual, and the Friars Minor Capuchin. Nevertheless, the "Earlier Rule" of 1221, with its far greater number of scriptural quotations, has remained a primary source of Franciscan spirituality.

12. *The Earlier Rule* 16:1-2, in *Francis and Clare: The Complete Works*, trans. Regis J. Armstrong, O.F.M. Cap. and Ignatius C. Brady, O.F.M., Classics of Western Spirituality (New York: Paulist, 1982), 121.

turned out to be an unsuccessful attempt to convert Sultan Malik-al-Kamil to Christianity.

A further characteristic of Francis's spirituality can best be illustrated by comparing him with Bernard of Clairvaux from the preceding century. Although Bernard would have preferred to remain always within his monastery, service to the church and society often saw him on the road, but even there his demeanor was so introspective that it was said he could travel from one town to another without having any sense of the kind of landscape he had traversed. Some aspects of his spirituality have been likened to the bare, whitewashed walls of a Cistercian oratory. Francis's spirituality, on the other hand, was much more sacramental in the sense that he readily saw features of the world around him as signs of God's presence. Perhaps his best-known composition is the "Canticle of Brother Sun," in which Francis invites all of creation to join him in praise of the Creator. It begins in the following way:

> Most High, all-powerful, good Lord,
> Yours are the praises, the glory, the honor, and all blessing.
> To You alone, Most High, do they belong,
> and no man is worthy to mention Your name.
> Praised be You, my Lord, with all your creatures,
> especially Sir Brother Sun,
> Who is the day and through whom You give us light.
> And he is beautiful and radiant with great splendor;
> and bears a likeness of You, Most High One.
> Praised be You, my Lord, through Sister Moon and the stars,
> in heaven You formed them clear and precious and beautiful.[13]

In the past hundred years at least five hundred articles and more than a dozen books have been published about this canticle, so clearly does it reflect the mystical vision of the saint. At least the following two points should be highlighted. First, although the popular image of Francis tends to be overly romantic and flowery, as though he had no appreciation of or acquaintance with the darker, harsher side of human life, as he neared his own death he added lines that realistically addressed death personified as "our Sister Bodily Death, / from whom no living man can escape. / Woe to those who die in mortal sin." Second, Francis clearly saw the various creatures around him as members of one family, to which he and all other human beings belonged. He could thus address the elements of wind, water, fire, and earth as his brothers and sisters, a fact that makes his having been named the patron saint of ecol-

13. Francis of Assisi, "The Canticle of Brother Sun," in *Francis and Clare*, 38.

ogy by Pope John Paul II especially fitting. Even though one will not find in Francis specific directives for the care of the environment, he offers our world something even more important and fundamental, a sense that human beings are not to be thought of as separate from the rest of creation, having some innate right to exploit it for their own ends, but rather as akin to the other creatures, each of which enjoys an intrinsic goodness in the sight of God apart from any usefulness it may have for humans.

Francis was able to love all of creation in large part because he did not cling to it. In fact, his love of poverty and simplicity earned him the title *Il Poverello*, the little poor man. After his death, however, varying interpretations of religious poverty led to sharp dissensions and even formal division among the friars. The person who most closely adhered to Francis's own ideal was not a friar but a woman, Clare (ca. 1193-1253), who was not yet twenty years old when she offered to Francis her solemn commitment to follow his way of life. Other women soon joined her at the church of San Damiano in Assisi, an edifice that Francis had once repaired with his own hands. For the remaining years of her life Clare remained superior of this monastic community, spending much time and effort in trying to secure papal approval of a stricter form of poverty than had been originally imposed on them by officials in the papal court. Finally, only two days before her death, Clare received a document in which Pope Innocent IV gave official approval to the rule she herself had written. It included a crucial chapter on "Not Having Possessions," which ended with the words that all who joined her community (which has since spread throughout the world and is commonly known as that of the Poor Clares) "are not to receive or hold onto any possessions or property [acquired] through an intermediary, or even anything that might reasonably be called property, except as much land as necessity requires for the integrity and the proper seclusion of the monastery; and this land is not to be cultivated except as a garden for the needs of the sisters."[14]

Along with her rule, we have letters that Clare sent to Agnes of Prague, a daughter of the king of Bohemia who had given up a life of royal luxury to enter a Poor Clare convent in the Bohemian capital. They reflect Clare's deep attraction to the poverty and humility of Christ and her desire to encourage such attraction in others. The last of these letters, written shortly before Clare died, is an especially beautiful piece of spiritual literature. Using the biblical image of a "mirror without blemish" (Wis 7:26), Clare urges Agnes to study that mirror each day, seeing within it "the poverty of Him Who was placed in a manger and wrapped in swaddling clothes," "the holy humility, the blessed

14. *The Rule of St. Clare* 6:5-6, in *Francis and Clare*, 219.

poverty, the untold labors and burdens which He endured for the redemption of all mankind," and "the ineffable charity which led Him to suffer on the wood of the Cross and die thereon the most shameful kind of death . . . From this moment, then, O queen of the heavenly King, let yourself be inflamed more strongly with the fervor of charity."[15] It is no exaggeration to say that the three practices mentioned in this passage—poverty, humility, and charity—remain foundational for the Poor Clares of our own day.

THE BEGUINES AND MEISTER ECKHART

Even as the foundation of the Poor Clares provided a way for women to follow Francis's way of radical poverty, other women were able to become nuns in the female branches of other religious orders, such as the Benedictines, Cistercians, and Dominicans. The mendicants even had lay groups associated with them, known variously as confraternities or Third Orders, whose members took promises or vows as a way of helping them attain holiness in secular society under the inspiration and spiritual guidance of one of the ecclesiastically approved religious orders. By the late twelfth century a different movement was also under way, especially in the Low Countries of northwestern Europe. Laywomen known as Beguines began living together in communities marked by poverty, celibacy, prayer, and service after the model of the Gospels, even though they were not affiliated with any religious order. This lack of affiliation inevitably led to suspicion on the part of church authorities, who occasionally issued warnings or even condemnations of the movement, although at other times they spoke in terms of cautious approval. The movement soon spread eastward into Germany, with more than two thousand such women living in Cologne by the middle of the thirteenth century.

What is especially important for our purposes is the fact that a few of the Beguines produced significant works of spiritual literature—treatises, poems, and letters—that have marked similarities with the work of some of the most prominent male authors of the period. In general, these women represent what the prominent church historian Bernard McGinn has called "vernacular theology," a third strand of medieval theology next to the monastic (as represented by someone like Bernard of Clairvaux) and the scholastic (which reached its apex in the writings of Thomas Aquinas). This vernacular theology and spirituality were characterized not simply by being written in vernacular languages (early forms of Dutch, French, and German) but by the

15. Clare of Assisi, "The Fourth Letter to Blessed Agnes of Prague," in *Francis and Clare*, 204-5.

fact that they broached new themes, or at least developed traditional themes in bold, new ways.

The central theme of union with God is especially instructive in this regard. We have already seen, from the time of Origen, how the scriptural text of the Song of Songs served as the foundation for reflections on union with God understood as a spousal union: the soul as bride seeks, and ideally attains, union with her divine Bridegroom. New Testament passages in which Christ is portrayed as a bridegroom, as in the parable of the ten bridesmaids (Mt 25:1-10), made such imagery seem natural in works like Bernard's sermons on the Song of Songs. It readily preserved a sense of divine transcendence, for however close the union, there remained a distinction between oneself and God, an "over against" to which St. Paul refers in writing that even in eternal life the elect will not be absorbed into or identified with God but will rather behold God "face to face" (1 Cor 13:12).

This sense of separateness, even to the slightest degree, is part of the pain to which spiritual writers often allude, occasionally calling it "the wound of love." Eventually a still more intimate union came to be affirmed, sometimes termed a "union without difference." Scriptural warrants for this were rarer but not totally lacking. St. Paul alludes at one place to a certain loss of selfhood and individual distinction when he writes that "it is no longer I who live, but it is Christ who lives in me" (Gal 2:20), while in the Fourth Gospel Jesus prays for his followers "that they may all be one. As you, Father, are in me and I am in you, may they also be in us" (Jn 17:21). Even more tellingly, the Letter to the Ephesians affirms that God "chose us in Christ before the foundation of the world to be holy and blameless before him in love" (Eph 1:4). If we creatures were somehow present and able to be chosen before the very creation of the world, this means that in some sense we *were* even before we existed as creatures in this realm of time and space. Such scriptural texts, few though they be, together with a conviction that this pre-temporal existence in the mind of God represents our truest self and that, because of the divine simplicity, this self is not distinct from God, led some of these Beguines to affirm what McGinn has called "*unitas indistinctionis*—the insistence that in the ground of reality there is absolute identity between God and the soul."[16]

We find this insistence, together with some of its ramifications for religious behavior, clearly taught in *The Mirror of Simple Souls*, written by a northern French Beguine named Marguerite Porete late in the thirteenth century. Porete writes that there are seven stages through which a soul passes

16. Bernard McGinn, introduction to *Meister Eckhart and the Beguine Mystics*, ed. Bernard McGinn (New York: Continuum, 1994), 12.

in its journey to God, beginning with a firm intent to keep the commandments of God until death and concluding with a seventh stage which will be attained only after death and cannot really be understood beforehand. While joined to its body on earth, the soul is keenly aware of its absolute difference from God, leading it to proclaim: "Lord, you are, and thus everything is perfected through you, and nothing is made without you. And I am not, and thus everything is made without me, and nothing is made through me."[17]

Knowing its own lowliness, the soul no longer desires even to will anything of its own. Whereas the more traditional teaching, as found for example in the works of William of St. Thierry (ca. 1085-1148), was that at the highest stage of the spiritual life the soul indeed has a will, but one that wills only what God wills, Porete went further and spoke of seeking the very annihilation of her own will. This annihilation itself is beyond the power of the soul. Rather, "it is the will of God which wills it in her. Which is why it appears that this Soul has no will without the will of God, who makes her will all that she ought to will."[18] If such annihilation takes place, then the soul has attained—or better, re-attained—the state in which it existed in the mind of God from all eternity. Porete teaches this with all possible clarity near the very end of her treatise, where she writes that at this stage

> the soul has nothing more to do for God than God does for her. Why? Because He is and she is not. She retains nothing more of herself in nothingness, because he is sufficient of Himself, that is, because He is and she is not. Thus she is stripped of all things because she is without existence, where she was before she was. Thus she has from God what He has, and she is what God is through the transformation of love, in that point in which she was before she flowed from the Goodness of God.[19]

Some of these expressions, such as the claim that at this stage the soul "is what God is," inevitably attracted the attention of church authorities, though a claim of this sort was rendered less daring by the following phrase explaining that the identity with God comes "through the transformation of love." What caused Porete much more serious problems were certain practical conclusions that she drew from her teaching about the annihilation of self-will, as when she wrote that such a soul "neither desires nor despises poverty nor tribulation, neither Mass nor sermon, neither fast nor prayer" and "no longer seeks God through penitence, nor through any sacrament of Holy Church."[20]

---

17. *Marguerite Porete: The Mirror of Simple Souls*, chap. 130, trans. Ellen L. Babinsky, Classics of Western Spirituality (New York: Paulist, 1993), 210-11.

18. Ibid., chap. 11 (p. 92).

19. Ibid., chap. 135 (p. 218).

20. Ibid., chap. 9 (p. 87) and chap. 85 (p. 160).

While a generous interpretation of these passages in our own day could conclude that "Marguerite's intention is to describe a spiritual life totally given over to the divine will, without any regard whatever for the ordinary cares and concerns of creaturehood,"[21] the eventual verdict of church authorities in her own time was severe. Near the beginning of the fourteenth century the bishop of Cambrai condemned Porete's treatise as heretical and had it publicly burned in her presence. That was only the beginning of her troubles. In 1308 Porete was arrested by the Dominican inquisitor, William of Paris, and judged guilty of having continued to propagate copies of her work after it had thus been condemned. Refusing to recant, she was burned at the stake in Paris on June 1, 1310.

Only a year after Porete underwent this harshest of punishments, one of the Dominican professorial chairs at the University of Paris was occupied by a man who has become one of the most frequently quoted spiritual writers of our day, Meister Eckhart (ca. 1260-ca. 1328). We do not even know his first name, for Meister is simply a title indicating that he had attained the highest academic degree and so had the right to teach courses of his own devising. Born near the German city of Erfurt, he entered the Order of Preachers while in his teens, studied in both Cologne and Paris, and subsequently spent the rest of his life alternating between academic, administrative, and pastoral assignments within his order.

Whether or not Eckhart was directly influenced by the writings of Marguerite Porete, there is no doubt that both of them shared certain key ideas about the nature of a human being's relationship with God. When writing of our existence in the realm of time and space, Eckhart insists on the absolute abyss that separates us from the transcendent God. If one claims that God is, then one will consistently have to claim that we are not, for in and of ourselves we are nothing apart from God's creative and conserving power. On the other hand, if one speaks of creatures as existing—as in one respect they clearly are—then one will just as consistently have to affirm that God is not: "He is as high above being as the highest angel is above a gnat. I would be speaking as incorrectly in calling God a being as if I called the sun pale or black."[22] At other times, however, Eckhart makes the most daring expressions of identity between creatures and God, as when he writes in another sermon:

> The Father gives birth to his Son in eternity, equal to himself . . . Yet I say more: He has given birth to him in my soul . . . The Father gives birth to his Son without ceasing; and I say more: He gives me birth, me, his Son

21. Ellen L. Babinsky, introduction to *Marguerite Porete*, 44.
22. Meister Eckhart, Sermon 9, in *Meister Eckhart: Teacher and Preacher*, ed. Bernard McGinn, Classics of Western Spiritualty (New York: Paulist, 1986), 256.

> and the same Son. I say more: He gives birth not only to me, his Son, but he gives birth to me as himself and himself as me, and to me as his being and nature. In the innermost source, there I spring out in the Holy Spirit, where there is one life and one being and one work. Everything God performs is one; therefore he gives me, his Son, birth without any distinction.[23]

Not surprisingly, such passages brought Eckhart under the same suspicion of heresy as had led to Marguerite Porete's execution. He was indeed brought to trial, first in Cologne at the behest of the archbishop of that city and then, after Eckhart had exercised his right to appeal to the pope, before the papal court at Avignon. He died in that city before Pope John XXII issued a decree condemning seventeen Eckhartian passages as heretical and another eleven as "very rash and suspect of heresy, although with many explanations and additions they might take on or possess a Catholic meaning."[24] We have enough material from the trials to see that one way in which Eckhart tried to defend himself was to claim that he was speaking from the perspective of eternity while his accusers were interpreting his works in temporal terms. Thus, during his trial in Cologne Eckhart's response to the charges brought against him included his statement that "every action of God is his substance, which is eternal. They [his accusers] do not understand what Augustine in the first book of the *Confessions* says of God: 'All tomorrows and beyond them, and all yesterdays and what is behind them, you are making today and have made today. What is it to me if someone does not understand this?'"[25]

Another way of explaining the boldness of some of his statements, such as the claim that God "gives birth to me as himself and himself as me," so that "he gives me, his Son, birth without any distinction," is to recall what we said earlier about the position that in some sense creatures have been in the mind of God from all eternity and that, because of the divine simplicity, they are in that respect identical with God. In fact, Eckhart makes this point quite often, especially in his Latin works, where he draws a distinction between an entity's virtual being (*esse virtuale*) and the formal being (*esse formale*) that accrues to it when it comes forth from God as a creature in time and space. Thus, in his *Commentary on John* Eckhart writes: "It is noteworthy that "before the foundation of the world" [Jn 17:24] everything in the universe was not mere

---

23. Meister Eckhart, Sermon 6, in *Meister Eckhart: The Essential Sermons, Commentaries, Treatises, and Defense*, trans. Edmund Colledge, O.S.A., and Bernard McGinn, Classics of Western Spirituality (New York: Paulist, 1981), 187-88.

24. Pope John XXII, *In agro dominico* (March 27, 1329), in *Meister Eckhart: The Essential Sermons*, 80.

25. Eckhart, "Response to the List of Fifty-nine Articles," in *Meister Eckhart: The Essential Sermons*, 76. The quotation from Augustine is from *Confessions* 1.6.3.

nothing, but was in possession of virtual existence,"[26] while in his *Commentary on Wisdom* he explains, "All things are in God as in the First Cause in an intellectual way and in the mind of the Maker. Therefore, they do not have any of their formal existence until they are causally produced and extracted on the outside in order to exist."[27]

The practical value for one's spiritual life that Eckhart found in teaching and preaching this doctrine lay in his conviction that a lively awareness that our truest being is in God, infinitely transcending the temporal order, will keep a person from being overcome by the inevitable vicissitudes of life on earth. One of his most widely read treatises was entitled *The Book of Divine Consolation.* Here he does not explicitly refer to the distinction between virtual being and formal being, but it is clearly the foundation of his teaching when he writes:

> In God there is no sorrow or suffering or affliction. If you want to be free of all affliction and suffering, hold fast to God and turn wholly to him and to no one else . . . If you preserved yourself as you were formed, in justice alone . . . then truly nothing could cause you suffering . . . Not unlikeness, not injustice, not anything made or created can cause suffering to one who is just, for everything that is created is as far beneath him as it is beneath God . . . [A]ll his being, living, knowing and loving is from God, is in God, is God.[28]

Here again one finds an expression that sounds overly bold: that all the "being, living, and knowing" of a person who turns wholly to God is not only *in* God but *is* God. If one accepts the distinction Eckhart makes between our virtual existence and our formal existence, one might readily reject the charge that he was a pantheist or autotheist (that is, one who claims, without qualification, that his or her very self is God). There is, however, another aspect of Eckhart's thought that is more troublesome. At a symposium on Eckhart's thought held a few years ago, the theologian Zachary Hayes raised some critical questions about the place of history in the Meister's thought. We have earlier alluded to the fact that proponents of what Bernard McGinn termed the *unitas indistinctionis* go beyond what St. Paul calls the face-to-face character of eternal life with God. Noting this, Hayes asked incisively:

> What does it mean when we view the "end" as a union not of two things that remain distinct, but as an absolute unity in which there is simply the

26. Eckhart, *Commentary on John* 1.45, in *Meister Eckhart: The Essential Sermons,* 137.
27. Eckhart, *Commentary on Wisdom* 21, in *Meister Eckhart: Teacher and Preacher*, 148.
28. Eckhart, *The Book of Divine Consolation* 1, in *Meister Eckhart: The Essential Sermons*, 211-12.

> One? [Eckhart writes,] "He who is one with God is 'one spirit' with God, the same existence." That is strong language. As a description of the end, it seems to coincide with what Eckhart had envisioned as the point of departure for his system: the undifferentiated Godhead, the mysterious origin of life. If creation emerges from a precreational oneness in the undifferentiated Godhead and returns to a final "postcreational" undifferentiated oneness in the Godhead, what is being said about history? If, after history is over, all is the same as "it was," is history just so much "sound and fury"? God gains nothing from it, for by definition, this is impossible. The creature seems to gain nothing from it, for it already "was" what it "becomes." What, then, is the point of creation and history at all?[29]

To ask those questions does not necessarily mean that they could not possibly be given a satisfactory answer from an Eckhartian perspective, but one would have to work at it. The point of creation was affirmed much more clearly and succinctly by the next spiritual master we will examine, an Englishwoman who has in recent years acquired just as avid a following as Eckhart.

JULIAN OF NORWICH

Thus far we have alluded to a number of different lifestyles lived by women during the first fourteen centuries of the church's history. The vast majority, of course, were wives and mothers, like Dhuoda. Macrina was an unmarried woman who led a quasi-monastic life within her own household, while Clare took formal religious vows as a nun and Marguerite Porete was but one of many Beguines in the late Middle Ages. Far less numerous than any of these were the anchoresses, women who lived a strictly enclosed life in a one- or two-room dwelling called an anchorhold, often built against the side wall of a church in such a way that an interior window opened up onto the sanctuary while an exterior window served as a means of communication with persons who came to seek the anchoress's counsel. Of all the medieval anchoresses, the one who has become best known in our own day is Julian of Norwich (ca. 1342-ca. 1416).

Almost everything we know about Julian comes from her own written work, the *Showing* (or *Revelations*), which has come down to us in two forms. The first, and shorter, was written soon after a vivid religious experience that she had when thirty years old. Apparently on the verge of death from some mysterious ailment, she had received the last rites from the parish priest and

29. Zachary Hayes, "Response to Bernard McGinn," in *God and Creation: An Ecumenical Symposium*, ed. David B. Burrell and Bernard McGinn (Notre Dame, Ind.: University of Notre Dame Press, 1990), 224.

was preparing to die when she suddenly recovered and, in the course of the next day and a half, underwent a series of sixteen "showings." Some of these were what she called "bodily visions" of Christ or of his mother Mary; some were "words formed in my understanding"; and still others were "spiritual visions" in which nothing was seen imaginatively but in which she gained special insight into one or another of the mysteries of the faith. In the short text of her treatise, Julian for the most part simply describes these experiences. If this were all that she left us, she would not stand out from many other medieval visionaries who left similar accounts of what they had seen or heard while in a state of ecstasy. Julian, however, continued to ponder the meaning of these showings over the next two decades, expanding her original work into the "long text" that allows us to place her in the ranks of the greatest of theologians. Three aspects of her teaching may be singled out as especially important for Christian spirituality today.

First, Julian was very comfortable speaking about what we might call "the maternal face of God." This was not original with her, for there are hints of this already in the Bible, as when God speaks to the people of Zion through the prophet Isaiah: "Can a woman forget her nursing child, or show no compassion for the child of her womb? Even these may forget, yet I will not forget you" (Is 49:15), or when Jesus laments over Jerusalem: "How often have I desired to gather your children together as a hen gathers her brood under her wings, and you were not willing!" (Mt 23:37). Picking up on such imagery, there were twelfth-century Cistercian abbots who wrote of "Jesus as mother,"[30] but none did so at as great a length as Julian or with reference to both the creative and the redemptive activity of God. She broaches this theme especially in chapters 57 through 63 of her long text, for example, when she draws a number of comparisons between our earthly mothers and Jesus as mother:

> The mother's service is nearest, readiest and surest: nearest because it is most natural, readiest because it is most loving, and surest because it is truest. No one might ever or could perform this office fully, except only him. We know that all our mothers bear us for pain and for death. O, what is that? But our true Mother Jesus, he alone bears us for joy and for endless life, blessed may he be . . .
>
> The mother can give her child to suck of her milk, but our precious Mother Jesus can feed us with himself, and does, most courteously and most tenderly, with the blessed sacrament, which is the precious food of true life . . .

30. See Caroline Walker Bynum, *Jesus as Mother: Studies in the Spirituality of the High Middle Ages* (Berkeley: University of California Press, 1982).

> The mother can lay her child tenderly to her breast, but our tender Mother Jesus can lead us easily into his blessed breast through his sweet open side, and show us there a part of the godhead and of the joys of heaven, with inner certainty of endless bliss.[31]

To be sure, such language as being led into Jesus' breast "through his sweet open side" may sound saccharine to many readers today, but the feeling of being protected by Christ and supported by knowledge of his love for his followers is one that Christians of all times can share with Julian.

A second aspect of her teaching that sets Julian apart from many spiritual writers is her very positive appreciation of the body and corporeality. For all that we might find admirable in the spirituality of Antony of Egypt, there are passages in Athanasius's *Life of Antony* that do not accord well with the image we see of Christ in the Gospels as someone who enjoyed eating and drinking with those who were scorned by the self-righteous. For example, Athanasius writes at one point that when Antony "was about to eat and sleep and provide for the other needs of the body, shame overcame him as he thought of the spiritual nature of the soul. Often when about to partake of food with many other monks, the thought of spiritual food came upon him and he would beg to be excused and went a long way from them, thinking that he should be ashamed to be seen eating by others."[32] It is noteworthy that Athanasius does not even specify what he means by "the other needs of the body." Altogether different, and far more wholesome, is Julian's attitude. Her reflection on the very first of the sixteen showings includes the following passage:

> The highest form of prayer is to the goodness of God, which comes down to us in our humblest needs . . . It is nearest in nature and promptest in grace, for it is the same grace which the soul seeks and always will, until we truly know our God, who has enclosed us all in himself.
>
> A man walks upright, and the food in his body is shut in as if in a well-made purse. When the time of his necessity comes, the purse is opened and then shut again, in most seemly fashion. And it is God who does this, as it is shown when he says that he comes down to us in our humblest needs. For he does not despise what he has made, nor does he disdain to serve us in the simplest natural functions of our body, for love of the soul which he created in his own likeness.[33]

---

31. Julian of Norwich, *Showings*, chap 61 (long text), trans. Edmund Colledge, O.S.A., and James Walsh, S.J., Classics of Western Spirituality (New York: Paulist, 1978), 297-98.

32. Athanasius, *Life of Antony* 45, trans. Robert T. Meyer, Ancient Christian Writers 10 (Westminster, Md.: Newman Press, 1978), 58.

33. Julian, *Showings*, chap. 6 (long text), 185-86. Not surprisingly, this passage does not appear in all of the manuscripts, but it is found in the earliest one, now in the Bibliothèque Nationale in Paris,

Third and last, Julian emphasizes, above all in the final chapter of her long text, that the entire reason why God created us and the rest of creation was love, a love that "was never abated and never will be." Moreover, this love is extended as fully to the greatest of sinners as to the holiest of saints, in the former case urging them to conversion, in the latter fostering fidelity and perseverance. Studies in the psychology of religion have shown the harm that is done to persons who consider themselves to be so sinful as to be deserving of nothing but divine wrath. As the Benedictine theologian Sebastian Moore has written, when someone hurts another or otherwise does something seriously wrong, it is easy and in some ways even natural to regard oneself as "a lousy, no-good person" from whom not much else could be expected. Moore notes that such a response is in fact a refusal to face the full situation, which is that in harming another, one is shrinking oneself: "When you hurt another person, your true self, the lover in you, goes into hiding, and uses every possible ruse to stay in hiding."[34] One of the great virtues of Julian's *Showings* is the way it encourages us to see the full picture and so avoid what in fact would be a cowardly self-denigration. Not denying the reality of sin and wrongdoing, Julian nevertheless knew that this does not constitute who we are at the deepest level and that in many respects our sins are the "happy fault" about which the church's liturgy sings at the paschal vigil each year. In Julian's words,

> we shall truly see in heaven without end that we have sinned grievously in this life; and notwithstanding this, we shall truly see that we were never hurt in [God's] love, nor were we ever of less value in his sight. And by the experience of this falling we shall have a great and marvelous knowledge of love in God without end; for enduring and marvelous is that love which cannot and will not be broken because of offenses.[35]

THE ICONS OF THE EASTERN CHURCH

For all of the depth of Julian's spirituality, there is at least one respect in which it is almost inevitably weak. Living as she did in a simple anchor-hold, with only a limited view into the interior of the church to which her dwelling was attached, she would have had little familiarity with religious art and so does,

---

and accordingly is part of the text as printed in both of the modern critical editions (those by James Walsh and Marion Glasscoe). It is easy to surmise that later, overly squeamish copyists would have omitted the passage.

34. Sebastian Moore, *The Crucified Jesus Is No Stranger* (New York: Seabury, 1977), 98.

35. Julian, *Showings*, chap. 61 (long text), 300.

in fact, make almost no allusions to it in her writing apart from brief references to the crucifix held before her eyes during the almost fatal illness of her thirtieth year. For most Christians, however, especially the millions who lived in the centuries before literacy became common, one of the privileged sources of spiritual wisdom was the visual arts. Paintings of Christ and other holy persons in the catacombs of Rome and similar frescoes on the walls of an ancient house church at Dura-Europos in Syria bear witness to the existence of such art from at least the late second and early third century, while the stained-glass windows of the medieval churches of Europe served as a Bible in pictures for the many worshipers who were unable to read. However, perhaps no aspect of Christian visual art has received as much attention in recent years as the icons of the Eastern churches.

The word "icon" itself simply means image, so even a statue in granite or marble is an icon, but the term is usually used of images painted (or "written") on wood panels, along with frescoes and mosaics on the walls and in the domes of churches. Genuine iconographers do not seek to be innovative but want only to pass on a sacred tradition dating back many centuries. One of their purposes was enunciated centuries ago by the great ascetic author Nilus of Sinai (d. ca. 430), who addressed the following words to a civil official who had built a church and was planning to embellish it with paintings: "Let the hand of the artist fill the church on both sides with pictures from the Old and New Testaments, in order that the illiterate, who cannot read the Divine Scriptures, should, by looking at the painted images, bring to mind the valiant deeds of those who served God with all sincerity and be themselves incited to rival the glorious and ever-memorable exploits through which they exchanged earth for heaven."[36] It would be wrong, however, to conclude from this that the only purpose of the icons was to instruct persons who were unable to read. Iconography is a fully liturgical art, one that is for all members of the church a privileged source of communication with the supernatural realm, a source of divine grace or sanctification, "a window into the supernatural world." This is why many members of the Eastern church even have in their homes an icon corner or shelf before which family prayers are offered, accompanied by burning incense and lighted candles.

Things were not always such. For more than a hundred years, beginning with a decree of the Byzantine emperor Leo III in 726, the iconoclasts ("image-breakers") held sway in the Eastern church, charging that those who venerated icons were guilty of idolatry. Many icons were destroyed and some

---

36. St. Nilus of Sinai, Letter to the Prefect Olympiodorus, quoted by Leonid Ouspensky, "The Meaning and Language of Icons," in Leonid Ouspensky and Valdimir Lossky, *The Meaning of Icons*, trans. G. E. H. Palmer and E. Kadloubovsky (Crestwood, N.Y.: St. Vladimir's Seminary Press, 1983), 26 n. 3.

of the iconographers put to death. Leading the opposition to the iconoclasts was John of Damascus (ca. 675-ca. 749). Living outside the borders of the Byzantine empire, he was able to write in defense of the icons without fear of retribution by the emperor, so he composed three forceful apologies against the iconoclasts. His major argument was based on the truth of the incarnation of the Son of God. John granted that "in former times God, who is without form or body, could never be depicted. But now when God is seen in the flesh conversing with men, I make an image of the God whom I see. I do not worship matter; I worship the Creator of matter who became matter for my sake . . . Never will I cease honoring the matter which wrought my salvation!"[37] Several decades after John's death, this and similar arguments were made at the Second Council of Nicaea (787), which decreed that the icons are a guarantee that the incarnation of the Word of God is true and not illusory. In fact, this council placed the icons on the same level as the symbol of the cross and the Gospels, for it held that the icons correspond to what the Gospels preach and narrate. As Basil the Great had written four centuries earlier, "What the word transmits through the ear, the painting silently shows through the image."[38] Even this ecumenical council did not finally resolve the controversy, which dragged on until 843, when the empress Theodora restored the icons, celebrating on the First Sunday of Lent a feast that is still kept in the Eastern church as "the Feast of Orthodoxy."

Among the many aspects of iconography that contribute to their spiritual power but are often overlooked by those not familiar with this kind of art is the fact that Christ and the saints are almost always turned toward the congregation, either full face or three-quarters, since to portray them in profile would to some degree break communion; depiction in profile is primarily allowed in the case of persons who have not yet attained sanctity. The prominent twentieth-century spiritual writer Henri Nouwen has some especially fine reflections on this point with regard to one of the most revered icons of the Russian Orthodox Church, Andrei Rublev's *Savior of Zvenigorod*, dating from the late fourteenth or early fifteenth century. Nouwen's study, although not as scholarly as many others, is based on careful research, but it reflects at the same time his own religious sensibility, as in the following passage:

> What finally makes seeing Rublev's icon such a profound spiritual experience are the eyes of the Savior. Their gaze is so mysterious and deep that any word which tries to describe them is inadequate . . . The Christ of

37. John of Damascus, *First Apology* 16, in *On the Divine Images: Three Apologies against Those Who Attack the Divine Images*, trans. David Anderson (Crestwood, N.Y.: St. Vladimir's Seminary Press, 1997), 23.

38. Basil the Great, "Discourse 19, On the Forty Martyrs," quoted by Ouspensky, "Meaning and Language of Icons," 30.

> Rublev looks directly at us and confronts us with his penetrating eyes . . . They are not severe or judgmental, but they see all that is. They form the true center of the icon . . . They are the eyes of God, who sees us in our most hidden places and loves us with a divine mercy.[39]

THE HESYCHASTS: SYMEON THE NEW THEOLOGIAN AND GREGORY PALAMAS

Scholars of Eastern Christian spirituality regularly point out that there are two primary ways of praying within that tradition.[40] One, called "iconic" and hence exemplified by (but not limited to) the icons themselves, makes full use of the imagination: symbols, ritual, poetry, music. The other way, "non-iconic," seeks to transcend images and discursive thought. An early representative of this latter way was Gregory of Nyssa with his emphasis on the incomprehensibility of God. Around the same time, and especially in monastic settings, there arose a form of prayer that came to be called "hesychastic," from the Greek word *hēsychia*, which designates a state of calm and silence resulting from the cessation of external noise and internal disturbance. In the Septuagint, the Greek word and its cognates appear in a number of texts, for example, Lamentations 3:26: "It is good that one should wait quietly for the salvation of the Lord." The church historian Sozomen (ca. 400-ca. 450) described the hermit monks of Egypt as "lovers of hesychia," not simply because they sought external quiet and solitude but also because they cultivated interior calm by trying to live without care and to hold fast to the "memory of God" by seeing the divine presence in all aspects of their daily life.

One special way in which these hermits maintained an awareness of God's presence was through practicing what was sometimes called "the prayer of a single word," according to which a word or short phrase was frequently repeated, sometimes in conjunction with the rhythm of one's breathing. Various phrases were advocated, but the one that became most common was "the Jesus Prayer," in which the petition of the blind beggar Bartimaeus in the Gospel (Mk 10:48) and that of the tax collector in Jesus' parable of the Pharisee and the tax collector (Lk 18:13) were combined and somewhat modified into the form, "Lord Jesus Christ, Son of God, have mercy on me, a sinner."

In the tenth century this form of prayer was avidly promulgated by a man who came to be known as Symeon the New Theologian (949-1042). While

39. Henri Nouwen, *Behold the Beauty of the Lord: Praying with Icons* (Notre Dame, Ind.: Ave Maria, 1987), 52-53.

40. See, e.g., Kallistos Ware, "The Spirituality of the Icon," in *The Study of Spirituality*, ed. Cheslyn Jones et al. (New York/Oxford: Oxford University Press, 1986), 198.

working as a civil servant in Constantinople, he followed the advice of his spiritual father to read the works of a fifth-century monk named Mark the Hermit. So impressed was Symeon by this material that he began spending his evenings in lengthy periods of prayer, from dusk till midnight, until on one occasion he had a profound experience of what he took to be divine light. Writing of himself in the third person, he described it thus:

> One day, as he stood and recited, "God, have mercy upon me, a sinner," uttering it with his mind rather than his mouth, suddenly a flood of divine radiance appeared from above and filled all the room. As this happened, the young man lost all awareness [of his surroundings] and forgot that he was in a house or that he was under a roof. He saw nothing but light all around him and did not know if he was standing on the ground . . . Oblivious of all the world, he was filled with tears and with ineffable joy and gladness . . .
>
> Once this vision was over and the young man . . . had come to himself, he was moved with joy and amazement. He wept with all his heart, and sweetness accompanied his tears.[41]

Soon thereafter Symeon became a monk at the Stoudion monastery in Constantinople and was eventually chosen to be its superior. His time in office was not entirely pleasant, for some of the monks vigorously opposed him for his mystical tendencies. Symeon eventually resigned as superior and moved to another monastery on the Asiatic side of the Bosphorus, but his writings became very influential for transmitting the tradition of hesychastic prayer to succeeding generations, especially for the thousands of monks who by this time had begun living on Mt. Athos, a peninsula in northeastern Greece that even today is considered the heart of Byzantine monasticism. There, in the thirteenth or fourteenth century, the monk Nicephorus wrote a treatise *On Vigilance and the Guarding of the Heart* in which he gave a detailed description of how one should pray the Jesus Prayer, including the need to find a quiet place, to lower one's head so as to be looking at the middle of the body, and to repeat the words of the prayer in such a way that gradually they move from the mind and lips into the heart.

One sees in Nicephorus's teaching a laudable attempt to avoid an overly intellectual kind of prayer, but the practice was not without its severe critics. Owing in part to exaggerated language used by some of the Athonite monks to describe their experience of union with God, the monk Barlaam, originally

41. Symeon the New Theologian, "Discourse 22: On Faith," in *Symeon the New Theologian: Discourses*, trans. C. J. deCatanzaro, Classics of Western Spirituality (New York: Paulist, 1980), 245-46.

from Calabria but residing in Constantinople, accused them of pretending to contemplate the essence of God with their physical eyes. Coming to the defense of his fellow Athonites was the monk Gregory Palamas (1296-1359). The controversy raged for many years, but Palamas was ultimately vindicated by three synods held in Constantinople between the years 1341 and 1351. The details of the controversy do not permit a simple summary, but one point should be stressed above all. The light or radiance that Symeon the New Theologian had experienced several centuries earlier and that many monks of Mt. Athos likewise claimed to have experienced was not, said Palamas, a physical light of the senses, but it could be perceived through the senses provided that they were transformed by the grace of the Holy Spirit. One of the strongest points in Palamas's favor was that such perception has a firm Gospel foundation in the account of Jesus' transfiguration on the mountain (traditionally considered to be Mt. Tabor, though it is not named in the Gospels). Palamas argued that just as Jesus' disciples Peter, James, and John were able to behold with their bodily eyes the divine radiance of their transfigured Lord (Mk 9:2-8 and parallels), it would be an inadmissible limitation on God's power to say that what occurred in New Testament times is no longer possible. In Palamas's words:

> Having testified to his vision of Christ's glory on the holy mountain—of a light which illumines, strange though it may be, the ears themselves (for they contemplated also a luminous cloud from which words reverberated)—Peter goes on to say, "This confirms the prophetic word" [2 Pet 1:19]. What is this prophetic word which the vision of light confirms for you, O contemplators of God? What if not that verse that God "wraps Himself in light as in a mantle" [Ps 104:2]? . . .
>
> Do you not see how this light shines even now in the hearts of the faithful and perfect? Do you not see how it is superior to the light of knowledge? It has nothing to do with that which comes from Hellenic studies . . . Indeed, this light of contemplation even differs from the light that comes from the holy Scriptures, whose light may be compared to "a lamp that shines in an obscure place" [2 Pet 1:19], whereas the light of mystical contemplation is compared to the star of the morning which shines in full daylight, that is to say, to the sun.[42]

In subsequent centuries, the most significant movement within this tradition of prayer was the so-called "Hesychast renaissance," which began in the

42. *Gregory Palamas: The Triads* 2.3.18, trans. Nicholas Gendle, Classics of Western Spirituality (New York: Paulist, 1983), 62-63.

latter part of the eighteenth century and resulted in a compilation of texts known as the *Philokalia*. Its two editors, Nicodemus of the Holy Mountain and Macarius of Corinth, intended the work for all Christians, and with its translation from the Greek into many other languages their wish has been largely fulfilled. Equally influential, though dependent on the *Philokalia*, is a shorter work from nineteenth-century Russia entitled *The Way of a Pilgrim*, purporting to be the account of how a simple pilgrim discovered the Jesus Prayer and the way in which its practice transformed his life.[43]

QUESTIONS FOR REFLECTION

1. Bernard's "affective mysticism" is evident when he writes that Jesus is "honey in the mouth, music in the ear, a song in the heart" and that "nothing else gives me joy when he is not with me." Many people in our own day are much more reserved about expressing religious feelings. Does Bernard have anything important to teach us in this regard?
2. Francis of Assisi took very seriously his claim of kinship with all creatures, calling them his brothers and sisters. Do you find a solid foundation for this kind of language, or are you inclined to dismiss it as overly romantic? What, if anything, do you think Francis has to offer the environmental movement today?
3. Writings of both Marguerite Porete and Meister Eckhart were judged heretical by church leaders in their day. What do you think are valid grounds for judging any work heretical? Do you agree with the judgments rendered against those two authors? Why or why not?
4. What might be the value of Julian's writing of Jesus as our mother? Is this something that could usefully be preached to congregations today? If so, how do you think it could most effectively be done?
5. As noted at the end of this chapter, both "iconic" and "non-iconic" ways of praying are common in the Eastern church. Granted that the two ways are not mutually exclusive, to which of the two are you more deeply drawn? If you were to teach that way to others, how would you go about doing so?

SUGGESTIONS FOR FURTHER READING AND STUDY

On the Cistercians and Bernard of Clairvaux

Bernard of Clairvaux, Sermon 26 on the Song of Songs. In idem, *On the Song of Songs II*, translated by Kilian Walsh, O.C.S.O., 58-73. Kalamazoo, Mich.: Cistercian

43. See *Writings from the Philokalia: On Prayer of the Heart*, trans. E. Kadloubovsky and G.H.E. Palmer (London: Faber & Faber, 1992) and *The Way of a Pilgrim*, trans. Olga Savin (Boston: Shambala, 1996).

Publications, 1976. All eighty-six of these sermons are available from this publisher, in four separate volumes.

Casey, Michael, O.C.S.O. "Cistercian Spirituality." In *The New Dictionary of Catholic Spirituality*, edited by Michael Downey, 173-82. Collegeville, Minn.: Liturgical Press, 1993.

On the Mendicants: Dominic, Francis, and Clare

Early Dominicans: Selected Writings. Edited and introduced by Simon Tugwell, O.P. Classics of Western Spirituality. New York: Paulist, 1982. See especially Tugwell's introduction (pp. 1-47) and Jean de Mailly's *Life of St. Dominic* (pp. 53-60).

Francis and Clare: The Complete Works. Edited and introduced by Regis Armstrong, O.F.M. Cap., and Ignatius Brady, O.F.M. Classics of Western Spirituality. New York: Paulist, 1982. See especially the editors' introductions to Francis and Clare (pp. 3-21 and 169-85), Francis's "Canticle of Brother Sun" (pp. 37-39), his *Earlier Rule* (pp. 107-35), and his *Testament* (pp. 153-56); and Clare's Letters to Blessed Agnes of Prague (pp. 189-206), her *Rule* (pp. 209-25), and her *Testament* (pp. 226-32).

Hellmann, J. A. Wayne. "The Spirituality of the Franciscans." In *Christian Spirituality: High Middle Ages and Reformation*, edited by Jill Raitt, 31-50. World Spirituality 17. New York: Crossroad, 1987.

Tugwell, Simon, O.P. "The Spirituality of the Dominicans." In *Christian Spirituality: High Middle Ages and Reformation*, edited by Jill Raitt, 15-31. World Spirituality 17. New York: Crossroad, 1987.

On the Beguines and Meister Eckhart

Marguerite Porete: The Mirror of Simple Souls. Translated and introduced by Ellen L. Babinsky. Classics of Western Spirituality. New York: Paulist, 1993. See especially Babinsky's introduction (pp. 5-61).

McGinn, Bernard, ed. *Meister Eckhart and the Beguine Mystics: Hadewijch of Brabant, Mechthild of Magdeburg, and Marguerite Porete*. New York: Continuum, 1994. See especially McGinn's introduction (pp. 1-14).

Meister Eckhart: The Essential Sermons, Commentaries, Treatises, and Defense. Translated and edited by Edmund Colledge, O.S.A., and Bernard McGinn. Classics of Western Spirituality. New York: Paulist, 1981. See especially McGinn's "Theological Summary" (pp. 24-61), Eckhart's Sermons 6 (pp. 185-89) and 52 (pp. 199-203), and his treatise *On Detachment* (pp. 285-94).

On Julian of Norwich

Julian of Norwich: Showings. Translated and introduced by Edmund Colledge, O.S.A., and James Walsh, S.J. Classics of Western Spirituality. New York: Paulist, 1978.

See especially chaps. 57-63 of the long text. Julian's work is also available in several other modern English translations, including *Revelations of Divine Love*, translated by Elizabeth Spearing (New York: Penguin, 1999), and *Revelation of Love*, translated by John Skinner (New York: Doubleday, Image Books, 1996).

Llewelyn, Robert, ed. *Julian: Woman of Our Day*. Mystic, Conn.: Twenty-third Publications, 1987. See especially Ritamary Bradley, "Julian on Prayer" (pp. 61-74).

On the Icons of the Eastern Church

Nouwen, Henri. *Behold the Beauty of the Lord: Praying with Icons*. Notre Dame, Ind.: Ave Maria, 1987.

Ouspensky, Leonid. "Icon and Art." In *Christian Spirituality: Origins to the Twelfth Century*, edited by Bernard McGinn and John Meyendorff, 382-94. World Spirituality 16. New York: Crossroad, 1985.

Ouspensky, Leonid, and Vladimir Lossky. *The Meaning of Icons*. Crestwood, N.Y.: St. Vladimir's Seminary Press, 1983.

Ware, Kallistos. "The Spirituality of the Icon." In *The Study of Spirituality*, ed. Cheslyn Jones et al., 195-98. New York/Oxford: Oxford University Press, 1986.

On the Hesychasts: Symeon the New Theologian and Gregory Palamas

Symeon the New Theologian: The Discourses. Translated by C. J. de Catanzaro. Introduced by George Maloney, S.J. Classics of Western Spirituality. New York: Paulist, 1980. See especially Maloney's introduction (pp. 1-36) and Symeon's "Discourse 22: On Faith" (pp. 243-53).

Gregory Palamas: The Triads. Edited and introduced by John Meyendorff. Translated by Nicholas Gendle. Classics of Western Spirituality. New York: Paulist, 1983. See especially Meyendorff's introduction (pp. 1-22) and the texts on deification in Christ (pp. 57-69).

Ware, Kallistos. "The Origins of the Jesus Prayer," "Symeon the New Theologian," "The Hesychasts," and "The Hesychast Renaissance." In *The Study of Spirituality*, ed. Cheslyn Jones et al., 175-84 and 235-58. New York/Oxford: Oxford University Press, 1986.

7

Reformation Spirituality, Protestant and Roman Catholic

WE HAVE ALREADY SEEN that at least by the fourth and fifth centuries Christianity had spread south into the African kingdoms of Ethiopia and Nubia. By the beginning of the seventh century the Christian faith had also begun spreading east of Persia, carried primarily by East Syrian monks, priests, and merchants following the Silk Road. In this way the Christian message had reached the Chinese city of Ch'ang-an, the imperial capital of the T'ang dynasty, by the year 635. Within two centuries, however, leading Confucian scholars had persuaded the emperor to preside over a nationalistic revival that led to a persecution of adherents of all nonindigenous religions: Manicheans, Buddhists, Zoroastrians, and Christians alike. In 845 the Christian religion was banned entirely, with monks and priests being forced to abandon their vocations, although some Christian communities survived, as was noted by the Italian merchant Marco Polo when he visited Beijing, the capital of the Mongol ruler Kublai Khan, around 1275. After Marco Polo's visit, several Franciscan missionaries also journeyed to China, but no permanent churches resulted from their efforts, and we last hear of any of them in 1360.[1] Another century and a half would pass before the Roman Catholic Church made any further attempts to establish a church of the Western (or Latin) rite in that part of the world. The effects of these later endeavors on Christian spirituality in Asia, as well as of similar efforts by various churches in Africa and the Americas, will be the focus of the final three chapters of this book.

At about the very time that this renewed missionary work had begun in Asia, the church in Europe itself was beginning to undergo a massive realignment in what is commonly called the Protestant Reformation, with profound effects for the understanding and practice of Christian spirituality. The

1. For further details about Christian expansion into Asia during this period, see Dale T. Irwin and Scott W. Sunquist, *History of the World Christian Movement*, vol. 1, *Earliest Christianity to 1453* (Maryknoll, N.Y.: Orbis Books, 2001), esp. chapters 25 and 35, on which the above paragraph relies.

Protestant reformers, however, were not the only European Christians who saw the need for church reform, so we will here be considering not only the work of Martin Luther, John Calvin, and Thomas Cranmer but also that of Ignatius of Loyola and Teresa of Avila. Moreover, since the following three chapters of this book will focus on Christian spirituality in other parts of the world, in this present chapter we will also discuss a few more recent European representatives of the spirituality taught and exemplified by some of the above-named reformers.

LUTHERAN SPIRITUALITY: MARTIN LUTHER AND DIETRICH BONHOEFFER

For many years, most Christians of the various Protestant churches avoided using the term "spirituality," and for quite understandable reasons. In the first chapter above, we referred to the Catholic theologian Walter Principe, who wrote that Christian spirituality refers to one's "striving for an ever more intense union with the Father through Jesus Christ by living in the Spirit." Such talk of "striving" sounds suspiciously like the "works righteousness" that traditional Protestant theology considers absolutely contrary to New Testament teaching. In fact, even Catholics would have to object to such a description of spirituality to the extent that it neglects to mention a truth common to all Christian churches, namely, that God's grace is the origin and foundation of our being in a right relationship with God. Many Protestants, however, are nowadays quite willing to speak of their tradition's spirituality, for they have found the term useful as a tool for describing a way of life based on faith as a gift of a loving God.

Theologically speaking, this right relationship is called "justification," a term taken from the realm of law and indicating that two parties are no longer in a state of enmity. Specifically, God is understood to render a verdict of acquittal toward sinners, who are thereby declared "just" (or "righteous"—in this context, the English words justification and righteousness are synonyms, since to be "justified" means precisely to be in a "right" relationship with God). The doctrine of justification lies at the very heart of the Christian faith, with the result that it was above all different understandings of this basic teaching that resulted in the disputes that led ultimately to the Protestant Reformation.

The first and surely the most influential of these reformers was Martin Luther (1483-1546). He was born of peasant stock in northeastern Germany, but his father Hans wanted all of his children to be as well educated and successful as possible. Recognizing Martin's intelligence, Hans sent him to some of the best schools in the country, including the University of Erfurt, from which Martin earned his master of arts degree in 1505. The next year he became an Augustinian friar in the same city and was ordained a priest only a year later, far more quickly than would be possible in the Catholic Church today. That same year, 1507, he began his theological studies and before long was told by his Augustinian superior, Johann von Staupitz, to work toward a doctorate in that field in preparation for a career as a theology professor at the University of Wittenberg. He began teaching there in 1512 and remained on the faculty at Wittenberg until the end of his life, lecturing primarily in the field of biblical exegesis.

Although Luther was outwardly successful as a budding scholar, his personal life was in turmoil. Nowhere is this described as starkly as in the preface to his Latin writings, which Luther wrote near the end of his life. That preface also gives a succinct description of how Luther had once arrived at a momentous change in his understanding of the doctrine of justification, which he came to consider to be the doctrine undergirding and governing all the others. Scholars debate the accuracy of some details of Luther's account, something not surprising when one considers that he is recounting things that occurred several decades earlier. Toward the end of the piece he recalls the years when he was giving courses at Wittenberg on various books of the Bible and how distressed he had been by what Paul wrote in the Letter to the Romans about "the righteousness of God" (Rom 1:17). He goes so far as to say that he actually "hated" the term, which he had been taught to understand as the "active" divine quality by which God is righteous and punishes the unrighteous sinner. What most afflicted Luther about the term was the sharp sense of his own sinfulness, for the passage continues with these striking words:

> Though I lived as a monk without reproach, I felt that I was a sinner before God with an extremely disturbed conscience. I could not believe that he was placated by my satisfaction. I did not love, yes, I hated the righteous God who punishes sinners, and secretly, if not blasphemously, certainly murmuring greatly, I was angry with God and said, "As if, indeed, it is not enough that miserable sinners, eternally lost through original sin, are crushed by every kind of calamity by the law of the Decalogue, without having God add pain to pain by the gospel and also by the gospel threatening us with his righteousness and wrath!" Thus I raged with a fierce and troubled conscience. Nevertheless, I beat importunately upon Paul at that place, most ardently desiring to know what St. Paul wanted.

> At last, by the mercy of God, meditating day and night, I gave heed to the context of the words, namely, "In it the righteousness of God is revealed, as it is written, 'He who through faith is righteous shall live.'" There I began to understand that the righteousness of God is that by which the righteous lives by a gift of God, namely by faith. And this is the meaning: the righteousness of God is revealed by the gospel, namely, the passive righteousness by which merciful God justifies us by faith, as it is written, "He who through faith is righteous shall live." Here I felt that I was altogether born again and had entered paradise itself through open gates.[2]

This insight led Luther to a sharp critique not only of the practice of indulgences, about which he had written the famous Ninety-Five Theses, but also of the very notion that any acts that humans perform could ever make a person righteous. Doctrinal battle lines were soon in place, disputations were held between representatives of the pope on the one hand and Luther and his supporters on the other, and soon the once scrupulously observant Augustinian friar found himself excommunicated. Within a decade tens of thousands of Germans had joined Luther, many monasteries and other religious houses stood closed, and the movement had spread to neighboring countries.

For our purposes, the challenge is to understand the implications of Luther's position for Protestant spirituality. The first and most important point is that such spirituality is not so much something one does as rather what is done for one by God, followed by an inevitable change in one's personal behavior. Faith itself is clearly taught to be a gift of God, not something that humans bring about. It consists not in doctrines one believes but in the conviction that God, in sheer and undeserved mercy, has effected reconciliation with sinners through the saving death of Jesus Christ. In one of his most irenic early writings, *The Freedom of a Christian*, Luther at times writes in the language of an ancient or medieval mystic like Origen or Bernard, as when he speaks of faith as that which "unites the soul with Christ as a bride is united with her bridegroom."[3] Just as in marriage between a man and a woman there is a mutual exchange of gifts, in an even more profound way this occurs in the relationship between Christ and his followers. In this exchange Christ takes their sin upon himself and in turn grants them his righteousness: "Christ is full of grace, life, and salvation. The soul is full of sins, death, and

---

2. Martin Luther, Preface to the Complete Edition of Luther's Latin Writings, in *Martin Luther's Basic Theological Writings*, ed. Timothy F. Lull, 2nd ed., with CD-ROM (Minneapolis: Fortress, 2005), 8-9.

3. Martin Luther, *Freedom of a Christian*, in *Martin Luther's Basic Theological Writings*, 397.

damnation. Now let faith come between them and sins, death, and damnation will be Christ's, while grace, life, and salvation will be the soul's; for if Christ is a bridegroom, he must take upon himself the things that are his bride's and bestow upon her the things that are his."[4]

What, then, of good works? Is one to take one's ease and be content with faith? By no means, Luther insists, but the works, while by no means justifying persons before God, will flow spontaneously from their faith and serve the welfare of others, helping them in their needs. It is in this sense that Luther explains that "faith is truly active through love [Gal 5:6], that is, it finds expression in works of the freest service, cheerfully and lovingly done, with which a man willingly serves another without hope of reward; and for himself he is satisfied with the fullness and wealth of his faith."[5]

When one considers that for centuries the undivided church had taught that the very beginning of faith, as well as its increase and even the desire to believe, can occur only as a gift of God,[6] and when one further considers the New Testament's teaching about the way good works naturally flow from a rightly ordered heart—as in Jesus' words that "the good person out of the good treasure of the heart produces good" (Lk 6:45)—one may wonder why the disputes and eventual division ever came about. There is no short answer to such a question, but there was definite need for reform in the church (as called for even by loyal Catholics like Erasmus of Rotterdam), and many admired Luther for refusing to take back anything he had written (including harsh condemnations of the papacy) when he was brought before Emperor Charles V and numerous other political and ecclesiastical potentates at Worms in southwestern Germany in the spring of 1521. Today, however, and largely as a result of intensive dialogue between representatives of the Lutheran and Roman Catholic Churches in the aftermath of the Second Vatican Council (1962-1965), a common understanding of justification has been reached. The "Joint Declaration on the Doctrine of Justification," officially signed at a ceremony in Augsburg on October 31, 1999, states that the two churches do not take the sixteenth-century condemnations lightly but adds that "in their respective histories our churches have come to new insights" that allow them to see those condemnations in a different light. Accordingly, both churches can now together confess that "by grace alone, in faith in Christ's saving work and not because of any merit on our part, we are accepted by God and receive the Holy Spirit, who renews our hearts while

4. Martin Luther, *Freedom of a Christian*, in *Martin Luther's Basic Theological Writings*, 397.
5. Ibid., 405.
6. See, e.g., the canons of the sixth-century Council of Orange.

equipping and calling us to good works."[7] The declaration concludes with the expressed hope that the Holy Spirit will "lead us further toward that visible unity which is Christ's will."

Just as Luther wanted to do away with what he considered harmful accretions that had taken root in the church over the preceding centuries, so too did a prominent Lutheran theologian of the twentieth century criticize attitudes and practices that had crept into his own church since the time of Luther. Dietrich Bonhoeffer (1906-1945) was born in Breslau, Germany, into a large and cultured family whose ancestors numbered theologians, professors, lawyers, and artists. Already in his early teens he had determined to study theology, which he did first at the University of Tübingen and later in Berlin. One of his best-known books, *The Cost of Discipleship*, is a forceful critique of the way Luther's understanding of God's grace had devolved into a caricature that Bonhoeffer called "cheap grace." By this he meant "the preaching of forgiveness without requiring repentance, baptism without church discipline, Communion without confession, absolution without personal confession. Cheap grace is grace without discipleship, grace without the cross, grace without Jesus Christ, living and incarnate."[8] Bonhoeffer insisted that when Luther said that grace alone can save, this claim included as its inevitable corollary an obligation to discipleship. Luther did not always need to mention this obligation explicitly, for it was clear to him that "this grace had cost him his very life," leading him "to the strictest following of Christ."[9]

It could just as correctly be said that this grace—"costly grace"—cost Bonhoeffer his very life as well, in an even more literal way. His spirituality, no less than Luther's, was not one of withdrawal into cloistered solitude but one of engagement. Though pacifist by nature, Bonhoeffer was appalled by the rise of the Nazi party in Germany and was actively involved in a group that tried to bring about a coup d'état during the 1930s and then, during the Second World War, tried to assassinate Hitler. It would have been altogether easy for Bonhoeffer to escape the consequences of such involvement. Having already spent a sabbatical year at Union Theological Seminary in New York before the Nazis came to power, he accepted an invitation to return there in 1939 for a summer appointment, with the possibility of remaining in the United States for the duration of a war that he clearly saw approaching. However, hardly had he arrived in New York when he began to doubt the

---

7. "Joint Declaration on the Doctrine of Justification," no. 15, in *Origins: CNS Documentary Service* 28, no. 8 (July 16, 1998): 122.

8. Dietrich Bonhoeffer, *The Cost of Discipleship*, trans. R. H. Fuller, rev. ed. (New York: Macmillan, 1963), 47.

9. Ibid., 53.

wisdom of having left Germany and so decided to return. As he wrote to the theologian Reinhold Neibuhr while sitting in the garden of the American friend who had secured the summer appointment for him,

> I have had time to think and to pray about my situation and that of my nation and to have God's will for me clarified. I have come to the conclusion that I have made a mistake in coming to America. I must live through this difficult period of our national history with the Christian people of Germany. I shall have no right to participate in the reconstruction of Christian life in Germany after the war if I do not share the trials of this time with my people . . . Christians in Germany will face the terrible alternative of either willing the defeat of their nation in order that Christian civilization may survive, or willing the victory of their nation and thereby destroying our civilization. I know which of these alternatives I must choose, but I cannot make that choice in security.[10]

In fact, Bonhoeffer was returning to an early death. Arrested by the Gestapo in the spring of 1943, he spent the final two years of his life in prison and was executed at the dreaded Flossenbürg extermination camp in Bavaria only weeks before the war in Europe ended. During those two years Bonhoeffer wrote many letters, which were later edited and published by his best friend, Eberhard Bethge. In one of the last letters, addressed to Bethge himself, Bonhoeffer wrote: "During the last year or so I've come to know and understand more and more the profound this-worldliness of Christianity . . . By this-worldliness I mean living unreservedly in life's duties, problems, successes and failures, experiences and perplexities. In so doing we throw ourselves completely into the arms of God, taking seriously not our own sufferings but those of God in the world—watching with Christ in Gethsemane. That, I think, is faith . . ."[11]

If Bonhoeffer had survived the war, he would surely have become a prominent professor and the author of many more books, but his influence has arguably been greater for the very "this-worldly" witness he gave by working with those who were actively trying to bring about the downfall of Hitler's regime and by being executed as a result of such activity. One of the central themes of Christian spirituality today is that it cannot stand aloof from the worlds of politics, economics, and other spheres that have at times been

---

10. Dietrich Bonhoeffer to Reinhold Niebuhr, July 1939, in Mary Bosanquet, *The Life and Death of Dietrich Bonhoeffer* (New York: Harper & Row, 1968), 217.

11. Dietrich Bonhoeffer to Eberhard Bethge, July 21, 1944, in idem, *Letters and Papers from Prison*, ed. Eberhard Bethge, trans. Reginald Fuller et al., enlarged ed. (New York: Macmillan, 1972), 369-70.

regarded as peripheral to the gospel. To be sure, one might disagree about particular tactics. One of Luther's essays, *On Temporal Authority, the Extent to which It Should Be Obeyed*, argues that even when secular authorities are acting in a manifestly unjust way and against the gospel, a Christian's resistance should take only the form of passive disobedience. In sensing the need to go beyond this form of resistance, Bonhoeffer did not deny that he was thereby having to abandon a sense of his own righteousness. In the words of one of his biographers,

> Step by step he was to be involved in a conspiracy which would require the abandonment of much that Christian life demands, expert lying built up into layer upon layer of closely-woven deception, and ultimately the willingness to murder. Bonhoeffer never for a moment regarded these evils as anything but what they were—evil. He accepted them as necessary.[12]

THE SPIRITUALITY OF JOHN CALVIN

Next to Luther, the most prominent of the Protestant Reformers was John Calvin (1509-1564). Born in Noyon, France, Calvin was trained as a lawyer at Orléans and Bourges, where he came into contact with the ideas of Luther and other first-generation reformers. In his early twenties he moved to Paris, where he became further acquainted with and accepting of these ideas. Critical remarks he made about the papacy in an oration at the Sorbonne so alarmed some of his friends that they warned him to flee France for his own safety. Calvin accordingly spent most of the rest of his life in Switzerland, first in Basel and then, in two separate periods, in Geneva, where he served as chief pastor of the city for twenty-three years.

As a second-generation leader in the Protestant Reformation, Calvin found in Switzerland a church already heavily influenced by Ulrich Zwingli (1484-1531), whose distrust of anything that could detract from the centrality of the Word led to positions considerably more radical than ones that Luther espoused. Whereas Luther did not feel that images in churches needed to be positively combated as dangerous, in the early summer of 1524 Zwingli and a group of his associates entered every church in Zurich and within two weeks stripped them of all art. Every standing altar was removed from the church, every painting was taken down and burned, and all crucifixes were removed, after which the walls were whitewashed to remove all

12. Bosanquet, *Life and Death of Dietrich Bonhoeffer*, 219-20.

traces of what had formerly adorned them. Churches in Calvin's Geneva were likewise much plainer than Lutheran ones in northern Germany. No portrayals of God in human form were allowed in the churches, not simply because this could lead something created to be confused with the Creator but more significantly because the transcendent God simply could not be portrayed.

This point about God's transcendence provides a useful entrée into Calvin's spirituality. Although he was a complex figure whose spirituality had many different aspects and whose way of expressing himself could differ radically from one context to the next, largely depending on whether he was addressing adversaries or like-minded followers, Calvin regularly emphasized how far the divine reality exceeds the power of the human mind to grasp it. As he writes in the first book of his major work, the *Institutes of the Christian Religion*, "[God's] essence is incomprehensible; hence, his divineness far escapes all human perception."[13] Humans can, however, know—or perhaps better, can experience—God through God's mighty acts, as when they experience thunder, one of Calvin's favorite metaphors. In one of his sermons on the Book of Deuteronomy, he said: "If we simply listen to natural thunder, we are seized with fear. Yet nothing is put into words; God only produces an indistinct rumbling. How would it be, then, if he should speak to us and reveal his glory? A human being cannot see God without dying or being consumed."[14]

This abyss between creatures and Creator was bridged, however, by Christ as mediator between God and human beings. Book 2 of the *Institutes* is on Jesus Christ as Redeemer, and here Calvin uses the same kind of language of exchange that we saw in Luther: "[The Mediator's] task was to restore us to God's grace so as to make of the children of men, children of God . . . Who could have done this had not the selfsame Son of God become the Son of man, and had not so taken what was ours as to impart what was his to us, and to make what was his by nature ours by grace?" (2.12.2). Although in the *Institutes* Calvin writes in a systematic and logical way, the twentieth-century Calvinist scholar Wilhelm Niesel was surely correct in claiming that the real foundation of Calvinism is the *unio mystica*, the union of Christ with the believer. In Niesel's words, "For Calvin . . . that joining together of Head and members, that indwelling of Christ in our hearts—in short, that mystical

13. John Calvin, *Institutes of the Christian Religion* 1.5.1 (1559 edition), in *Calvin's Institutes: A New Compend*, ed. Hugh T. Kerr (Louisville: Westminster John Knox Press, 1989), 24. Subsequent parenthetical references to this work indicate the number of the book, the chapter, and the section.

14. Calvin, Sermon 43 on Deuteronomy, quoted by William J. Bouwsma, "The Spirituality of John Calvin," in *Christian Spirituality: High Middle Ages and Reformation*, ed. Jill Raitt, World Spirituality 17 (New York: Crossroad, 1987), 323.

union is fundamental. We do not, therefore, contemplate him outside ourselves from afar in order that his righteousness may be imputed to us, but because we put on Christ and are engrafted into his body—in short because he deigns to make us one with him."[15]

If one uses this term *unio mystica*, however, it must be understood as mediated through the church, above all through preaching and the celebration of the Lord's Supper. As another Calvinist scholar has noted, "for Calvin the reading and preaching of the Word is the way in which Christ comes to us and shares himself with us . . . So totally did Calvin see the reading and preaching of the Word as a single indissoluble event (and not one a commentary on the other) that his Liturgy contains no provision for the reading of the Word; it simply assumes that reading and preaching will be a single act."[16] Nor did Calvin want this aspect of the liturgy to be separated from the celebration of the Lord's Supper, for this is another way in which Christ comes to share himself with his people. Under Zwingli's influence the Lord's Supper had already been reduced to being celebrated only a few times a year, something against which Calvin protested all his life, though largely in vain. He writes of Christ as "the only food of our soul" (4.17.1), and although he, like the other Protestant reformers, rejected the Catholic terminology of "transubstantiation" with regard to the eucharist, and although he claimed that "this mystery of Christ's secret union with the devout is by nature incomprehensible" (4.17.1), he certainly believed in the real presence of Christ in the Supper and spoke of this with almost childlike simplicity: "Now, if anyone should ask me how this takes place, I shall not be ashamed to confess that it is a secret too lofty for either my mind to comprehend or my words to declare. And, to speak more plainly, I rather experience than understand it. Therefore, I here embrace without controversy the truth of God in which I may safely rest. He declares his flesh the food of my soul, his blood its drink. I offer my soul to him to be fed with such food" (4.17.32).

Calvin expected Christians thus nourished with the Word through sermon and sacrament to be active throughout society, entering the realms of politics, scientific endeavor, and the arts. Indeed, he reserved some of his highest praise for those who serve in civil government: "No one ought to doubt that civil authority is a calling, not only holy and lawful before God, but also the most sacred and by far the most honorable of all callings in the whole life of mortal men" (4.20.4). This ideal seemed within reach in a soci-

15. Wilhelm Niesel, *Reformed Symbolics* (Edinburgh: Oliver & Boyd, 1962), 182, quoted by Howard G. Hageman, "Reformed Spirituality," in *Protestant Spiritual Traditions* (New York: Paulist, 1986), 60-61.

16. Hageman, "Reformed Spirituality," 66.

ety like that of Calvin's Geneva, where church and commonwealth were mutually inclusive. It is not so readily obtainable in societies that proclaim the separation of church and state, a difficulty that is frankly acknowledged by some contemporary authors within this tradition. As one of them has asked with reference to his own country: "What happens to Reformed piety when Church and State are 'separate,' or faith and culture are at cross-purposes? Or where the prevailing ethos is no longer Protestant, or even Christian? ... In other words, how does [one] manage to live in terms of Reformed commitments and values in the America we increasingly know today?"[17]

ANGLICAN SPIRITUALITY: *THE BOOK OF COMMON PRAYER* AND EVELYN UNDERHILL

Wherever and in whatever form it took root, the Protestant Reformation emphasized the priesthood of all believers as distinct from a two-tiered order in which those who were ordained and/or living under religious vows were regarded as *ipso facto* leading a holier way of life. The particular way in which this emphasis was manifested in the Church of England will provide a helpful focus for our discussion of Anglican spirituality.

In 1534 King Henry VIII obtained from Parliament the Act of Supremacy, creating a national church separate from Rome and naming the king as protector and sole supreme head of the church and clergy of England. This was the decisive moment of the English Reformation. Many of the monasteries were subsequently dissolved, with their buildings often taken apart and the stones used for the construction of grand homes for the nobility nearby. Henry had already named Thomas Cranmer archbishop of Canterbury, and it was under Cranmer's leadership that the liturgical life of the church was reformed. Although many persons regard the Middle Ages in the West as an age of faith, there were definite deficiencies in the liturgical practice of that era. Whereas in the time of Augustine of Hippo the congregation shared with him a common language, Latin, the rise of the various Romance languages in subsequent centuries meant that Latin became more and more the reserve of an educated elite. Since the prayers of the Mass continued to be in that language, it was no longer possible for most members of the congregation to participate fully in the celebration; many of them accordingly turned to various private devotions (such as the rosary) while the priest recited the eucharistic prayer. While the use of vernacular languages in the

17. T. Hartley Hall IV, "The Shape of Reformed Piety," in *Spiritual Traditions for the Contemporary Church*, ed. Robin Maas and Gabriel O'Donnell, O.P. (Nashville: Abingdon, 1990), 217.

liturgy became more and more common throughout the churches of the Protestant Reformation, in England this went hand-in-hand with a further change, the publication of *The Book of Common Prayer.*

This book brought together in one volume all the public rites of the church. In addition, it provided a structure for the regular public reading of the Bible, in such a way that the New Testament would be read through three times in the course of each year and the First Testament once. These two books were the only ones needed for the public services. Although the fact is not evident at first sight, *The Book of Common Prayer* (often referred to simply as the Prayer Book) owes much to the pattern of common prayer found in the *Rule of Benedict*, for what Cranmer basically did was combine Benedict's two morning services of Vigils and Lauds into Morning Prayer (or "Matins") and the two Benedictine services that end the day—Vespers and Compline—into Evening Prayer ("Evensong"). Both the structure and the language of the prayers owe much to Cranmer's work, with some of them having been composed by him, others superbly translated from the Latin prayers that had been in use for centuries. Although members of each parish were expected to pray these together in church, especially on Sundays, they were also encouraged to use the book as the focal point of their spirituality throughout the week. Martin Thornton, former chancellor of Truro Cathedral, has expressed the real significance of *The Book of Common Prayer* for Anglican spirituality in the following words:

> The Prayer Book was not a shiny volume to be borrowed from a shelf on entering the church and carefully replaced on leaving. It was a beloved and battered personal possession, a lifelong companion and guide, to be carried from church to kitchen, to living room, to bedside table. It was a symbol of the domestic emphasis, providing spiritual stimulus, moral guidance, meditative material and family prayer.[18]

When the Prayer Book was taken from one's home to the church on Sundays, it was not only so that one could take part in the parish celebration of Morning Prayer or Evensong. The full Sunday morning service as Cranmer envisioned it continued after Matins with the Great Litany and the eucharist. Although he had made certain revisions in the Mass as it had been celebrated in the Middle Ages, the basic structure remained: a service of the Word of God, including a sermon, followed by the Holy Communion, with both the bread and the cup offered to the communicants after the priest had prayed

18. Martin Thornton, "The Caroline Divines and the Cambridge Platonists," in *The Study of Spirituality*, ed. Cheslyn Jones et al. (New York/Oxford: Oxford University Press, 1986), 435.

the Great Thanksgiving. For Cranmer, it was above all the eucharist that served as a bridge to a life of "good works," another essential aspect of Anglican spirituality. This link is especially clear in some of the traditional prayers known as collects, such as the following:

> O Lord our heavenly Father, whose blessed Son came not to be ministered unto but to minister: Bless, we beseech thee, all who, following in his steps, give themselves to the service of others; that with wisdom, patience, and courage, they may minister in his name to the suffering, the friendless, and the needy; for the love of him who laid down his life for us, the same thy Son our Savior Jesus Christ, who liveth and reigneth with thee and the Holy Spirit, one God, for ever and ever. *Amen.*[19]

As an indication of the unsurpassed importance of the eucharist in the spirituality of many Christians, there is an eloquent paragraph from the pen of a twentieth-century Anglican liturgist, Dom Gregory Dix. Near the end of his lengthy study of the historical development of the eucharistic rite, he describes some of the many different occasions that Christians have traditionally marked by the celebration of the eucharist. Both Anglicans and Roman Catholics, as well as members of other churches that have retained this sacrament, can readily affirm what Dix wrote about why Christians have regularly sought to fulfill Christ's command, "Do this in remembrance of me" (Lk 22:19):

> Was ever another command so obeyed? . . . Men have found no better thing than this to do for kings at their crowning or for criminals going to the scaffold; for armies in triumph or for a bride and bridegroom in a little country church; for the proclamation of a dogma or for a good crop of wheat; for the wisdom of the Parliament of a mighty nation or for a sick old woman afraid to die; . . . furtively, by an exiled bishop who had hewn timber all day in a prison camp near Murmansk; gorgeously, for the canonization of S. Joan of Arc—one could fill many pages with the reasons why men have done this, and not tell a hundredth part of them. And best of all, week by week and month by month, on a hundred thousand successive Sundays, faithfully, unfailingly, across all the parishes of christendom, the pastors have done this just to make the plebs sancta Dei—the holy common people of God.[20]

---

19. *The Book of Common Prayer . . . According to the Use of The Episcopal Church* (New York: Church Hymnal Corporation and Seabury Press, 1979), 209.
20. Dom Gregory Dix, *The Shape of the Liturgy* (London: Dacre Press, 1945), 744.

Even the most reverent celebration of liturgical rites will not, however, by itself keep alive the spiritual life of a people. Teaching is also necessary, and in more recent times one of the most influential teachers in the Anglican Church was a laywoman, Evelyn Underhill (1875-1941). Born into a prosperous English family, Underhill grew up in London with parents who were not of a strong religious persuasion. As a young woman, she had little appreciation of institutional religion but was drawn toward the study of mysticism as found in various traditions throughout the world. Being self-taught in philosophy, psychology, and religious studies, Underhill began work on her first study of mysticism in 1907. When it was published four years later under the title *Mysticism*, she became immediately well known.[21] In the words of one scholar, the book's originality "lay in the fact that it redefined what it is to be human and what it is to be religious," while its popularity "stemmed from the fact that it carved out a new subject, made it intelligible, and interpreted it with convincing power."[22]

Gradually, and largely through the guidance of astute spiritual directors like the Roman Catholic layman Friedrich von Hügel and the Anglican priest Reginald Somerset Ward, Underhill became more open to the importance of membership in a church (what she sometimes called "corporate religious life") and participation in its liturgy. In her late forties she began regularly attending services in the Church of England and soon was being asked to conduct retreats, including ones for Anglican clergy. Although still able to draw upon her vast knowledge of mysticism in all of the world's religions, she now focused mainly on the Christian tradition, emphasizing above all the call to love God and one's neighbor and the need for regular times of quiet, contemplative prayer if one is to avoid "the starved life" of the merely "Social Christian." She concluded one of her finest retreat conferences with the words: "I emphasize this [need of a balanced life], because its realization seems to me to be a desperate modern need; a need exhibited supremely in our languid and ineffectual spirituality, but also in the too busy, too entirely active and hurried life of the artist, the reformer and the teacher."[23] It was such teaching, and the books and articles that complemented these retreat conferences, that led the former archbishop of Canterbury Michael Ramsey to say that it was primarily Evelyn Underhill who kept spiritual life alive in the Anglican Church in the period between the two World Wars.

---

21. Evelyn Underhill, *Mysticism: A Study in the Nature and Development of Man's Spiritual Consciousness* (London: Methuen, 1911). This work went through many revised editions and is still in print from various publishers.

22. Dana Greene, *Evelyn Underhill: Artist of the Infinite Life* (New York: Crossroad, 1990), 54.

23. Evelyn Underhill, "The Life of the Spirit in the Individual," in eadem, *The Life of the Spirit and the Life of To-day* (London: Methuen, 1922), 160.

IGNATIAN SPIRITUALITY: IGNATIUS OF LOYOLA AND KARL RAHNER

In the opening pages of this chapter we noted that it was not only the Protestant Reformers like Luther and Calvin who saw the need for reform of the church in the late medieval and early modern periods. What was once regularly called the Counter-Reformation is now more properly called the Catholic Reformation, implying that it was seen to be necessary by many Roman Catholics even apart from the rise of the Protestant churches. One of the earliest and most influential leaders of this reformation was a Spaniard, Ignatius of Loyola (1491-1556), who did indeed seek to "counter" inroads made by Lutherans and Calvinists but who was motivated primarily by a simple desire to advance the kingdom of Christ as he understood it.

The story of Ignatius's conversion from a self-centered way of life is about as dramatic as one could wish. Ignatius was born into a noble family, and his only goal as a young man was to become a dashing soldier and a ladies' man. His leg was broken by a cannonball during the siege of the town of Pamplona, and he was considerately taken by his French captors to his family's nearby castle to recuperate. At this time, Ignatius was still so vain that he had his wounded leg broken once more and reset in the hope of correcting a limp. To help pass the time during his lengthy recuperation, he asked in vain for books of chivalry and had to settle for two volumes of a very different sort: a book of meditations on the life of Christ and one containing lives of the saints. Gradually he noticed that although tales of chivalrous exploits were pleasant to think about at the time he was pondering them, such thoughts afterwards left him feeling dry and empty, whereas reading about the lives of Francis of Assisi and Dominic Guzmán delighted him not only at the time but long afterward as well. Writing of himself in the third person when he was prevailed upon to compose his autobiography years later, he recalled that "not only was he consoled when he had these thoughts [about the saints], but even after putting them aside he remained satisfied and joyful. He did not notice this [at first], however; nor did he stop to ponder the distinction until the time when his eyes were opened a little, and he began to marvel at the difference and to reflect upon it, realizing from experience that some thoughts left him sad and others joyful. Little by little he came to recognize the difference between the spirits that were stirring, one from the devil, the other from God."[24] Although Ignatius could not have known it at the time,

24. Ignatius of Loyola, *The Autobiography* 8, in *Ignatius of Loyola:* The Spiritual Exercises *and Selected Works*, ed. George E. Ganss, S.J., Classics of Western Spirituality (New York: Paulist, 1991), 71.

this insight was to lie at the core of one of the most influential works of Christian spirituality ever written, his *Spiritual Exercises*.

The *Exercises* evolved slowly over the course of the following years, during which Ignatius first spent some months largely in solitude in the Spanish town of Manresa, then visited the Holy Land in the unrealizable hope of remaining there, and eventually got the best education possible at schools in Spain and Paris. The text of the *Exercises* is divided into four sections called "weeks," although this term does not rigidly refer to periods of seven days but rather to stages of ongoing conversion through which the "exercitant" is to be brought with the help of an insightful spiritual guide or director. The principal reason for undertaking the exercises is to find clarity about God's will for oneself, above all (though not exclusively) with regard to the choice of a state in life. To facilitate this end, the person making the exercises does not even have to read the work, for it serves primarily as a guidebook for the director. The director, in turn, is not to influence the decision of the exercitant by suggesting a particular course of action but is only to help him or her discern God's will, at times using the principles for the discernment of spirits that Ignatius had first discovered while recuperating from his wound.

This search for God's will is emphasized at the very beginning of the work, in what Ignatius calls the "Principle and Foundation," where he writes that our whole aim in life is to praise, reverence, and serve God and thereby come to salvation. We are therefore to use all things on earth only as means to this end, not seeking health rather than sickness, wealth rather than poverty, or honor rather than dishonor, but instead desiring and choosing only what is more conducive to the end for which we have been created. Through a series of carefully sequenced meditations, in which Ignatius recommends using all the powers of one's imagination (such as seeing oneself as present at particular scenes from the Gospels), the exercitant is gradually brought to make a "sound and good election" concerning whatever matter is under consideration, and then to solidify this choice through various ways of praying. In this final part of the *Exercises* Ignatius reaches the fitting climax of the four weeks with his "Contemplation to Attain Love," whose aim is to bring the exercitant to offer his or her whole self back to God. This contemplation includes the following beautiful prayer: "Take, Lord, and receive all my liberty, my memory, my understanding, and all my will—all that I have and possess. You, Lord, have given all that to me. I now give it back to you, O Lord. All of it is yours. Dispose of it according to your will. Give me your love and your grace, for that is enough for me."[25]

While studying in Paris, Ignatius had gathered a small group of followers,

25. Ignatius of Loyola, *Spiritual Exercises* no. 234; Ganss p. 177.

the core of what eventually became the Society of Jesus, commonly called the Jesuits. Ignatius's final years were spent in Rome, formulating the constitutions of this new form of religious life that, to the consternation of his critics, no longer required the members to pray the Liturgy of the Hours in common, an innovation that made them more available for service wherever and whenever needed. Already in Ignatius's lifetime some Jesuits had departed for missionary work in all parts of the then-known world, while others remained in Europe to work as pastors, teachers, theologians, natural scientists, and spiritual directors for influential laypersons.

Because of the skill with which Ignatius crafted the constitutions of the Society, he has often been regarded primarily as an efficient bureaucrat, but in fact he cannot be properly understood apart from his profound mystical bent, which centered on his devotion to the Trinity and his conviction that human beings can have direct experience of God. His autobiography contains various references to such experiences in his own life, such as the following one, which occurred while he was still residing at Manresa shortly after his conversion:

> Once he was going out of devotion to a church situated a little more than a mile from Manresa; . . . As he went along occupied with his devotions, he sat down for a little while with his face toward the river [the Cardoner], which ran down below. While he was seated there, the eyes of his understanding began to be opened; not that he saw any vision, but he understood and learnt many things, both spiritual matters and matters of faith and scholarship, and this with so great an enlightenment that everything seemed new to him . . . This was such that in the whole course of his life, after completing sixty-two years, even if he gathered up all the various helps he may have had from God and all the various things he has known, even adding them all together, he does not think he had got as much as at that one time.[26]

This experience, which is commonly called an intellectual vision because there was no imaginative component to it, remained normative for the rest of Ignatius's life, for he afterward saw everything in a new light. In later years, when asked why he had established this or that feature in the Society of Jesus, he would often reply that it was "because of what I saw at Manresa." As one of today's leading Jesuit scholars points out, this does not mean that Ignatius there saw everything about the future religious institute worked out in detail, but rather that he saw "the new course his life was to take, and the conse-

---

26. Ignatius of Loyola, *Autobiography* 30; Ganss p. 81.

quences in a general way. He was not to remain a solitary pilgrim imitating the saints in prayer and penance, but to labor with Christ for the salvation of others."[27]

As noted above, among the tens of thousands of Jesuits who have served the church since the founding of the Society in 1540, there have been many theologians. In the past hundred years, the most influential of these has been the German Jesuit Karl Rahner (1904-1984). His massive output of books and essays, many of the latter collected and published in English translation as his *Theological Investigations*, cover almost every topic of systematic and pastoral theology, with some important essays in moral theology as well. For our present purposes, it is especially helpful to note how clearly Rahner saw into the heart of Ignatius's spirituality, namely, the possibility of directly experiencing God, even if not always in as memorable a way as in the intellectual vision that Ignatius had while seated along the bank of the Cardoner. Rahner would emphasize this possibility whenever he himself gave the *Spiritual Exercises* to groups of fellow Jesuits, but nowhere did he do so as strikingly as in a short piece in which he imagined Ignatius speaking to Jesuits of our own time. Rahner/Ignatius wrote:

> When I claim to have known God at first hand, I do not intend here to add to my assertion a theological treatise on the nature of such a direct experience of God . . . All I say is I knew God, nameless and unfathomable, silent and yet near, bestowing himself upon me in his Trinity. I knew God beyond all concrete imaginings. I knew Him clearly in such nearness and grace as is impossible to confound or mistake . . .
>
> One things remains certain: it is possible for man to know God. And your cure of souls must keep this goal in mind, always, at every step, unwaveringly. If you fill up the barns of man's consciousness only with your very learned and up-to-date theology, which ultimately engenders nothing but a fearful torrent of words, if you were to train men only for piety, as zealous subjects of the ecclesiastical establishment, if you were to make the people in the Church no more than obedient subjects of a distant God . . . if you were not to help them finally to abandon all tangible assurances and isolated insights and go with confidence towards the inconceivable, where there are no longer paths . . . if you were not to help thus, then you would have either forgotten or betrayed my "spirituality" in your so-called cure of souls and missionary task.[28]

27. George E. Ganss, S.J., general introduction to *Ignatius of Loyola*, 31.

28. Karl Rahner, "Ignatius of Loyola Speaks to a Modern Jesuit," in idem, *Ignatius of Loyola*, trans. Rosaleen Ockenden (London: Collins, 1979), 11, 14.

Elsewhere in his writings, Rahner went into much more detail about just what he meant by such terms as "experience of God," "experience of grace," and "mystical experience," all of which he used more or less synonymously. Unlike the striking experience that Ignatius had while sitting next to the Cardoner, the experiences that Rahner describes are much more mundane but are, for that very reason, probably more meaningful for the many persons for whom Ignatius's experience may sound quite foreign.

In the background of all that Rahner says about experiencing God is the still more basic experience of transcendence. By this latter term he simply means that as soon as we experience ourselves as the limited beings that we in so many ways obviously are, we have already overstepped these boundaries and are reaching out beyond ourselves toward that which cannot be comprehended or circumscribed. Religious believers, of course, understand the "whereunto" of this omnipresent transcending movement of the human mind to be the all-holy God. This allows Rahner to argue that the experience of transcendence is always also the experience of God in the midst of ordinary life. For this reason, most of the examples he gives of the experience of God are drawn from the nitty-gritty of what he calls "everyday mysticism." At times he provides long lists of specific ways of acting in everyday life that he says are in fact experiences of God or of the Holy Spirit: such actions as being really good to someone from whom there is no sign of appreciation or gratitude, or renouncing something without receiving recognition from others or even a feeling of inward satisfaction, or making a decision purely in the light of the inmost dictates of one's conscience without being able to make the decision understandable to others. When we truly act in such ways, "*there* is God and his liberating grace. There we find what we Christians call the Holy Spirit of God . . . There is the mysticism of everyday life, the discovery of God in all things; there is the sober intoxication of the Spirit, of which the Fathers and the liturgy speak [and] which we cannot reject or despise, because it is real."[29]

CARMELITE SPIRITUALITY: TERESA OF AVILA AND THÉRÈSE OF LISIEUX

Although Karl Rahner was not primarily a historical theologian, he did know very well the works of the main figures in the history of Christian spiritual-

29. Karl Rahner, "Experiencing the Spirit," in idem, *The Practice of Faith: A Handbook of Contemporary Spirituality*, ed. Karl Lehmann and Albert Raffelt (New York: Crossroad, 1984), 84. This essay first appeared in *The Spirit in the Church*, trans. John Griffiths (London: Search Press, 1979), 11-22.

ity and wrote some important essays about them, including one about the founder of the Carmelite reform, Teresa of Avila (1515-1582). In a piece that he composed in 1970 on the occasion of Teresa's being named a doctor of the church (that is, an approved teacher of the highest rank), Rahner said that in our time it is more urgent than ever to have a theology and an initiation into the personal experience of God and that Teresa and her fellow reformer John of the Cross "are thoroughly good and almost irreplaceable teachers of this sort of theology and initiation, particularly adept at making this personal experience of God intelligible."[30]

Although Teresa's work has had immense influence throughout the church, her original intent was quite modest. Having entered a Spanish Carmelite convent governed by a rule of life that had been considerably mitigated from the one given to her Carmelite forebears while they were still living on Mount Carmel in the Holy Land in the thirteenth century, Teresa eventually received permission for herself and a few like-minded sisters to live under the original rule. The idea caught on beyond her expectations, so that before long, and in the face of considerable opposition, she was traversing Spain to found monasteries of the Carmelite reform, its members known as "discalced" because the original rule forbade the wearing of shoes.

Even if Teresa had done only this, she would be an important figure in church history, but she has attained even greater stature because of her writings. Whereas some authors labor over their work, constantly revising what they have penned, Teresa—writing for the most part under obedience to her spiritual directors—would spend only a relatively short time composing these works, hardly ever looking back to see what she had written the previous day and occasionally using terms in somewhat different senses from one treatise to the next. Her masterpiece, *The Interior Castle*, was written in merely two months in the latter half of 1577. In her totally frank and open way, she begins its first chapter by saying that she had asked the Lord to give her help in the writing "because I wasn't able to think of anything to say nor did I know how to begin to carry out this obedience."[31] There then came into her mind the image according to which she structured the entire work—the soul as a crystalline castle in which there are many dwelling places, with the divine King residing in the very center. The spiritual journey is thus described as a

30. Karl Rahner, "Teresa of Avila: Doctor of the Church," in idem, *Opportunities for Faith: Elements of a Modern Spirituality*, trans. Edward Quinn (New York: Seabury, 1974), 125.

31. Teresa of Avila, *The Interior Castle* 1.1.1, in *The Collected Works of St. Teresa of Avila*, vol. 2, trans. Kieran Kavanaugh, O.C.D., and Otilio Rodriguez, O.C.D. (Washington, D.C.: Institute of Carmelite Studies, 1980), 283. The treatise is divided into seven major parts, each corresponding to a set of "dwelling places." Subsequent parenthetical references to this work indicate the number of the dwelling places, the chapter, and the paragraph.

prayerful journey within, marked by less and less effort on the human being's part as the action of God's grace becomes more and more pronounced. A crucial turning point comes at the Fourth Dwelling Places, which for Teresa marks the transition to contemplative or mystical prayer in what she calls the prayer of quiet. To help explain the difference between such prayer and the kind that preceded she turns to another image, that of ways of providing water for two troughs. One trough is filled with water brought from far away "through many aqueducts and the use of much ingenuity" on our part, while "with the other the source of the water is right there, and the trough fills without any noise" (4.2.3). The former way leads to the kind of consolation that we might derive from our own efforts, "using creatures to help our meditation, and tiring the intellect" (ibid.), while the latter way signifies the prayer of quiet, a supernatural favor or delight that God alone can bring about and that is marked by "the greatest peace and quiet and sweetness in the very interior part of ourselves" (4.2.4).

Reading only those quotations could be misleading, for one might get the impression that for Teresa contemplative prayer is marked simply by feelings of peace and contentment. Nothing could be farther from the truth. Throughout her treatise she insists that what really matters is living in accord with God's will, which is synonymous with a fruitful love of God and one's neighbor. In the very same part of the treatise in which she speaks of the "quiet and sweetness" of the prayer of quiet, Teresa also writes that "the important thing is not to think much but to love much; and so do that which best stirs you to love. Perhaps we don't know what love is. I wouldn't be very surprised, because it doesn't consist in great delight but in desiring with strong determination to please God in everything, in striving, insofar as possible, not to offend Him, and in asking Him for the advancement of the honor and glory of His Son and the increase of the Catholic Church" (4.1.7). Even when she reaches the end of the treatise and speaks of the culminating state of "spiritual marriage," whereby the soul is permanently united with the divine Bridegroom, she insists that the whole purpose of this state is not quiet rest but fruitful activity: "O my sisters! How forgetful this soul, in which the Lord dwells in so particular a way, should be of its own rest, how little it should care for its honor, and how far it should be from wanting esteem in anything! . . . All its concern is taken up with how to please Him more and how or where it will show Him the love it bears Him. This is the reason for prayer, my daughters, the purpose of this spiritual marriage: the birth always of good works, good works" (7.4.6).

One further passage will illustrate the very practical, down-to-earth nature of Teresa's spiritual doctrine. In another of her works, *The Way of Perfection*, she includes a lengthy set of reflections on the Lord's Prayer. Although she is writing in the first instance for members of her own Discalced Carmelite community, the advice she gives is applicable to anyone, but above all to those who might mistakenly think that persons who have advanced far in the ways of prayer will be withdrawn and unapproachable. When commenting on the phrase "lead us not into temptation," Teresa writes:

> Sisters, strive as much as you can, without offense to God, to be affable and understanding in such a way that everyone you talk to will love your conversation and desire your manner of living and acting, and not be frightened and intimidated by virtue. This is very important for religious; the holier they are the more sociable they are with their Sisters. And even though you may feel very distressed if all your Sisters' conversations do not go as you would like them to, never turn away from them if you want to help your Sisters and be loved. This is what we must strive for earnestly, to be affable, agreeable, and pleasing to persons with whom we deal . . .[32]

Teresa's reform quickly spread to other countries, including neighboring France. There, in the town of Lisieux in Normandy, lived one of Teresa's many namesakes, Thérèse of the Child Jesus (1873-1897). In some respects the two women were quite different in personality: Teresa was outgoing, ready even to perform a flamenco dance to cheer up a sister who seemed depressed, whereas Thérèse was so shy that she did not easily mix with the other students at the school she attended for five years as a day boarder. Her desire to enter the Carmelite convent in Lisieux came to her early in life, from the time that two of her older sisters had joined that community. She herself, with a dogged perseverance that included petitioning not only the local bishop but even the pope while on a pilgrimage to Rome with her father and her sister Céline, finally obtained permission to enter the Carmel while still only fifteen years old. In the remaining nine and a half years of her life, brought to an early end by tuberculosis, she made rapid strides in holiness, ones that were nevertheless so unobtrusive that as she lay dying some members of the community wondered aloud what they could find to say about her on the obituary notices that would be sent to other convents. The heroic character of her virtue, which she always attributed to God's grace, is nevertheless evident from the three autobiographical manuscripts written at the request of various members of the Lisieux Carmel. These three, published

32. Teresa of Avila, *The Way of Perfection* 41.7, in *The Collected Works of St. Teresa of Avila*, vol. 2, trans. Kieran Kavanaugh, O.C.D., and Otilio Rodriguez, O.C.D. (Washington, D.C.: Institute of Carmelite Studies, 1980), 199-200.

after her death under the single title *Story of a Soul*, rapidly became a best-seller, translated into many languages and leading not only to her early canonization as a saint but to her being declared, like her patron Teresa of Avila, a doctor of the church.

Since Thérèse's preferred spiritual reading centered more and more on the Gospels as she grew older, it is not surprising that she regularly expressed her spiritual teaching in evangelical terms. Taking the central Christian commandment to be Jesus' injunction, "Love one another as I have loved you" (Jn 15:12), she tried to live this out in ways that did not attract the attention of others but demanded a lot of herself. She writes, for example, that there was one member of the community whose character and behavior displeased her so much that she was tempted to give in to the natural antipathy that she experienced and avoid that sister. In fact, she did just the opposite: "I told myself that charity must not consist in feelings but in works; then I set myself to doing for this Sister what I would do for the person I loved the most . . . I wasn't content simply with praying very much for this Sister who gave me so many struggles, but I took care to render her all the services possible, and when I was tempted to answer her back in a disagreeable manner, I was content with giving her my most friendly smile, and with changing the subject of the conversation."[33] Although Thérèse does not refer very often to the teaching of St. Teresa of Avila, in such behavior she most definitely followed her patron's teaching about the central place of love in the Christian life.

Still another aspect of Thérèse's spirituality ought to be mentioned for its continuing relevance. Both as a young girl and as a Carmelite nun, she regularly expressed her yearning for heaven, her true home. Then, during Holy Week of 1896, she not only had the first signs of life-threatening tuberculosis but, almost simultaneously, an evaporation of any sense of heaven's reality. With a frankness that led her to fear she had written too much, she spoke of feeling that her soul was invaded by the thickest darkness, while death personified said to her: "You are dreaming about the light, about a fatherland embalmed in the sweetest perfumes; you are dreaming about the *eternal* possession of the Creator of all these marvels; you believe that one day you will walk out of this fog that surrounds you! Advance, advance; rejoice in death which will give you not what you hope for but a night still more profound, the night of nothingness" (213).

This trial of faith remained with Thérèse for the final year and a half of her life on earth. She writes that she had never before made as many acts of

33. *Story of a Soul: The Autobiography of Saint Thérèse of Lisieux*, trans. John Clarke, O.C.D., 3rd ed. (Washington, D.C.: Institute of Carmelite Studies, 1996), 222-23. Subsequent parenthetical references to this work indicate the page number of this edition.

faith as during this period, nor did she complain of having had taken away what had been the joy of her life. Addressing her prioress, Mother Marie de Gonzague, she wrote: "Never have I felt before this, dear Mother, how sweet and merciful the Lord really is, for He did not send me this trial until the moment I was capable of bearing it. A little earlier I believe it would have plunged me into a state of discouragement. Now it is taking away everything that could be a natural satisfaction in my desire for heaven. Dear Mother, it seems to me now that nothing could prevent me from flying away, for I no longer have any great desires except that of loving to the point of dying of love" (214).

Those who have already read some of Thérèse's own writings will have noted that, in accordance with the kind of religious language common in France in the late nineteenth century, some of her expressions seem cloying, as when she writes about herself as "a little flower" and her siblings as lilies, two of whom had already been planted in the soil of the Lisieux Carmel by Christ:

> It was He who had her born in a holy soil, impregnated with a *virginal perfume.* It was He, too, who had her preceded by eight Lilies of dazzling whiteness. In His love He wished to preserve His little flower from the world's poisoned breath. Hardly had her petals begun to unfold when this divine Savior transplanted her to Mount Carmel where already two Lilies, who had taken care of her in the springtime of her life, spread their sweet perfume. (15-16)

Such language has made it difficult for some persons to read *Story of a Soul.* Thérèse was, however, one of the strongest and, yes, toughest saints who ever lived. The only proper response to the difficulties some may feel about her language was given some years ago in a fine biographical study of Thérèse by the late Barry Ulanov of Columbia University. He wrote: "If we, in reading her, are foolish enough to stop at the signs of tenderness, and to be affronted by their occasional stickiness or stuffiness or girlish exaggeration, then we will be guilty of almost every possible sin against the Thérèsian canon. We will ourselves have stopped at surfaces and we will have judged by surfaces . . . We will have turned unlovingly from one of the great displays of love of the modern world."[34]

It may surprise some readers to learn that this woman, who never left the

---

34. Barry Ulanov, *The Making of a Modern Saint: A Biographical Study of Thérèse of Lisieux* (Garden City, N.Y.: Doubleday, 1966), 359.

grounds of the Lisieux Carmel after her entrance there at the age of fifteen, was named co-patron of the missions by the Catholic Church, along with the sixteenth-century Jesuit missionary Francis Xavier. Thérèse did, however, have a keen interest in the missions, exchanging letters with several missionaries and praying fervently for the success of their work. Indeed, she herself had volunteered to be transferred to the Carmel in Saigon and was prevented from going there only because of her poor health. By her time the Christian faith had been proclaimed among the Vietnamese for more than two and a half centuries, having first been brought to that land by French Jesuit missionaries, the most prominent of whom was Alexandre de Rhodes. His work, and that of two other early missionaries to countries in Asia, will be discussed at the beginning of the next chapter.

QUESTIONS FOR REFLECTION

1. What practical effect do you think Luther's teaching about the relationship between faith and good works has had on the Lutheran understanding of Christian spirituality? Do you find any causal relationship between the way he spoke about "justification by faith alone" and the emergence of what Bonhoeffer later criticized as "cheap grace"? Do you accept Bonhoeffer's description of faith as "to throw ourselves completely into the arms of God"?
2. Do you agree with Calvin's calling the exercise of civil authority "the most sacred and by far the most honorable of all callings in the whole life of mortal men"? Why do you think many people do not consider this vocation especially sacred or honorable?
3. How important do you consider Evelyn Underhill's remarks about the "desperate modern need" for a balanced life in the face of what she believed to be the overly busy and hurried lifestyle of many people today? In your own experience, does participating in liturgical worship help restore such balance?
4. Karl Rahner locates the core of Ignatian spirituality in the reality of direct experience of God, an experience that some persons today would consider impossible. What does the phrase "experience of God" mean to you? Do you agree with Ignatius and Rahner about the possibility of this kind of direct experience?
5. Teresa of Avila wrote that it is very important for Christians to be affable and understanding: "The holier they are, the more sociable they are . . ." Did this, or anything else in Teresa's work, significantly alter your understanding of Christian spirituality?
6. Some authors have suggested that the way Thérèse of Lisieux dealt with her trial of faith is especially relevant in our time, when many persons regard religious faith as quaint or irrelevant. Other authors focus more on the way

Thérèse lived out the Gospel commandment of love. What in her spiritual teaching strikes you as most significant?

SUGGESTIONS FOR FURTHER READING AND STUDY

On Lutheran Spirituality

Bonhoeffer, Dietrich. *The Cost of Discipleship*. New York: Simon & Schuster, 1976. See especially chap. 1, "Costly Grace" (pp. 45-60) and chap. 2, "The Call to Discipleship" (pp. 61-86).

Lienhard, Marc. "Luther and the Beginnings of the Reformation." In *Christian Spirituality: High Middle Ages and Reformation*, edited by Jill Raitt, 268-99. World Spirituality 17. New York: Crossroad, 1987.

Martin Luther's Basic Theological Writings. Edited by Timothy F. Lull. 2nd ed. Minneapolis: Fortress, 2005. See especially "Autobiographical Fragments" (pp. 2-11) and *The Freedom of a Christian* (pp. 386-411).

Senn, Frank C. "Lutheran Spirituality." In *Protestant Spiritual Traditions*, ed. Frank C. Senn, 9-54. New York: Paulist, 1986.

On the Spirituality of John Calvin

Hageman, Howard G. "Reformed Spirituality." In *Protestant Spiritual Traditions*, edited by Frank C. Senn, 55-79. New York: Paulist, 1986.

Hall, T. Hartley, IV. "The Shape of Reformed Piety." In *Spiritual Traditions for the Contemporary Church*, edited by Robin Maas and Gabriel O'Donnell, O.P., 202-21. Nashville: Abingdon, 1990.

John Calvin: Selections from His Writings. Edited by John Dillenberger. American Academy of Religion Aids for the Study of Religion 2. Missoula, Mont.: Scholars Press, 1975. See especially the selections from the 1536 edition of the *Institutes of Christian Religion* (pp. 267-317) and the "First Sermon on Pentecost" (pp. 560-73).

On Anglican Spirituality

Evelyn Underhill: Modern Guide to the Ancient Quest for the Holy. Edited by Dana Greene. Albany: State University of New York Press, 1988. See especially the following pieces by Underhill: "The Authority of Personal Experience" (pp. 117-31), "Prayer" (pp. 133-44), and "God and Spirit" (pp. 177-90).

Wakefield, Gordon S. "Anglican Spirituality." In *Christian Spirituality: Post-Reformation and Modern*, edited by Louis Dupré and Don E. Saliers, 257-93. World Spirituality 18. New York: Crossroad, 1989.

Wall, John N. "Anglican Spirituality: A Historical Introduction." In *Spiritual Tradi-*

tions for the Contemporary Church, edited by Robin Maas and Gabriel O'Donnell, O.P., 269-86. Nashville: Abingdon, 1990.

On Ignatian Spirituality

Ignatius of Loyola: The Spiritual Exercises *and Selected Works*. Edited by George E. Ganss, S.J. Classics of Western Spirituality. New York: Paulist, 1991. See especially *The Autobiography* (pp. 65-111) and *The Spiritual Exercises* (pp. 113-82).

O'Malley, John. "Early Jesuit Spirituality: Spain and Italy." In *Christian Spirituality: Post-Reformation and Modern*, edited by Louis Dupré and Don E. Saliers, 3-27. World Spirituality 18. New York: Crossroad, 1989.

Rahner, Karl. "Ignatius of Loyola Speaks to a Modern Jesuit." In idem, *Ignatius of Loyola,* 9-38. Translated by Rosaleen Ockenden. London: Collins, 1979.

Wiseman, James A., "'I Have Experienced God': Religious Experience in the Theology of Karl Rahner." *American Benedictine Review* 44 (1993): 22-57.

On Carmelite Spirituality

The Collected Works of St. Teresa of Avila, vol. 2. Translated by Kieran Kavanaugh, O.C.D., and Otilio Rodriguez, O.C.D. Washington, D.C.: Institute of Carmelite Studies, 1980. See especially chaps. 41-42 of *The Way of Perfection* (pp. 196-204) and the First, Fourth, and Seventh Dwelling Places of *The Interior Castle* (pp. 283-96, 316-34, and 427-50).

Kavanaugh, Kieran. "Spanish Sixteenth Century: Carmel and Surrounding Movements." In *Christian Spirituality: Post-Reformation and Modern*, edited by Louis Dupré and Don E. Saliers, 69-92. World Spirituality 18. New York: Crossroad, 1989.

May, Gerald G. *The Dark Night of the Soul: A Psychiatrist Explores the Connection between Darkness and Spiritual Growth*. San Francisco: Harper, 2003.

Payne, Steven, O.C.D. "The Tradition of Prayer in Teresa and John of the Cross." In *Spiritual Traditions for the Contemporary Church*, edited by Robin Maas and Gabriel O'Donnell, O.P., 235-58. Nashville: Abingdon, 1990.

Thérèse of Lisieux. *Story of a Soul: The Autobiography of Saint Thérèse of Lisieux*. Translated by John Clarke, O.C.D. 3rd ed. Washington, D.C.: Institute of Carmelite Studies, 1996. See especially chap. 9, "My Vocation is Love" (185-200) and chap. 10, "The Trial of Faith" (203-29).

8

Asian Christian Spirituality

IN ADDITION TO ALEXANDRE DE RHODES (1591-1660), mentioned at the end of the previous chapter as a principal founder of Vietnamese Christianity, two other early Jesuit missionaries to Asia are especially well known for their attempts to inculturate[1] Christianity into Asian society and to bring indigenous Asian traditions into line with Christian faith: Roberto de Nobili (1577-1656) arrived in India in 1605 and spent the rest of his life there, while Matteo Ricci (1552-1610) took up residence in China in 1583, eventually becoming so honored that his grave outside the city walls of Beijing was a gift of the emperor. Ricci, the earliest of the three, wore the robes of a Confucian scholar and argued forcefully that the traditional Confucian veneration of ancestors—such as the offering of food and incense before the wooden tablets on which the ancestors' names and other data were written—was a pious but not superstitious rite. Considering such veneration to be compatible with Christian faith, he saw no need to forbid converts to practice it. De Nobili, similarly intent on distinguishing between the essentials of Christianity and its European trappings, which most of his fellow missionaries would not abandon, adopted the garb and vegetarian diet of an Indian *sannyasi* (renunciant), became the first European to acquire firsthand knowledge of the Vedas and of the Sanskrit language in which they were written, and allowed converts of the Brahmin caste to retain the characteristic thread worn from the left shoulder across the breast. Like de Nobili and Ricci, de Rhodes was assiduous in learning the native language and was altogether willing to dress in native garb. He was, in fact, so keen to have Christian converts appear no different from their fellow Vietnamese that he persuaded them not to wear religious objects that would set them culturally apart. He also sought to

1. Inculturation is not mere adaptation, with representatives of the communicator culture taking all the initiative. "No longer is the communicator culture active and the receptor culture passive; it is a two-way street, with deliberate giving and receiving at both ends. The message is not something initially possessed by one and lacked by the other: it will be more fully discovered in the interchange" (Frank de Graeve, "Roberto de Nobili: A Bold Attempt at Inculturation?" in *Religion in the Pacific Era*, ed. Frank K. Finn and Tyler Hendricks [New York: Paragon House, 1985], 33).

invest with Christian meanings any traditional Vietnamese practices that he did not consider morally objectionable. For example, the Vietnamese had the custom of erecting, on the evening of the last day of the year, a bamboo pole in front of their houses in order to invite their deceased parents to come share in the New Year celebration. Although de Rhodes considered some aspects of this practice superstitious, it was so important culturally that he retained the custom but gave it a Christian meaning by affixing a crucifix rather than a wicker basket containing nuts and money to the top of the pole.[2]

Regarding what we are calling Asian Christian spirituality, however, it must be said that these attempts at inculturation, laudable though they were as missionary methods well ahead of their time, were accompanied by a theology and spirituality that remained basically European, largely unaffected by any elements that might have been drawn from Asian cultures. All three of these men, in varying degrees, were critical of the indigenous religious traditions they found in their host countries, as is quite apparent in their own writings. Three of de Nobili's most important treatises, written in Tamil and recently translated into English,[3] contain very little that is positive about what we would call Hindu religious texts, doctrines, and ritual practices. In the words of one of the translators of these treatises by de Nobili, they "do not reflect a sympathetic attitude. Rather, a sense of superiority is evident, as he sought to prove his religion right and other religions wrong."[4] Another scholar writes that de Nobili "never tells us directly what, if anything, he had learned about religion from these people in the forty years he lived among them. Although we might not have expected loud praises of Hinduism, it nevertheless strikes one as odd that we cannot discover any explicit, positive appreciation of Hindu religiosity per se."[5]

Ricci, to be sure, was complimentary toward Confucianism, whose doctrine he considered to be generally compatible with Christian faith. By emphasizing this compatibility, he was in fact able to obtain a fair and open hearing for his own proclamation of the gospel. Of other aspects of Chinese religion, however, he had nothing positive to say. His diary, found among his papers after his death, was translated from Italian into Latin and given a nar-

---

2. For further details about de Rhodes's missionary strategies, see Peter C. Phan, *Mission and Catechesis: Alexandre de Rhodes and Inculturation in Seventeenth-Century Vietnam* (Maryknoll, N.Y.: Orbis Books, 1998), esp. chap. 3 (pp. 69-106).

3. Roberto de Nobili, S.J., *Preaching Wisdom to the Wise: Three Treatises*, trans. Anand Amaladass, S.J., and Francis X. Clooney, S.J. (St. Louis: Institute of Jesuit Sources, 2000).

4. Anand Amaladass, S.J., introduction to *Preaching Wisdom to the Wise*, 36.

5. Francis X. Clooney, S.J., "Roberto de Nobili, Adaptation and the Reasonable Interpretation of Religion," *Missiology* 18 (1990): 26.

rative format by a fellow Jesuit, Nicola Trigault, who published it in 1615. In the section describing Ricci's edition of a Compendium of Christian Doctrine, Trigault wrote that the book "provided a refutation of all the Chinese religious sects, excepting the one founded on the natural law, as developed by their Prince of Philosophers, Confucius ... The book proved to be a thorn in the side of the idol worshippers, because it stripped them of arms to defend their own vain doctrines."[6]

Of the three missionaries, de Rhodes was the most negatively disposed toward the religions he encountered in Asia. In his *Catechismus*, published in Vietnamese in romanized script, he wrote that three religions had infiltrated Vietnam from China and that all three were blatantly false. Of the Buddha he wrote: "By means of his falsehoods and magical practices he made the people so foolish as to adopt the worship of idols, promising those who worship idols that they, though they may be of the lowest social rank in this world, will be born again as children of kings in the transmigration of souls." The second of these religions, Daoism, "venerates demons and consists mainly in sorcery; it does not render Lao Tzu any cult and is wrapped in thickest obscurity." As for Confucianism, its founder either knew the supreme Creator and Lord or he did not. If Confucius did know him, he should have told his disciples; not having done so, "he could be neither good nor holy but rather perverse and evil." On the other hand, "if he did not know the supreme God, principle and source of all goodness, how could he have been holy and good? Consequently, there is no reason to call him a saint, much less to pay him the honors due to the Lord of heaven alone." De Rhodes then sums up this section of his catechism with the words: "Many other errors have been derived from these three religions as from poisoned sources, but it is unnecessary to refute them one by one. Suffice it to know what their sources are in order to perceive their falsehood."[7]

It would be several more centuries before there emerged anything like a genuinely Asian Christian spirituality—or better, spiritualities, for even within a single country, much less among several countries, there has been considerable variety. Just as throughout the rest of this book, our presentation will therefore have to be severely selective. We will be looking at a few prominent attempts to develop inculturated spiritualities in three Asian countries, beginning with India and then moving east.

6. *China in the Sixteenth Century: The Journals of Matthew Ricci: 1583-1610*, trans. Louis J. Gallagher, S.J. (New York: Random House, 1953), 448-49.

7. Alexandre de Rhodes, *Catechismus*, "The Fourth Day," in Phan, *Mission and Catechesis*, 250-53.

INDIAN CHRISTIAN SPIRITUALITIES: ABHISHIKTANANDA AND BEDE GRIFFITHS

Whereas Roberto de Nobili went to India as a missionary and remained one throughout his life, the life of the French monk who came to be known by his adopted Indian name Abhishiktananda ("Bliss of the Anointed One") followed a very different trajectory. Henri Le Saux (1910-1973) was born in Brittany, the eldest of seven children. After studying for several years as a diocesan seminarian he entered the Benedictine community of Sainte-Anne-de-Kergonan not far from his family home. A letter he wrote to the novice master a year before his eventual entry sounds a theme that would characterize his deepest desire for the rest of his life: "What has drawn me [to the monastery] from the beginning, and what still leads me on, is the hope of finding there the presence of God more immediately than anywhere else."[8] In his early years as a monk he served the community as librarian and as a teacher of patristics for the novices, but even before his final profession and priestly ordination he was making reference in his letters and diary to a growing desire to go to India in the hope of helping Christianize that land just as Benedictine monks had fashioned a Christian Europe centuries earlier. He eventually obtained his abbot's permission to explore this possibility and, after some disappointments, got a favorable response from a bishop in the South Indian state of Tamil Nadu. Jules Monchanin, a French diocesan priest who was already living in that diocese, took Le Saux's arrival as the answer to his prayers for a kindred spirit with whom he could start an ashram, that is, a religious retreat where disciples would gather around a teacher or guru. The two men accordingly began living in simple huts at a site called Shantivanam ("Forest of Peace") along the banks of the Cavery River. It was at this time that Le Saux took the Indian name by which he increasingly became known (and which will be used of him in the following paragraphs).

When not at the ashram, Abhishiktananda could regularly be found visiting Christian or Hindu sites in the area. One of the latter sites, Mount Arunachala, had a particularly profound effect on him, for it was at the foot of this sacred mountain that the Hindu sage Sri Ramana Maharshi lived with his disciples. This sage's quiet smile, the profound concentration of his disciples, and the haunting beauty of the Vedic chants sung each morning and evening were for Abhishiktananda "a call which pierced through everything,

8. Henri Le Saux to the novice master at Kergonan, December 4, 1928, in James Stuart, *Swami Abhishiktananda: His Life Told through His Letters* (Delhi: I.S.P.C.K., 1989), 3.

rent it in pieces and opened a mighty abyss . . . New as [these experiences] were, their hold on me was already too strong for it ever to be possible for me to disown them."[9] He now began spending weeks at a time in solitude in one of the caves that dot the sides of the mountain, where he underwent an overpowering sense of his inmost self together with the conviction that this self, the deepest core of his being, was ultimately one with the Absolute. He claimed that such experience, so prominent in the advaitic ("non-dual") texts of the Hindu Upanishads, is likewise present in the Gospels, as in Jesus' words, "The Father and I are one" (Jn 10:30).

Abhishiktananda thus did not at all consider advaitic experience to be uniquely Indian. Indeed, he felt that it had been undergone by many of the Christian mystics of Europe, though usually expressed by them inadequately because they were fettered by an inconvenient terminology overly dependent on Hellenistic and scholastic categories: "If only they had been familiar with Vedantic thought, they would have expressed themselves quite naturally in advaitic language, as do their Indian counterparts. Indeed, some of them did so, since at times experience is so strong that it shatters all restrictions—but they had to pay dearly for not following the beaten track. [Meister] Eckhart was condemned, [Marguerite] Porete was burned at the stake, and even John of the Cross was regarded with suspicion."[10]

Not surprisingly, Abhishiktananda himself came under suspicion, often finding it impossible to get ecclesiastical permission to publish some of his works; much of what he wrote was published only posthumously. He was at times distraught not only by such censorship but by confusion about his own religious identity: Was he still genuinely Christian (even though he continued to pray the Liturgy of the Hours and to celebrate Mass)? How, if at all, could his Christian and Hindu leanings be reconciled with each other? The heart of the problem lay in what he called "the advaitic dilemma": "In this annihilating experience [of *advaita*] one is no longer able to project in front of oneself anything whatsoever, to recognize any other 'pole' to which to refer oneself and to give the name of God." The sense of *relationship* with God as expressed, for example, by St. Paul's "face to face" (1 Cor 13:12), vanishes when "one is so forcibly seized by the mystery that one can no longer utter either a 'Thou' or an 'I.'"[11] Toward the end of his life, however, and especially in the five months between a near-fatal heart attack and his death following

9. Abhishiktananda, *The Secret of Arunachala* (Delhi: I.S.P.C.K., 1979), 9.

10. Abhishiktananda, *Saccidananda: A Christian Approach to Advaitic Experience*, rev. ed. (Delhi: I.S.P.C.K., 1984), 78.

11. Abhishiktananda, "Experience of God in Eastern Religions," *Cistercian Studies* 9 (1974): 151-52.

a second attack, Abhishiktananda experienced once again something of the equanimity that he had known as a young monk at Kergonan. It is not that he had come to clear answers to questions raised by his religious quest, but rather that he became increasingly content to live, and live joyfully, in the face of the divine mystery by which he sometimes said he felt "enveloped." Accordingly, his spirituality, like that of some other figures studied earlier in this book—especially Gregory of Nyssa, Meister Eckhart, and Marguerite Porete—was stalwartly apophatic, and like all apophatic mystics he inclined more and more to silence. Indeed, he believed that India's major contribution to the spirituality of the rest of the Christian world was precisely its emphasis on silence, exemplified above all in the lives of its many hermit sages:

> India has taken with utter seriousness this word that tradition has adopted from Psalm 64: *silentium tibi laus: Thy praise is silence.*
>
> The Christian of the West and of the East, whom a temporary acculturation has all too often cut off from the well-springs of his prayer, must re-learn this silence of the soul before God from eternal India . . .
>
> . . . As long as God—or the Mystery—is led back to the name that a group of humans give to Him or to the notion of Him fashioned by them, as long as His unnameableness is still a concept, an idea—the apophatism of theology—it is quite difficult for the believer . . . to recognize everywhere the total mystery of this Presence. Only when the soul has undergone the experience that the Name beyond all names can be pronounced only in the silence of the Spirit, does one become capable of this total openness which permits one to perceive the Mystery in its sign . . .[12]

This emphasis on silence was innately congenial to Abhishiktananda, who sometimes spent whole weeks in silent retreat, but he also had a genuine appreciation of the importance of the church's liturgy. Through retreat conferences and writings, especially after the Second Vatican Council and its call for liturgical reform, he tried his utmost to lead others to see the importance of having liturgical prayer rooted in contemplative experience. One of his finest books, entitled simply *Prayer*, contains the following reflections on the liturgy in the postconciliar era:

> Now that all structures and formulas are being challenged, where can the Christian find the firm footing that he needs ... except in the funda-

12. Abhishitkananda, "India's Contribution to Christian Prayer," in idem, *The Eyes of Light* (Denville, N.J.: Dimension Books, 1983), 40-41, 43.

> mental experience of the Presence in himself, all around him, in everything and beyond everything?
>
> Liturgy should express above all that inner experience . . . New forms of prayer should stress the inner mystery and the wonder of the Presence (on which the traditional forms were all too silent!), and should help Christians to taste it and long for it, so that in their petitions they beg for a deeper knowledge of these realities rather than for deliverance from those vague spiritual and temporal dangers to which the old forms so often refer. Meditative chants after the readings, enabling the worshipper to savour the mystery, should be drawn not only from biblical sources but also from texts in the "cosmic covenant," whose authors have experienced the mystery and have expressed it in terms capable of arousing a like hunger in their brethren . . . Then only will the Church's liturgy recover its proper function in Christian life and the old reproach which contrasted its legalism and ritualism with the spontaneity and the depth of true prayer, be no longer heard.[13]

After Jules Monchanin died in 1957, Abhishiktananda felt more and more drawn to abandon the ashram at Shantivanam and live in the north of India, especially in a hermitage along the banks of the Ganges, where he began spending more and more time with each passing year. He left the ashram for good in 1968, turning it over to an English monk, Bede Griffiths (1906-1993), and two of the latter's companions. Although Abhishiktananda and Griffiths were in some ways similar—Europeans who had left their monasteries in order to take up a contemplative way of life in India—they were quite different in the ways in which they fostered an Indian Christian spirituality. We will highlight some of these differences in the following paragraphs about Griffiths.

Born on December 17, 1906, into a middle-class English family, Griffiths' spiritual journey took him from a vague agnosticism during his teens to nature mysticism (or what he called a "kind of worship of nature") while at Oxford University and from there to the Church of England and eventually to Roman Catholicism, a journey described by him in his first book, *The Golden String*.[14] Shortly after being received into the Catholic Church he entered the Benedictine monastic community at Prinknash Abbey in Gloucestershire, later remarking that this was the only place in England

13. Abhishiktannda, *Prayer* (Philadelphia: Westminster, 1973), 49.

14. Bede Griffiths, *The Golden String: An Autobiography*, 2nd ed. (Springfield, Ill.: Templegate, 1980).

where he had really felt at home. The abbey was, however, not to remain his permanent home. While there he began a serious study of Eastern scriptures, including the *Bhagavad Gita* and the Upanishads. This reading, plus conversations with a disciple of Carl Jung who had opened a yoga and meditation center in London, enkindled in Griffiths a strong desire to go to India. His motivation, unlike that of Henri Le Saux, was not primarily to be a missionary but, as he himself often said, to find "the other half of my soul," a half that would be characterized by the intuitive and the contemplative over against what he perceived as the excessive rationalism and aggressive activism of the West.

Griffiths' dream came to fruition in the mid-1950s, when he obtained permission to accept the invitation of an Indian priest to help establish a monastery in the vicinity of the South Indian city of Bangalore. Although this experiment failed, he remained in India, first at a Cistercian ashram in Kerala state and then at Shantivanam as the successor of Abhishiktananda. Whereas the latter had been unable to attract any permanent members of the community, possibly because candidates sensed his own ambivalence about Shantivanam, Griffiths did attract vocations; by the time of his death in 1993 the community had about fifteen members, all of them Indian with the exception of Griffiths himself.

There was an even more significant difference in the spirituality of the two men. We have already noticed Abhishiktananda's years-long grappling with "the advaitic dilemma," which made it difficult for him to see how advaitic experience could be shown to be compatible with such basic Christian doctrines as the Trinity.[15] In fact, toward the end of his life, when he had been invited to give a lecture on the Trinity to the Jesuit theological faculty at Delhi, he was filled with misgivings, writing in a letter to his closest disciple: "I am a little anxious about these lectures requested by Delhi . . . What can I say now? Lead them toward the 'open sea,' with all moorings severed? . . . Nothing comes that is worth saying."[16]

Griffiths, on the other hand, always relished speaking about the Trinity, believing this doctrine to be precisely the way to answer the advaitic dilemma. In *A New Vision of Reality*, the work that many consider the most masterful synthesis of his thought, he writes: "The Hindu in his deepest experience of *advaita* knows God in an identity of being. 'I am Brahman,' 'Thou art that.' The Christian experiences God in a communion of being, a

15. He did attempt this in his book *Saccidananda: A Christian Approach to Advaitic Experience* (see n. 10 above), but he became dissatisfied with this work even before he had finished writing it.

16. Abhishiktananda to Marc Chaduc, April 8 and 11, 1973, in Stuart, *Swami Abhishiktananda*, 326.

relationship of love, in which there is nonetheless perfect unity of being."[17] This relationship of love is rooted in the Trinity and is in fact "the reflection of the life of the Godhead, where the Father and the Son give themselves totally in love and are united in the Spirit in an unfathomable unity. So the interpersonal relationships within the Trinity are the model and exemplar of all interpersonal relationships on earth and ultimately also of all interrelationships in the whole creation."[18] There is unity here, but it is unity-in-distinction, a kind of unity that characterizes not only the Godhead but also our own relationship to the triune God. When we lose ourselves in that abyss of love, we find ourselves.

This losing-and-finding was played out in a striking way in the final months of Griffiths' own life. Two strokes, one in December 1992 and the other in February 1993, brought about what one of his closest acquaintances called an "embellishment" of his whole person, while another friend expressed the change in the following words:

> I have never seen him so affectionate and loving. He draws people to himself and hugs them. After he greeted Asha [Russill] with a great hug and tears of joy, he took my hands, kissed them and drew me down to himself, kissed me on the cheek and held me down with a hug and embrace that I shall never forget and always cherish. It was as if the other part of his soul that he had come to find in India broke through the proper English manner like a torrent of love and joy.[19]

A final point about Griffiths should be made explicit, even though it has been alluded to in the preceding paragraphs. Although he never agonized over his Christian identity in the way Abhishiktananda did at times, he was also insistent that the church needed to be in dialogue with representatives of the other world religions. He feared that to one degree or another all of the great religious traditions had become fossilized and that renewal would best come about through their developing vital relationships with one another. This was a common theme in his writings, as in the following passage from an article for a British journal:

> We are not seeking a syncretism in which each religion will lose its own individuality, but an organic growth in which each religion has to purify

17. Bede Griffiths, *A New Vision of Reality: Western Science, Eastern Mysticism and Christian Faith* (Springfield, Ill.: Templegate, 1990), 220.

18. Ibid., 254.

19. Father John Kilian, letter to friends, May 10, 1993, quoted by Shirley du Boulay, *Beyond the Darkness: A Biography of Bede Griffiths* (New York: Doubleday, 1998), 260.

itself and discover its inmost depth and significance and then relate itself to the inner depth of the other traditions. Perhaps it will never be achieved in this world, but it is the one way in which we can advance today towards that unity in truth which is the ultimate goal of mankind.[20]

Like other pioneers in interreligious dialogue and spirituality, both Abhishiktananda and Bede Griffiths have had their critics and detractors, but they also continue to have considerable influence, both through their writings and through organizations that have been established to preserve and promote their visions of a Christian spirituality appropriate for our time, especially in India and other parts of the non-European world.[21]

JAPANESE CHRISTIAN SPIRITUALITIES: KAZOH KITAMORI AND SHUSAKU ENDO

In the first chapter of this book we referred to David Tracy's statement that works of fiction can open our minds and imaginations to new and possibly transformative ways of being-in-the-world. The two authors to be considered in this present section—one a theologian conversant with Japanese drama and the other a novelist—illustrate the validity of Tracy's point. During some of the darkest days in Japan's history, when the Japanese people were enduring the bombings that led to the unconditional surrender of their government and the end of the Second World War, the Lutheran theologian Kazoh Kitamori (1916-1998) was writing the first strictly theological Japanese book ever to be translated into English. Kitamori's *Theology of the Pain of God*, whose first Japanese edition appeared in 1946, is the author's explicit attempt to "approach the Bible from a fresh point of view,"[22] freed from the particularity of most Western theology, which he faults for its vision of an impassible, immutable, totally self-sufficient God derived largely from certain currents of ancient philosophy. If the church's theologians had allowed themselves to be influenced by Greek tragedy and not only by Greek philosophy, argues Kitamori, they would likely have followed the Hebrew prophets in proclaiming that pain is inseparable from God and is not merely an anthropomorphic or

20. Bede Griffiths, "The One Mystery," *The Tablet*, March 9, 1974, quoted by du Boulay, *Beyond the Darkness*, 183.

21. The Abhishiktananda Society is headquartered in Varanasi, India, and publishes a bulletin entitled *Setu*. The Bede Griffiths Trust is headquartered at New Camaldoli Hermitage in Big Sur, California; its bulletin is entitled *The Golden String*.

22. Kazoh Kitamori, *Theology of the Pain of God*, trans. M. E. Bratcher (Richmond, Va.: John Knox, 1965), 8. Subsequent parenthetical references to this book indicate the page number.

mythological way of speaking about an impassible God. This does not mean that pain exists in God as "a substance." Rather, it denotes a relationship—God's constant love toward human beings even in their unlovable sinfulness, as expressed in God's word about wayward Ephraim in Jeremiah 31:20: "Therefore my heart is pained for him." (Kitamori also provides Luther's translation: *Darum bricht mir mein Herz*, "Therefore my heart is broken.") In the New Testament, the pain of God has a further meaning: not only God's love for the unlovable (as in Jeremiah and other prophets) but also God's sending the beloved Son to make atonement. Kitamori finds this most clearly expressed in the fifth chapter of the Letter to the Romans, where Paul writes: "Rarely will anyone die for a righteous person—though perhaps for a good person someone might actually dare to die. But God proves his love for us in that while we were still sinners Christ died for us" (Rom 5:7-8).

Since Kitamori holds that the main reason why Western theologians understood prophetic references to God's pain only metaphorically is that they were too influenced by the "typical Greek way of thinking," the Japanese theologian's whole project could be described as an attempt to "advance one step beyond the position of the Greco-Roman churches" (132). He begins this attempt by turning to literature, especially the classical drama of his native land, the kind of source largely ignored by Western theology. Kitamori reflects above all on Japanese tragedies, whose basic principle is *tsurasa*, the feeling of inevitable fate and sorrow that hangs over human life and that is realized "when one suffers and dies, or makes his beloved son suffer and die, for the sake of loving and making others live" (135). Among the tragedies to which he refers is *The Temple School*, in which the character Matsuomaru is a retainer for a feudal lord whose son and heir is being sought by the lord's enemies. When the latter narrow their search to a school for boys housed in a Buddhist temple, Matsuomaru knows that the only way to save the heir's life is to substitute his own son, so he sends him to the temple school and thus to his death. To console his wife, Matsuomaru says to her: "Rejoice, my dear. Our son has been of service to our lord" (134). Kitamori concludes his analysis of Japanese drama with these words:

> It is our conviction that the pain which is the only concern for Japanese tragedy corresponds most aptly with the pain of God, which is the main subject of this book . . . Thus the Japanese mind, which has seen the deepest heart of his fellowman in pain, will come to see the deepest heart of the Absolute God in pain. Those of us who have been given the land of Japan as the 'boundaries of habitation' will serve God with all our hearts, bearing the sense of pain as we attempt to comprehend the image and view of

> God. By so doing, one decisive aspect of God's nature, which was overlooked by the Greek churches, will be recovered by the churches of our country. (136)

Although in his book Kitamori does not dwell at length on the spiritual or moral implications of this understanding of God, he does say enough to indicate how significant these are. He writes that on a purely psychological level it is impossible to feel another's pain as intensely as one feels one's own, or to love one's neighbor as intensely as a parent loves his or her child, but on a theological or spiritual level this does occur when we become "imitators of God's love" (123) and love others as faithfully as God has done:

> We can give to a suffering neighbor our love with an intensity equal to what we feel in our own pain only when we and that neighbor rest in the pain of God. That is, when we are both 'of the same body . . . in Christ' (Eph 3:6). Love for our neighbor becomes real for the first time when we walk in the way which God has shown us. Since we and our suffering neighbor are joined together when we are both embraced in the pain of God, we can feel our neighbor's pain as intensely as our own. (86)

Whereas the Lutheran Kitamori turned to the classical drama of his country to help elucidate his theology of the pain of God, that theology has subsequently been carried back into the world of literature by the Catholic novelist Shusaku Endo (1923-1996), whom many consider the leading writer in Japan during the last half of the twentieth century. Baptized at age eleven, Endo once said in an interview that the Catholicism of his youth was like a ready-made suit that did not properly fit his own body, leaving him with the choice of either making it fit or discarding it and finding another that fit. As the years went by he found that it had become so much a part of him that he could not throw it off. Nevertheless, "From the time I first began to write novels even to the present day, this confrontation of my Catholic self with the self that lies underneath has . . . echoed and reechoed in my work. I felt that I had to find some way to reconcile the two."[23]

Like Kitamori, Endo sought to present an understanding of God to which the Japanese mentality would be responsive. That he did so primarily in works of fiction rather than in theological treatises laid his work open to many divergent and sometimes mutually exclusive interpretations. This is

23. Quoted by William Johnston in his translator's preface to *Silence* (New York: Taplinger, 1980), xix. Subsequent parenthetical references to this book indicate the page number.

especially true of his best-known novel, *Silence*, but the following paragraphs represent a reading of that work that is in accord not only with key passages in the novel itself but with what Endo wrote in some of his works of non-fiction.[24] This reading likewise corresponds to and advances the kind of Japanese Christian spirituality projected in Kitamori's *Theology of the Pain of God.*

The main character in Endo's book, the Portuguese missionary Sebastian Rodrigues, is fictional but is based on a historical figure, Giuseppe Chiara, who arrived in Japan in 1643 at a time when Christians were undergoing severe persecution because the empire's chief minister, Hideyoshi, suspected that the missionaries had come to Japan in order to change the government and gain possession of the land. In order to make peasant Christians apostatize, extremely cruel tortures were devised, the worst of which was being hung upside down from a gallows over a pit filled with excrement and other filth. Most of the martyrs survived in the pit only a few days, although there is evidence that some lingered in excruciating pain for as long as two weeks. In the novel, Rodrigues is eventually captured and urged to apostatize both by his interpreter and by Christovao Ferreira, who was in actual fact the Portuguese Jesuit provincial who had some years earlier become the first missionary to apostatize, to the great dismay of his fellow Christians. The act of apostasy was signified by trampling on a small metal image of Christ's face affixed to a wooden plank and called a *fumie*. Rodrigues knows that if he tramples on the image, he will not only save his own life but will win the release of the peasants hanging in the pit. Up to this point, Rodrigues has been troubled by the silence of God in the midst of so much horrific suffering on the part of the martyrs. He keeps asking himself, "Why is God continually silent while those groaning voices [from the pit] go on?" (254-55). Finally, having been handed the *fumie* he brings it close to his eyes, then places it on the floor and raises his foot. Unlike the interpreter's repeated claim that the trampling will be only a formality, signifying nothing, Rodrigues knows it is much more than that, but he also finds that the divine silence is broken in a most shocking way:

> He will now trample on what he has considered the most beautiful thing in his life, on what he has believed most pure, on what is filled with the ideals and the dreams of man. How his foot aches! And then the Christ in bronze speaks to the priest: "Trample! Trample! I more than anyone know

24. See, e.g., his preface to the American edition of *A Life of Jesus*, trans. Richard A. Schuchert, S.J. (New York: Paulist, 1978).

> of the pain in your foot. Trample! It was to be trampled on by men that I was born into this world. It was to share men's pain that I carried my cross." (259)

Many readers, both in Japan and elsewhere, were troubled by this. Endo's translator writes that some of the "old Christians" of Japan felt that Endo "had been less than fair to the indomitable courage of their heroic ancestors" (xxii), many of whom had gone to a martyr's death singing joyfully and hopefully that they were on their way "to the temple of Paradise," ultimately victorious over the magistrates who had tried to get them to apostatize. Endo, however, does not take the step of having the Portuguese missionary continue to stand firm instead of apostatizing and thereby having the peasants released from the pit. What changes Rodrigues's mind is a change in his vision. In the words of one perceptive critic, Brett Dewey,

> we read about how Rodrigues learns to see Jesus differently. First we read of Rodrigues' reflection on Jesus as the paragon of beauty and perfection. This vision of Christ dominated his life as a child. While in Japan, he meditates on Jesus' face regularly, and that meditation begins to take a different form. In the end, Jesus appears before Rodrigues not as ideal beauty or cosmic perfector, but as a haggard face burdened with the trials of the world. Compassion for this face leads Rodrigues to stomp on the *fumie*. Endo reflects that the true vocation of the Church, then, is to be moved to compassion and to suffer with God and the peasantry of the world.[25]

This understanding of the Christian vocation is portrayed not only in the words that Rodrigues hears Christ speaking from the *fumie* but also in the novel's appendix, which shows Rodrigues, now known as Apostate Paul, as the head servant of a subterranean Christian community in which even the weakest and most cowardly are welcomed back into the fold. As Dewey writes, "There is a place for weakness and forgiveness in the community. Endo shows us that the church is made of redeemed Peters and Judases; it is a broken community whose triumph is in the shared suffering with God."[26] This insight reflects a statement made years earlier by Kazoh Kitamori, that "For us, the imitators of God's love . . . forgiveness is everything. Even though our love . . . is defeated and has become a 'lost love' . . . we must love our fel-

25. Brett R. Dewey, "Suffering the Patient Victory of God: Shusaku Endo and the Lessons of a Japanese Catholic," *Quodlibet: Online Journal of Christian Theology and Philosophy* 6, no. 1 (Jan.-Mar. 2004), http://www.Quodlibet.net.

26. Ibid.

lowmen with unchanging faithfulness as God has done."[27] As we have seen throughout this book, the touchstone of Christian spirituality is the practice of love, including love of "the weakest and most cowardly."

FILIPINO CHRISTIAN SPIRITUALITY: MARY JOHN MANANZAN

Despite the warm reception that Kitamori's theology of the pain of God was given in many quarters, the book was criticized by some as being too vague about just how we and our neighbor can come to "rest in the pain of God." Other critics, even more forcefully, objected that it effectively ignored the victimized, the oppressed, "the absent in history." That charge could not be made about the person we have chosen as a representative of Christian spirituality in the Philippines. Mary John Mananzan was born in 1937 into a middle-class family in the province of Pangasinan. When she was ten years old the family moved to Manila, where she received elementary, secondary, and tertiary education at schools run by Benedictine sisters. She decided to enter that Benedictine community at age nineteen and, after a further ten years there, was sent abroad for graduate studies in theology and philosophy in Germany and at the Pontifical Gregorian University in Rome, becoming the first woman to receive a doctorate at the latter institution. Once back in Manila, Mananzan was entrusted with a number of responsible positions, including the deanship and later the presidency of St. Scholastica's College, the school where she had earlier received her bachelor's degree. In 2004 she was elected the religious superior of her community. She has also held important positions in the Ecumenical Association of Third World Theologians and in Gabriela, a federation of Filipina women which she cofounded and whose aim is to promote the place of women in that society. Of course, many persons have held similar positions of administrative authority. What has made Mananzan a prominent spokesperson for Filipino Christian spirituality is the articulate way in which she has linked the practice of spirituality with commitment to justice. When once asked by the editor of a festschrift to answer the question, "What is the most important spiritual question of our time?" she replied: "I have come to the conclusion that it is still the question of justice."[28]

---

27. Kitamori, *Theology of the Pain of God*, 123.

28. Mary John Mananzan, O.S.B., "Globalization and the Perennial Question of Justice," in *Spiritual Questions for the Twenty-First Century: Essay in Honor of Joan D. Chittister*, ed. Mary Hembrow Snyder (Maryknoll, N.Y.: Orbis Books, 2001), 153.

How Mananzan came to this conclusion goes back to her early days in religious life. Martial law had been imposed by the Marcos regime in 1972, with strikes prohibited. In a wine factory called La Tondeña the working conditions were so bad that six hundred workers went on strike anyway. Mananzan and four of the other sisters went out shortly before midnight to support the strikers. In an interview she later described the events of that night in these words: "I call this experience the Baptism of Fire because this was the first time I had witnessed military brutality. I mean they were really beating up these workers. Bloody . . . That was a terrible experience for me. It made me think, 'O my God, I have to help these people. I have to be one with them. They are struggling for justice.' So that was how it began."[29] Another spur to her social awakening came from her study of Filipino history, in which she learned that prior to Spanish colonization women in the Philippines had a high standing in their society, enjoying relatively equal status with men as regards inheritance rights, political leadership, and service in the religious sphere (as *babaylan*, priestesses). This has led her to focus especially on issues of justice for women.

Although Mananzan and many other Filipino theologians have been inspired by the liberation theology propounded in the works of Gustavo Gutierrez and other Latin Americans (to be studied in the final chapter of this book), she writes that the Filipinos "prefer to have their theology called theology of struggle rather than liberation theology. It is not so much a theology about struggle but in the context of struggle—the struggle of the great majority of the Filipino people for justice."[30] Within this context of struggle, Mananzan has singled out various characteristics of what she calls "a spirituality for our times." Four of these characteristics in particular will enable us to obtain an overview of Filipino Christian spirituality as she and a great many of her associates understand it: (1) prophetic, (2) integral, (3) contemplative, and (4) paschal.[31]

By "prophetic spirituality" Mananzan means one "that is convinced of the good news it has to announce and has the courage to denounce what it considers the bad news" (159). Among "the bad news" are some particular aspects of globalization. She realizes that this latter term has various meanings, not

---

29. Mary John Mananzan, "Sister of Action," http://www.multiworld.org/m_versity/changemak/sister.htm.

30. Mary John Mananzan, "Paschal Mystery from a Philippine Perspective," in *Any Room for Christ in Asia?* (*Concilium* 1993/2), ed. Leonardo Boff and Virgil Elizondo (Maryknoll, N.Y.: Orbis Books; London: SCM, 1993), 90.

31. These are among a total of seven characteristics discussed in her article "Globalization and the Perennial Question of Justice" (see n. 28 above). Parenthetical references to this article indicate the page number.

all of them negative. When it refers to the networking going on internationally in all fields, whereby people can share their insights and the results of their research through conferences or the Internet, it can only be affirmed, for "true international solidarity cannot but be positive" (153). But she also notes a more sinister side to the phenomenon of globalization, with wealth being concentrated in fewer and fewer hands and the economy of third world countries coming more and more under the control of foreign, multinational corporations. A comprehensive study by the United Nations Development Fund concluded that globalization in this sense has widened the gap between rich and poor, resulting in "an export-oriented, import-dependent, foreign-investment-controlled, and debt-ridden economy" (154) for a country like the Philippines.

Mananzan, who has served in various executive roles for the Ecumenical Association of Third World Theologians, notes that members of this ecumenical association actually see globalization as a kind of "new religion," with its high priests (such as officials of the International Monetary Fund), its doctrines and dogmas (import liberalization and deregulation), its temples (the super mega-malls), and its victims on the altar of sacrifice (the marginalized poor who are the majority of the world's population). She accordingly has joined her voice to others in that association in calling for a prophetic theology "that will critique prince and priest, market and mammon, multinationals and war merchants and all hegemony and all plunder of the poor. It will call into question the silence of religions and churches as children die of hunger . . . due to imperialist policies of superpowers or local magnates. It will call into question the centuries-old oppression of women at home and in society" (157-58).

For Mananzan, a second characteristic of a spirituality appropriate for our times is that it be "integral," that is, transcending dichotomies such as body/soul, sacred/profane, and contemplative/active. An experience she had after speaking in front of ten thousand people urging them to oppose a hike in the price of oil serves well to illustrate this point. When she had finished speaking, a policeman came up to her and asked, "Aren't you a Sister." After she said she was, he went on: "So why are you talking about the oil price hike? You are a Sister. You ought to take care of the souls of the people. Why don't you talk about mortal sin, purgatory, hell?"[32] It is to dispel this narrow notion of Christian spirituality that Mananzan regularly insists that the gospel message is for the liberation of the whole human being, not only from sin, death, and hell but from everything that dehumanizes: exploitation of the weak,

32. Mananzan, "Sister in Action."

oppression, poverty, destruction of the environment. In her words, "We need to integrate our relationships with God, with ourselves, with others, and with the planet. [Integral spirituality] is inclusive and resists exclusion of peoples for any reason, be it class, race, gender, or any other" (159).

Third, Mananzan speaks of the need for a "contemplative spirituality," by which she means one that "emphasizes moments of reflection, meditation, and contemplation—being present to the Presence, a constant awareness of the absolute within us, who is the inexhaustible source of joy, love and energy and makes us committed but carefree" (160). From what has been said in the preceding paragraphs, one might have gotten the impression that Mananzan sees no place for contemplative practice in Christian spirituality, but that is far from being the case. While she clearly recognizes that there can and should be a contemplative aspect to the life of any Christian, the emphasis on this in the Benedictine way of life was a major factor in her joining that religious order. As she said in the earlier-mentioned interview, "You become a nun not in order to teach, you become a nun because there is a certain style of life: prayer, community life. The work is just a part of it, but the most important thing is that you want to live a life of prayer, a life of contemplation, a certain kind of community life, together with others. And what you get from that you put into practice whatever you are doing, whether it is in school, hospital, or social action." She notes that the contemplative attitude that she has imbibed from living according to the *Rule of Benedict* since her late teens has given her a perspective that prevents any particular cause or activity from becoming all-consuming.

To understand what Mananzan means by the fourth characteristic of a contemporary Christian spirituality—that it be paschal ("an Easter spirituality")—it is important to know something of the way Christianity came to the Philippines. In the case of countries like India, China, and Japan, Christian missionaries found well-developed traditions already in place: Hindu, Confucian, Daoist, Buddhist, and Shintoist. Not so in the Philippines, where the indigenous peoples, having no highly structured religion of their own, readily embraced Christianity, although it is questionable whether many of them truly assimilated it. What made the deepest impression on the native people were certain practices and devotions that the sixteenth- and seventeenth-century missionaries brought from their native Spain, such as the reading of the Passion Narrative and the reenactment of the suffering and death of Christ during Holy Week services.[33] As an explanation of why this aspect of the

33. Mananzan, "Paschal Mystery from a Philippine Perspective," 87.

paschal mystery, rather than the resurrection, received such emphasis, one social scientist has written:

> In a country where poverty, deprivation and oppression are the common lot of the masses, where typhoons and earthquakes frequently occur, it is not surprising that the image of the Crucified One, head bowed, mouth agape in excruciating agony, provides consolation and an outlet for pent-up emotions of sympathy and tragedy for the ignorant and the heavy-laden . . . In the sight of the cross, Christians live in acceptance and trust in the suffering God who remains faithful in his love for sinful human beings.[34]

Correspondingly, the resurrection of Christ has been relatively ignored in Filipino spirituality. Another scholar has commented on this as follows:

> The omission [of the resurrection] seems characteristic of the whole Filipino Catholicism. A look at Holy Week traditions can tell a lot of the story. No matter what clergy today may be saying to the crowds about the importance of Easter, nearly every parishioner you speak with has spent his/her religious energy by Good Friday night. The main event, plainly, is over. Even for so-called educated Filipinos, Easter apparently comes as a supplement, maybe even as an inconvenience.[35]

This subordinating of Easter to Good Friday is evident even in Filipino religious art, for in a survey of the preferred image of Christ among grassroots Filipinos, that of the crucified Christ ranked first. In some rural parishes during Holy Week, young men make superficial blade cuts on their backs and flagellate themselves or let someone else whip them in imitation of Christ's being scourged at the pillar. Some men actually have themselves crucified with nails—living crucifixes.[36] How extreme and misguided such devotion is becomes all the more evident when one considers the earliest Christian art. For the first four centuries of our era there were no crucifixes at all, a fact regularly explained by art historians as connected with the apostolic and early patristic emphasis on the risen Christ's victory over sin and death. One such

---

34. Benigno Beltran, *The Christology of the Inarticulate: An Inquiry into the Filipino Understanding of Jesus the Christ* (Manila: Divine Word Publications, 1987), 123, quoted by Mananzan, "Paschal Mystery from a Philippine Perspective," 88.

35. James Ebner, F.S.C., "God: A Problem in Filipino Catholicism," *Vision* 4, no. 1 (1978): 19, quoted by Mananzan, "Paschal Mystery from a Philippine Perspective," 88.

36. Mananzan, "Paschal Mystery from a Philippine Perspective," 88-89.

historian has surmised that in those early centuries "any depiction of Christ crucified would have been regarded as a kind of anachronism."[37] Later church councils began advocating depictions of the crucifixion as an effective way of counteracting docetic denials of Christ's full humanity.

There is no doubt that crucifixes sculpted or painted by great artists like Giovanni Cimabue in the thirteenth century or Matthias Grünewald in the sixteenth have played a valuable role in the history of Christian piety, but it is also true that an overabundance of such images can limit our understanding of Christ's redeeming activity to what occurred in his suffering and death. Redemption entails our living "in Christ," to use a phrase that St. Paul employs dozens of times to encapsulate what being a follower of Jesus is all about. Now the Christ in whom we are called to live is the risen, exalted, glorified Christ, no longer a "Man of Sorrows" but the one whom the Letter to the Ephesians describes as "seated at [God's] right hand in the heavenly places, far above all rule and authority and power and dominion, and above every name that is named, not only in this age but also in the age to come" (Eph 1:20-21). Accordingly, Paul may be said never to have thought of Christ's redemptive death without simultaneously thinking of his salutary resurrection. In the words of the eminent Scripture scholar Joseph A. Fitzmyer, "the cross and the resurrection are two intimately connected phases of the same salvific event."[38] The church's liturgy brings out this connection by speaking of the one paschal mystery, celebrated indeed over the course of several days at the end of Holy Week but really one event: the commemoration and celebration of Christ's passing from death to new life as the first-born of many brothers and sisters. To whatever extent people focus almost all of their spiritual energy on Good Friday, to that extent their understanding of the mystery is short-circuited, with one possible negative effect being a sense that their own suffering is positively willed by God and that it is therefore right simply to accept patiently the injustices they are experiencing.

To help overcome this truncated view of Easter and of Christian spirituality itself, Mananzan regularly calls for "an Easter spirituality" in her talks and writings, describing it as "a spirituality that transcends Good Friday, that is infected with the fearless joy of Easter. It resists the forces of death and promotes the enhancement of life. It feasts more than it fasts … It is not cold asceticism but a celebration of life" (160). Our next chapter, on African Christian spirituality, will provide still further and at times even more vibrant examples of a spirituality that is a celebration of life.

37. Cyril Pocknee, *Christ and Crucifix in Christian Worship and Devotion* (London: Mowbray, 1962), 38.

38. Joseph A. Fitzmyer, S.J., *Romans: A New Translation with Introduction and Commentary*, Anchor Bible 33 (New York: Doubleday, 1993), 389.

QUESTIONS FOR REFLECTION

1. Few Christian missionaries today would regard other religions as deriving from what Alexandre de Rhodes called "poisoned sources," but they would also normally not refrain from noting inadequacies and even errors in these religions. By what criteria can one best separate "the wheat from the chaff" in religious traditions that differ from one's own?
2. How would you express in your own words what Abhishiktananda meant by "the advaitic dilemma"? Bede Griffiths was not as troubled by this dilemma as was Abhishiktananda. Do you think this was because Griffiths had a better appreciation of the doctrine of the Trinity as the key to resolve the dilemma, or might it be that he had not experienced *advaita* in as profound and unsettling a way as had the French monk?
3. Griffiths went to India in search of what he called "the other half of my soul." In what circumstances do you think a geographical move to another culture would be spiritually helpful for a person? What could be done to recover this "other half of one's soul" if a person finds it simply impossible to move elsewhere?
4. This chapter's section on Kazoh Kitamori and Shusaku Endo discusses the way in which works of literature (in this case, classical dramas and a novel) can provoke a transformed understanding of God and of one's calling as a Christian. Why might works of fiction do this more effectively than theological treatises? Are there some particular literary works that have had this kind of effect on your own theology and spirituality?
5. What do you consider the most significant aspect of Mary John Mananzan's attempt to develop a spirituality appropriate for Filipino society? Of the four characteristics of spirituality discussed in this part of the chapter (prophetic, integral, contemplative, and paschal), which do you consider most needed in your own society or culture?

SUGGESTIONS FOR FURTHER READING AND STUDY

On Indian Christian Spiritualities

Abhishiktananda. *The Eyes of Light*. Denville, N.J.: Dimension Books, 1983. See especially chap. 2, "India's Contribution to Christian Prayer" (pp. 35-47).

———. *Prayer*. Rev. ed. Philadelphia: Westminster, 1973.

Boulay, Shirley du. *The Cave of the Heart: The Life of Swami Abhishiktananda*. Maryknoll, N.Y.: Orbis Books, 2005.

Griffiths, Bede. *The Golden String: An Autobiography*. 2nd ed. Springfield, Ill.: Templegate, 1980. See especially chap. 10, "Catholicism" (pp. 165-79) and "Epilogue: Heaven's Gate" (pp. 180-89).

———. *A New Vision of Reality: Western Science, Eastern Mysticism and Christian Faith.* Springfield, Ill.: Templegate, 1989. See especially chap. 13, "The New Age" (pp. 276-96).

Bruteau, Beatrice, comp. *The Other Half of My Soul: Bede Griffiths and the Hindu-Christian Dialogue.* Wheaton, Ill.: Quest Books; Madras, India: Adyar, 1996. See esp. Wayne Teasdale's introduction, "Bede Griffiths as Visionary Guide" (pp. 2-24).

Wiseman, James A., O.S.B. "Enveloped by Mystery: The Spiritual Journey of Henri Le Saux/Abhishiktananda." *Église et Théologie* 23 (1992): 241-60.

On Japanese Christian Spiritualities

Cavanaugh, William. "Absolute Moral Norms and Human Suffering: An Apocalyptic Reading of Endo's *Silence.*" *Logos: A Journal of Catholic Thought and Culture* 2 (Summer 1999): 96-116.

Christianity and Literature 48, no. 2 (Winter 1999). This entire issue is devoted to articles about Shusaku Endo. See especially the piece by his widow, Junko Endo, "Reflections on Shusaku Endo and *Silence*" (pp. 145-48).

Endo, Shusaku. *Silence.* Translated by William Johnston. New York: Taplinger, 1980.

Kitamori, Kazoh. *Theology of the Pain of God.* Translated by M. E. Bratcher. Richmond, Va.: John Knox Press, 1965. See especially chap. 11, "The Pain of God and Gospel History" (pp. 128-38).

McWilliams, Warren. "The Pain of God in the Theology of Kazoh Kitamori." *Perspectives in Religious Studies* 8 (1981): 184-200.

Otto, Randall E. "Japanese Religion and Kazoh Kitamori's Theology of the Pain of God." *Encounter* 52 (1991): 33-48.

On the Filipino Christian Spirituality of Mary John Mananzan

Mananzan, Mary John. "Globalization and the Perennial Question of Justice." In *Spiritual Questions for the Twenty-First Century: Essays in Honor of Joan D. Chittister*, edited by Mary Hembrow Snyder, 153-61. Maryknoll, N.Y.: Orbis Books, 2001.

———. "Paschal Mystery from a Philippine Perspective." In *Any Room for Christ in Asia?* (*Concilium* 1993/2), edited by Leonardo Boff and Virgil Elizondo, 86-94. Maryknoll, N.Y.: Orbis Books, 1993.

———, ed. *Women and Religion.* Manila: St. Scholastica's College, 1998. See especially the following pieces by Mananzan: "Women and Religion" (pp. 1-12), "The Religious Woman Today and Integral Evangelization" (pp. 60-72), and "Towards an Asian Feminist Theology" (pp. 92-102).

9

African Christian Spirituality

As the world's second largest continent, Africa is marked by cultural, geographical, and linguistic diversity—as many as one thousand separate and distinct languages are spoken on this continent! Even so, there are only three major religious traditions predominant in Africa: Christianity, Islam, and what is commonly called African Traditional Religion. The northernmost third of the continent is primarily Muslim (with the exception of Ethiopia, where the majority of the people are members of the Ethiopian Orthodox Church, whose uninterrupted history goes back at least to the middle of the fourth century). Even in the Muslim countries of North Africa, however, there are some vibrant Christian communities, one of the most remarkable being in the desert of Scetis south of Alexandria, where there have been monks since the days of Antony of Egypt. In 1985 one of the world's leading liturgical scholars, Robert Taft, S.J., visited the monastery of St. Macarius there and wrote a fascinating account of his ten-day stay. In addition to providing a fairly detailed description of the daily round of activities at the monastery, he wrote of the spirit of the community, which has preserved the same ideal of fraternal love and hospitality that marked the lives of the early monks who were discussed in the fourth chapter of this book. Toward the end of his account, Taft noted that "this community cannot fail to impress one by its spirit of quiet recollection and spontaneous, open friendliness. There is a great, unaffected simplicity to human relations here . . . Their uniform kindliness, cheerfulness, and calm joy are too constant and too general to be superficial or affected. Nor is this spirit reserved to the members of the community, like some Gnosticism of the initiated. It was, as of old, a joy to be shared with all."[1] Far to the south of Scetis, in the other two-thirds of the continent known as sub-Saharan Africa, the majority of the population is Christian, although there remain many practitioners of African Traditional Religion as well as a growing number of Muslims and, on the east

1. Robert Taft, S.J., "A Pilgrimage to the Origins of Religious Life: The Fathers of the Desert Today," *American Benedictine Review* 36 (1985): 141.

coast, Hindus whose forebears had sailed over from India. This present chapter will therefore focus on the lands south of the Sahara Desert.

AFRICAN TRADITIONAL RELIGION

Christian missionaries from Portugal and Spain came to the coasts of what are now the countries of Ghana and Angola in the fifteenth and sixteenth centuries and led some of the native peoples to embrace Christianity, but then came a lull in missionary activity, which resumed in earnest only in the nineteenth century as part of what has been called "the scramble for Africa." Just as missionaries had accompanied colonizing forces in Asia, so too did they arrive in Africa at the time when European countries—primarily England, France, Belgium, and Germany—began acquiring colonies there. These missionaries, both Protestant and Catholic, did not arrive in a religious vacuum, as though the religious sensibility of the Africans was a kind of blank sheet or *tabula rasa*. Instead, what they encountered was African Traditional Religion. Since this, like all primal religions, was passed down from generation to generation orally rather than in writing, it was not rigidly standardized throughout the continent, nor is there any reason to think that its various manifestations have not changed over the course of the centuries. For this reason, some scholars prefer to speak of this tradition in the plural: African Traditional Religions. There are, however, so many common characteristics in the native religious beliefs and practices of sub-Saharan Africa that most scholars use the singular, as we will be doing here.

Although none of those common characteristics are unique to Africa and although the number of those that could be listed varies considerably from study to study, as an ensemble they do provide a reasonably accurate description of the traditional religion. The following five features regularly appear in accounts given by native African scholars: (1) belief in a supreme being; (2) belief in other spiritual beings, including ancestors, who can mediate between humans living on earth and the supreme being; (3) a strong sense of family and community; (4) rituals marked by song, dance, and spontaneous prayer; and (5) a sense of the sanctity of nature and the environment. Since these five marks have in one way or another influenced the practice of Christian spirituality among Africans, something more should be said about each.

The prominent African theologian John Mbiti has made the forthright claim that "All African peoples believe in God. They take this belief for granted. It is at the centre of African Religion and dominates all its other beliefs."[2] In what could be considered a parallel to the apophatic tradition in Christian thought, many Africans consider this supreme being to be so transcendent as not even to be able to be named, or at least not to have the name spoken casually or revealed to outsiders. In this sense, God is considered the creator of the universe and the ultimate source of all life but is not thought to be concerned about the everyday happenings and activities of men and women on earth. For this reason, prayers are often addressed to beings who stand midway between the creator God and human beings.

The number and nature of these intermediate beings vary from place to place, but in most African cultures the role of the ancestors is very prominent. We have already touched on the significance of the veneration of ancestors in connection with the work of Matteo Ricci in China in the late sixteenth and early seventeenth centuries. Just as in China (and elsewhere in Asia), so too in Africa there is among most people a keen sense that those who have died are not truly dead and that it is altogether possible and desirable to maintain communion with them. Since the ways in which this is done vary, a specific example will help clarify what is meant by what anthropologists call "the cult of ancestors."

Among the mountain people of northern Cameroon, each male head of a family possesses a jar called a *Baba* or *pra* that represents his father or grandfather and is believed to be the residence of the latter's soul. The *Baba* is kept in the most privileged place in the home, and when prayers are recited over it, those praying speak as though they are talking to an actual person, for the jar "is a vital bond that permits the ancestors to communicate with the living and to exercise their immediate and direct influence."[3] This cult, which may also include the pouring of libations and the sacrifice of domestic animals, is part of an overall vision of kinship that undergirds every sector of traditional African society. This includes kinship with nonhuman and even inanimate objects, as is poignantly expressed in a poem by the Senegalese poet Birago Diop:

> Those who are dead are never gone:
>   they are there in the thickening shadow.
> The dead are not under the earth:
>   they are in the tree that rustles,
>   they are in the wood that groans;

---

2. John S. Mbiti, *Introduction to African Religion*, 2nd rev. ed. (London: Heinemann, 1991), 45.

3. Jean-Marc Éla, *My Faith as an African*, trans. John Pairman Brown and Susan Perry (Maryknoll, N.Y.: Orbis Books; London: Geoffrey Chapman, 1988), 16.

Those who are dead are never gone:
    they are in the breast of the woman,
    they are in the child who is wailing
    and in the firebrand that flames.
The dead are not under the earth:
    they are in the forest,
    they are in the house.
The dead are not dead.[4]

This second characteristic leads directly into the third, namely, the centrality of one's family and community as the place to be born, live, and die. In the words of Chris Nwaka Egbulem, an African Dominican priest, "Being born into a family inserts a person into a kind of current, and it is identification with that family and community that determines the nature of one's existence and survival," so much so that "it could be said that the African is incomplete when alone" and becomes fully a person only in association with other persons.[5] This ideal is more readily realized in village life, where the people normally live in extended families, than in the large cities, but even for urbanites the yearning for community remains. Another African Catholic priest, James C. Okoye, writes: "The African is a person-in-community. One of the deepest yearnings is to rediscover true community and solidarity amid the social changes of modern life."[6]

Among the most powerful bonds holding family and community together in African Traditional Religion is our fourth characteristic, ritual, which is generally much more vibrant than that found in northern Europe or North America. A leading African liturgist has written that religious ritual "makes the acting community experience the anchor of its existence. The community therefore participates in transcendent reality. It expresses and realizes this experience of its foundation through ritual. Religious ritual can thus be called the highest point of ritual action, for in it resides the community's self-discovery."[7] Such rituals are often held outdoors, perhaps at a waterfall, grove, cave, or other spot considered especially sacred. They mark not only certain

4. Birago Diop, quoted by Ogbu U. Kalu, "Ancestral Spirituality and Society in Africa," in *African Spirituality: Forms, Meanings, and Expressions*, ed. Jacob K. Olupona, World Spirituality 3 (New York: Crossroad, 2000), 54.

5. Chris Nwaka Egbulem, O.P., "African Spirituality," in *The New Dictionary of Catholic Spirituality*, ed. Michael Downey (Collegeville, Minn.: Liturgical Press, 1993), 19.

6. James C. Okoye, C.S.Sp., "African Theology," in *Dictionary of Mission: Theology, History, Perspectives*, ed. Karl Müller, S.V.D., et al., trans. Francis Mansfield, S.V.D., et al. (Maryknoll, N.Y.: Orbis Books, 1997), 15.

7. Elochukwu E. Uzukwu, C.S.Sp., *Worship as Body Language: Introduction to Christian Worship; An African Orientation* (Collegeville, Minn.: Liturgical Press, 1997), 43.

seasons of the year (such as the time for planting or harvesting) but also significant stages in a person's life, above all one's birth, initiation into adulthood at the onset of puberty, marriage, times of sickness, and eventual death (which is not really death!). Since African Traditional Religion is not based on written scriptures but is transmitted orally, the prayers and the recounting of myths, stories, and proverbs are spoken or chanted extemporaneously, while the community's songs are regularly accompanied by dancing and instrumental music, especially drumming.

How different this is from many Western forms of worship is evident. We noted in chapter 4 that some Christian ascetics experienced a certain shame about the body, even preferring not to be seen by others when partaking of food. This is in accord with the ancient Platonic ideal that admires a "godlike" mastery of mind (or soul) over body. Quite different is the African experience of the body, which is not at all seen as a kind of prison for the soul. Rather, "the body is the center of the total manifestation of the person in gestures . . . The African executes bodily in the dance the complex nature of African rhythm as expressed in music."[8] In other words, "Dance is an integral part of African life. The African dances when a child is born, during puberty rites, marriage, funerals, religious ceremonies, festivals, and for recreation. Africans also use dance idioms to express hostility, cooperation, friendship, and expectation . . . [Thus,] dance provides interactional resources during which profound statements are made by individuals or groups."[9]

In African Traditional Religion these rituals, whether or not dance is included, are usually performed in the open air rather than in buildings. There are various reasons for the relative absence of cultic buildings. In many parts of the continent, building materials and techniques are not suitable to the construction of vast edifices that would rival the cathedrals of medieval Europe, while in the tropical zone that covers much of sub-Saharan Africa the climate makes it much more difficult than in temperate zones to tolerate gatherings in enclosed spaces. The more fundamental reason, however, has been pointed out by a prominent French anthropologist, who observes that in Africa the sacred calendar of the traditional religion "is founded on the processional rhythm of the stars and the seasons, on the movement and cycle of the year, and on the succession and metamorphosis of natural events." Accordingly, "the idea of a public religious edifice specifically intended as a place where people can come into contact with the Invisible can be of little interest to the African . . . [who instead] will seek in nature to achieve har-

8. Ibid., 10-13.

9. Pashington Obeng, "Asante Catholicism: An African Appropriation of the Roman Catholic Religion," in *African Spirituality*, 380.

mony with the divine."[10] A sense of the sacred quality of the natural world is accordingly another fundamental characteristic of this religion.

CHRISTIAN SPIRITUALITY IN SUB-SAHARAN AFRICA

Against the background of this brief survey of some major characteristics of African Traditional Religion, we now turn to African Christian spirituality. After discussing the way in which missionaries up to the middle of the twentieth century tended to regard the religious tradition they found among the native peoples, we will look at the significant change in attitude and approach that has occurred more recently, especially in matters of religious ritual. A subsequent section of this chapter will consider the struggle for social justice as another crucial aspect of Christian spirituality in Africa in recent times, and a final section will discuss the rise of the African Independent Churches and the ways in which they differ from the mainline denominations that came to the continent from abroad.

Although there were exceptions, many Christian missionaries from the late fifteenth century up to around the middle of the twentieth tended to regard African Traditional Religion as simply misguided and riddled with errors. Africans who wished to become Christian were therefore required to abandon their ancestral religion. A professor who for years taught at the University of Durban in South Africa minced no words in describing the attitude of such missionaries and other foreigners:

> Everything African was seen as hardly of any significance; thinking was here seen as based on "pre-logical mentality," that is, not really evolutionized; their achievements were treated as if next to nothing, their social systems not worth maintaining. African life was described as irrational, the Western culture as based on the so-called superiority of the science-oriented Western world; the one "primitive" and "traditional," the other so-called civilized or modern.[11]

As one would expect, the attitude of those Westerners who had brought not only a new religion but also a new way of governing civil society had profound effects on the Africans, much of it dramatized in what became one of the most widely read and highly acclaimed novels of the twentieth century,

---

10. Dominique Zahan, *The Religion, Spirituality, and Thought of Traditional Africa*, trans. Kate Ezra and Lawrence M. Martin (Chicago/London: University of Chicago Press, 1979), 19-20.
11. G. C. Oosthuizen, "The Task of African Traditional Religion," in *African Spirituality*, 278.

Chinua Achebe's *Things Fall Apart*. Taking the title of his book from a famous poem by William Butler Yeats, this African author portrays the dissolution of life in a Nigerian community over the course of some years. Near the beginning of the third and final part of the novel, Achebe has one of the characters say: "The white man is very clever. He came quietly and peaceably with his religion. We were amused at his foolishness and allowed him to stay. Now he has won our brothers, and our clan can no longer act like one. He has put a knife on the things that held us together and we have fallen apart."[12] Even more harshly, other Africans used to say during the colonial era: "When the white man came, he had the Bible and we had the land. Now we have the Bible and he has the land."

However, the blanket dismissal of African Traditional Religion on the part of missionaries and others from the West is no longer nearly as prevalent as it was in the past. In the Roman Catholic Church, a changed attitude became apparent by mid-twentieth century when Pope Pius XII emphasized what had in fact been common practice in the church in much earlier times, such as when the peoples of northern Europe were evangelized in the first millennium: "The Church from the beginning down to our time has always followed this wise practice: let not the Gospel on being introduced into any new land destroy or extinguish whatever its people possess that is naturally good, just or beautiful."[13] This kind of papal admonition led Catholic missionaries to seek out those beliefs and practices in traditional religions that were "good, just or beautiful," even as they also recognized the need to oppose baneful practices such as human sacrifice. Pope Pius XII's words were echoed even more forcefully a few decades later in one of the groundbreaking documents of the Second Vatican Council, *Nostra Aetate*, the Declaration on the Church's Relationship to Other Religions, promulgated by Pope Paul VI in October 1965. In one of the most frequently quoted sentences from the entire council, section 2 of the declaration ends with the words: "Let Christians, while witnessing to their own faith and way of life, acknowledge, preserve and encourage the spiritual and moral truths found among non-Christians, also their social life and culture."

Although that conciliar document does not specifically name African Traditional Religion (as it does name Hinduism, Buddhism, Islam, and Judaism), Pope Paul VI made up for this omission in a talk he gave at a gathering of African bishops in Kampala, Uganda, in July 1969, the first time a

12. Chinua Achebe, *Things Fall Apart* (New York: Fawcett Crest, 1969), 162. The quoted passage is found at the end of chap. 20.

13. Pope Pius XII, encyclical *Evangelii Praecones* (June 2, 1951), quoted by Karl Müller, S.V.D., "Inculturation," in *Dictionary of Mission*, 199.

pope had ever traveled to sub-Saharan Africa. After urging the bishops to uphold the faith of the church, Paul VI went on to say:

> The expression, that is, the language and mode of manifesting this one faith, may be manifold . . . From this point of view, a certain pluralism is not only legitimate but desirable. An adaptation of the Christian life in the fields of pastoral, ritual, didactic and spiritual activities is not only possible, it is even favored by the Church. The liturgical renewal is a living example of this. And in this sense you may, and you must, have an African Christianity.[14]

Liturgical Inculturation

Because Paul VI singled out the liturgical renewal as "a living example" of this desirable kind of pluralism, and because ritual is, as we have seen, so central an aspect of African Traditional Religion, we will now look at several instances in which Roman Catholic liturgists and church leaders have fashioned rites that are intended to be authentically African while yet remaining truly Catholic. The first will be from the diocese of Kumasi in Ghana; the second, from the Democratic Republic of the Congo, formerly known as Zaire.

Although the principal liturgical rite in Roman Catholicism is the celebration of the eucharist (or Mass), there are many other forms of devotion that have developed over the centuries, some of them closely related to the eucharistic liturgy. In the thirteenth century a feast known as Corpus Christi ("the Body of Christ") was celebrated first in the diocese of Liège in the Low Countries, but it soon spread throughout the Catholic world and was frequently marked by festive processions in which the consecrated host was carried through the streets of a city or town in a gold or silver vessel known as a monstrance. In the universal liturgical calendar of the Roman Catholic Church this feast is celebrated shortly after Pentecost, while another feast, that of Christ the King, falls on the last Sunday of the church's liturgical year (always in late November). In the diocese of Kumasi, populated mainly by people of the Asante tribe, these two feasts have been combined into one, celebrated on that final Sunday of the ecclesiastical calendar. As the consecrated host, revered by Catholics as the sacramental body of Christ, is carried through the streets, Christ is honored as the great *ohene* (king) with ritual acts

14. Pope Paul VI, "The African Church Today," *The Pope Speaks* 14 (1969): 218-19.

of singing and dancing performed by a variety of actors at different locations along the route of the procession. Before 1970, the music was provided by a European-style brass band, but since that time the musical instruments have been African: drums, flutes, shakers, and xylophones. As the bishop noted in an interview in the 1970s, "when we were using a brass band to accompany Christ, many people did not know what we were doing. Now that we use Asante instruments . . . even non-Christians know at least that we are presenting Christ as the ultimate *ohene*."[15] This change was fully in accord with what he and his fellow bishops in the Ghana Bishops Conference had said in the aftermath of the Second Vatican Council's constitution on the liturgy: "The mystery of the incarnation demands that Christianity be inculturated . . . In view of this, African thought patterns, life-style, dress, ways of celebrating, art, music, preferences for colour and materials, etc., must be reflected in our being church and incorporated in our Christian liturgy, catechesis and theologies."[16]

As noted earlier, dance (even in the context of religious ritual) is not exclusively a means of conveying praise or thanksgiving to God. Even here, the symbolic gestures may express criticism of the behavior of one or another of the onlookers. At one of the Corpus Christi celebrations in Kumasi, a woman dancer not only used the standard gestures for requesting permission from Jesus Christ, enthroned in the monstrance, to dance and for seeking guidance, protection, and courage from God; she also used other gestures to indicate her displeasure at what she considered the arrogant behavior of a particular priest who was standing by. A person who observed this later commented: "Within the intended purpose of Asante Corpus Christi, with its prefabricated cast of characters, there emerges a range of possibilities for women dancers to articulate and redefine power relations and their identities. The above example shows that within each seemingly unchanging celebration of Corpus Christi lies the critical variable of the current psychosocial concerns of the participants."[17] Although one might at first hearing feel that the scolding gesture of that dancer lay outside the realm of Christian spirituality, in fact her behavior could be considered to be quite in accord with Jesus' teaching in the Gospel about the need to correct those who are behaving badly (Mt 18:15).

Far better known than that Africanized way of celebrating Corpus Christi in a particular diocese is what is usually called the Zairean Mass or the

---

15. Bishop Peter Sarpong, quoted by Obeng, "Asante Catholicism," in *African Spirituality*, 384.
16. Ghana Bishops Conference, quoted in Obeng, "Asante Catholicism," 375.
17. Obeng, "Asante Catholicism," 385-86.

Zairean Rite, its official name being *The Roman Missal for the Dioceses of Zaire*. The Catholic Church in that country has in fact been in the forefront of efforts to incarnate the faith in an African setting. Well before the Second Vatican Council the bishops of Zaire had publicly recognized the need to elaborate an authentically African liturgy sensitive to the needs and aspirations of their congregations. When the council's Constitution on the Sacred Liturgy opened up the possibility for such elaboration, these bishops took full advantage of the opportunity, obtaining permission from the Vatican's Congregation for Divine Worship to set up a special liturgical commission in Zaire to integrate the new Order of Mass (*Ordo Missae*) into the life of their dioceses. From 1970 through the mid-1980s the work of refining a proposed text of the rite went on simultaneously with liturgical experimentation in various parishes. Vatican approval of the Zairean rite of the eucharist was given in 1988, with four major changes from the Order of Mass that had been promulgated for the universal church in 1969. The rationale for each of these changes illustrates the way an appropriate inculturation was carried out.

First, the Zairean Mass begins not with the penitential rite but with an invocation of the saints and ancestors in the form of a litany. The liturgical commission's study of traditional African rituals had shown that celebration normally begins with "rites of contact," devised to express the worshipers' sense of the transcendent and their own creatureliness. The opening invocation is precisely such a rite of contact, helping to establish a creative link between the past and present. Even though some liturgists regret the absence of the actual names of any particular ancestors in the published rite, the very fact that the ancestors are invoked has gone a long way toward incorporating this central aspect of African spirituality into the celebration of the Zairean Mass.

Second, the penitential rite has been placed after the proclamation of the readings from the Lectionary and the recitation or chanting of the creed, just before the General Intercessions. This, too, better corresponds to the rhythm of traditional African rituals, where the rites of purification occur only after certain preparatory rituals have taken place. A further reason for the relocation of this rite was given in one of the background documents used in preparing the text of the rite: "The penitential act is placed after the liturgy of the word in order to bring out the fact that it is the word of God which reveals to us that we are sinners. It is also this word which arouses in us the motivation for our conversion."[18] This penitential rite is a somewhat extended version of the triple formula that normally begins the Mass in the

18. Quoted by Raymond Moloney, "The Zairean Mass and Inculturation," *Worship* 62 (1988): 437.

Roman rite. It concludes with the sprinkling of the congregation with holy water and the exchange of the sign of peace, whose relocation to this place in the Mass is more in accord with Jesus' injunction, "When you are offering your gift at the altar, if you remember that your brother or sister has something against you, leave your gift there before the altar and go; first be reconciled to your brother or sister, and then come and offer your gift" (Mt 5:23-24).

The third major change concerns that offering of gifts, an important African tradition. Many different kinds of gifts, including foodstuffs intended for the poor, are brought forward in a rhythmic procession of song and dance, while the words used in presenting the gifts bear marks of originality instead of being the repetition of stereotyped formulas. Dancing occurs not only here at the Offertory but also at the beginning and end of Mass and before the proclamation of the Gospel. Its significance, as well as the danger of its possibly taking on an exaggerated importance, is captured well in the following observations of the Jesuit priest Raymond Moloney, who was visiting Zaire while in Africa on a teaching assignment in Kenya:

> The sense of bodily rhythm is a unique gift of the people of Africa, and it would be denying a basic instinct of the people not to incorporate it into the liturgy. Englebert Mveng has observed that dance is the sole expression of mysticism in African religion. Clearly this is a challenge fraught with difficulties, and sometimes, I am told, it has got out of hand, turning some pastors against the Zairean Mass. However, where there is a firm hand at the helm, the effect is truly impressive. In the Masses in which I took part, the entrance and exit processions, the gospel and offertory processions, were all carried out in a solemn rhythmic way, more a movement than a dance, with all the people clapping hands and singing.[19]

The fourth major change is in the eucharistic prayer itself. Although the prayer is basically a modification of the second prayer of the usual Roman rite, it is normally sung, with nine acclamations accorded to the congregation at various places within the prayer in addition to the opening dialogue of the preface and the concluding doxology. Moloney found the effect of this to be "an overwhelming impression of a prayer offered by the whole people of God. The chant I have heard in Lingala, the local language of Kinshasa, is a very simple but beautiful native creation, lending itself admirably to the alternation between celebrant and people."[20]

---

19. Moloney, "Zairean Mass," 439.
20. Ibid., 438.

Moloney's comment brings out another very important point. It is one thing to read the text of the Zairean Mass, for like most liturgical texts it may strike one as quite formal and rigid on the printed page, but it is something else to experience an actual celebration of the Mass, described by one liturgist as "full of life, spontaneous, responding to local sentiments, artistic, and rich with religious symbolisms ... So much ground has been covered in Zaire, and this Mass is offering a new vision of what the African Church is offering to the world-church."[21] This is why the many people who do not have the possibility of participating in such a celebration in person would do well to experience it at least on videotape or DVD.[22]

One further point should be made with reference to this and all other attempts at liturgical inculturation in African countries. One of the most widely quoted lines from the Second Vatican Council comes at the beginning of section 10 of *Sacrosanctum Concilium*, the council's Constitution on the Sacred Liturgy: "The liturgy is the summit toward which the activity of the Church is directed; it is also the fount from which all her power flows." Part of the power flowing from this liturgical fount is intended to bring about effective activity for the promotion of peace and justice within civil society. The very country in which the Zairean Mass is celebrated has gone through especially tumultuous times since it attained independence from Belgium in 1960. In fact, the name of the country has been changed four times since then, always in connection with changes of government that have regularly been accompanied by violence. During the thirty-year rule of the president and dictator Mobuto Sese Seko, there was much economic exploitation and corruption, with the country undergoing such deterioration that he was finally forced from office and sent into exile. During the time when Mobuto was still in charge, the members of the diocesan synod of Kinshasa expressed the close connection between liturgy and social justice when they proclaimed the following about the Zairean Mass: "The desire expressed on all sides to continue the effort of creativity and inculturation manifests the profound need to relate the rite to life, and the will to find in liturgical experience the strength and the means of cohesion necessary for daily commitment to justice and truth, so that all Christians may assume their responsibility for the Kingdom of God."[23] We accordingly turn now to this other crucial aspect of

---

21. Chris Nwaka Egbulem, "An African Interpretation of Liturgical Inculturation: The *Rite Zairois*," in *A Promise of Presence: Studies in Honor of David N. Power, O.M.I.*, ed. Michael Downey and Richard Fragomeni (Washington, D.C.: Pastoral Press, 1992), 247-48.

22. See, e.g., *The Dancing Church Around the World: DVD Collection by Thomas A. Kane* (Tomaso Production, 2004). Further information is available at http://www.thedancingchurch.com.

23. Quoted by Moloney, "The Zairean Mass," 441.

African Christian spirituality, the struggle for justice. In doing so, we will focus on the work of two church leaders, the Catholic archbishop Martin-Léonard Bakole wa Ilunga of Zaire and the Anglican archbishop Desmond Tutu of South Africa.

The Struggle for Justice

Archbishop Bakole wa Ilunga, born in 1920, served as archbishop of Kananga from 1967 until his retirement in 1997. When he died three years later there was a great outpouring of grief because so many people realized that their country had lost a great leader, one who spoke honestly and unflinchingly about the many problems that they all faced and who went directly to the root of those problems, all for the purpose of showing his people the paths that would lead effectively to liberation. In his book on third-world spirituality, he observes that two basic ambitions had inspired the people of his country since they attained independence from Belgium. First, they wanted to develop the material values that the colonizers had brought with them, such as material goods from foreign markets and improved medical care, while on the other hand and simultaneously they sought to win back their traditional values, their spontaneity and human dignity. In asking how they stood with regard to these two ambitions, he gave a blunt analysis, even claiming that "if our ancestors could return and see what is going on in our society, they would not believe they were in Africa, nor would they recognize their descendants."[24] Specifically, as regards the second of these ambitions:

> We sing of the value of life—but children are dying of malnutrition; people practice abortion nowadays as though they were simply getting rid of an object and not a human life. We give speeches about solidarity—but we have no concern for our common assets, which we waste in our greed, and even within our own families we abandon the widow, the orphan, those we brand as witches, and so on . . . Festivals, dance, music have always been part of the authentic African; they were the expression and not the source of our vitality and our trust in life despite any difficulties. But for many, festivals have become drinking bouts, and bring not fulfillment or vital joy but reduction to the level of the animals. (17)

24. Bakole wa Ilunga, *Paths of Liberation: A Third World Spirituality*, trans. Matthew J. O'Connell (Maryknoll, N.Y.: Orbis Books, 1984), 17. Subsequent parenthetical references to this work indicate the page number.

Turning to the other ambition, the desire to develop the country into a modern state, the archbishop observed that even when practical plans have been drawn up and new equipment imported from abroad, "in most instances, the undertakings bear no direct relation to the various needs of the population; they are disconnected enterprises that bring profit to a few people and serve primarily the interests of foreign capital and a very small privileged class of our fellow citizens" (18). In all this, he said, "*we are far from being true Africans*. If so, then we cannot put the blame for the situation on the colonial tyranny. No, we must blame ourselves, because we abandon all that was finest in our traditions or we cling to what was ambiguous in them" (17).

Rather than refuse to face up to the reality or grow discouraged, he urged his fellow citizens to engage in a sober critique while yet retaining confidence in their ability to make effective changes in a wretched situation: "Many small acts of neglect and selfishness form a chain, and the end-result is a corrupt society that cannot assure the happiness of each individual . . . The heart of the problem afflicting our society is, then, human beings who are the slaves of their passions, of their desires to possess, enjoy, and dominate. This interior slavery is what makes us vulnerable to domination by foreigners and prevents us from controlling our own destiny" (36). In sum, "Our society needs prophets: men and women who allow themselves to be wholly drawn by the will of God and have the courage to bear witness to that will, in word and action, before their fellow citizens" (213). Archbishop Bakole wa Ilunga was himself a prophet of that sort, and for this reason was deeply mourned at the time of his death.

An even better known prophet has been the Anglican archbishop Desmond Tutu, who helped lead a struggle against a societal evil that was, if anything, still worse than any that had afflicted Zaire. The first apartheid laws of the Republic of South Africa were passed in 1948 as an extension of segregationist laws established by previous white-minority governments in that country, the aim being to segregate the races as much as possible. By 1990, largely in response both to protests within that country and from around the world and also to economic sanctions imposed by other countries, the legal basis for apartheid had been largely repealed. A multiracial, multiparty transitional government was set up in 1993, and at the end of April in the following year the first truly democratic elections in the history of South Africa were held, with the former political prisoner Nelson Mandela being elected president. All during the preceding decades of protest, one of the strongest voices was that of Desmond Tutu.

Ordained a priest of the Anglican Church in 1961, Tutu became the first black African dean of Johannesburg in 1975. He also served as general secretary of the South African Council of Churches from 1978 to 1984, and became archbishop of Capetown (and thus the Anglican primate of South Africa) in 1986, a position he held for the next ten years. After retiring from the archbishopric, Tutu headed the country's Truth and Reconciliation Commission (1996-2003), whose responsibility was to investigate human rights abuses in the apartheid era and, on the basis of honest admissions of guilt by those guilty of human rights violations during those years, to promote reconciliation among the races. For his tireless efforts to end the evil of apartheid in a nonviolent way, Tutu was awarded the Nobel Peace Prize in 1984 and has subsequently been honored with numerous other awards.

Like Archbishop Bakole wa Ilunga of Zaire, Archbishop Tutu has always insisted that genuine Christian spirituality necessarily includes working for justice and peace. In a talk given at Pretoria University in 1981, he said: "The Church must be ever ready to wash the disciples' feet, a serving Church, not a triumphalistic Church, biased in favour of the powerless to be their voice, to be in solidarity with the poor and oppressed, the marginalized ones—yes, preaching the Gospel of reconciliation but working for justice first, since there can never be real reconciliation without justice."[25] Sounding the same theme of liberation as that preached by the Zairean archbishop, Tutu said in another statement that apartheid "is evil, totally and without remainder," but that "the Gospel of Jesus Christ our Lord is subversive of all injustice and evil, oppression and exploitation . . . God is on the side of the oppressed and the downtrodden" and is "the liberator God of the Exodus, who leads his people out of every kind of bondage: spiritual, political, social and economic. Nothing will thwart him from achieving the goal of the liberation of all his people and the whole of his creation."[26] Convinced of the justice of his cause, Tutu showed no fear whatever of the South African government, correctly predicting in 1982 that "the government will fail completely, for it is ranging itself on the side of evil, injustice and oppression. The government is not God, just ordinary human beings who very soon, like other tyrants before them, will bite the dust" (58).

When Tutu's prediction came true, he neither gloated over nor sought revenge on his former oppressors, but rather rejoiced with the people of all races in his country. Referring to the huge lines waiting to vote in the historic election of April 27-28, 1994, he said: "They stood in the voting queues

25. Desmond Tutu, *Hope and Suffering: Sermons and Speeches*, comp. Mothobi Mutloatse (Grand Rapids: Eerdmans, 1984), 86.

26. Desmond Tutu, *The Rainbow People of God: The Making of a Peaceful Revolution*, ed. John Allen (New York: Doubleday, 1994), 56. Subsequent parenthetical references to this book indicate the page number.

together—white, black, Colored, Indian—and they discovered that they were compatriots. White South Africans found that a heavy weight of guilt had been lifted from their shoulders. They are discovering what we used to tell them—that freedom is indivisible, that black liberation inexorably meant white liberation . . . It is a victory for all South Africans" (263-64). Two weeks later, as Nelson Mandela was inaugurated president, Tutu was asked to close the religious part of the proceedings with a prayer that included the following lines: "Thank you, O God, that you have chosen this your servant to be the first President of a democratic South Africa where all of us, black and white together, will count, not because of irrelevancies such as race, gender, status or skin color but because of our intrinsic worth as those created in your own image, as redeemed by the precious blood of Jesus, as being sanctified by the Holy Spirit" (268-69).

Without directly intending to, church leaders like Desmond Tutu and Bakole wa Ilunga have won great respect for their churches throughout Africa and have in this way helped increase the number of persons wishing to be members of the Anglican or Roman Catholic Church. Growth has also been experienced by other mainstream churches that were implanted in African soil by foreign missionaries who have gradually turned over their leadership roles to native Africans. However, there is a further aspect to ecclesial spirituality on that continent that is not so well known in other parts of the world and yet has had great impact on Christian spirituality there. This is the movement of the African Independent Churches, to which we now turn in the final section of this chapter.

The Independent Churches

The earliest of the African Independent Churches (AICs) began in 1862 in what was then called the Gold Coast, present-day Ghana. Since then the movement has mushroomed, with more than ten thousand such communities or churches being found throughout the continent, with names like the Christ Apostolic Church, the Cherubim and Seraphim, and the Celestial Church of Christ. Many of them split off from one or another of the historic mission churches, while others arose on their own, but their common aim has been to provide a form of Christian belief and practice more in accord with African culture than seemed possible in the mission churches.[27]

---

27. See the useful "Database of African Independent Churches and Leaders," maintained by the Southern African Missiological Society, at http://www.geocities.com/missionalia/aicdb.htm.

The vast number of these churches means that there is inevitably a lot of diversity, but certain generalizations may nevertheless be made. For one thing, many of their members sensed that the historic mission churches were too influenced by the secularization of Western culture and demanded too little of their members. It was not enough to have weekly worship on Sunday, so many of the AICs offer daily services, including in a special way services for the healing of physical or mental illnesses. A number of them also require fairly strict asceticism, such as abstention from all alcoholic beverages and certain foods, together with the wearing of distinctive garb (in some cases a white cassock similar to ones worn by Catholic missionaries). On the other hand, some of the AICs permit polygamy, which is quite prevalent in certain parts of Africa; their leaders regularly turn to the example of the biblical patriarchs to justify the practice. Indeed, in all of the independent churches the Bible enjoys pride of place for determining the will of God, but there is usually a reliance on some other forms of discerning God's intentions as well: visions, dreams, and reliance on the utterances of persons considered to be possessed by the Holy Spirit. Indeed, many of these churches were founded by Spirit-filled charismatic figures, both men and women, whose divine calling was recognized by their communities on the basis of their extraordinary experiences and holy lives.

A particularly prominent group of independent churches in Nigeria is known as Aladura, a Yoruba word that means "owners of prayer." Their ideal has been summed up in the following words:

> The central conviction of the Aladura, which they share with many other prophetic churches elsewhere, is the belief that fervent prayer attains specific goals, such as good health, or children. In some cases, their confidence in prayer is so great that they reject both traditional and western medicine. They believe that God speaks to the faithful in dreams and visions, and that blessings are often won by fasting, and have retained from traditional religion a belief in the reality of witchcraft.[28]

Within many of the AICs there is also an emphasis on sacred places, not only a church building with its surrounding plot of land, sometimes called "The Mercy Land," but also open-air worship sites or even the homes of individual members of the church. Many of these churches have relatively small memberships, which is in certain respects an advantage. One scholar of

28. Elizabeth Isichei, *A History of Christianity in Africa: From Antiquity to the Present* (Grand Rapids: Eerdmans; Lawrenceville, N.J.: Africa World Press, 1995), 282.

the movement points out that "one of the most original values in African religious traditions is the community sense of Africans," a sense that is often not palpable in the large congregations found in some of the historic churches. The latter, with their large numbers and a limited numbers of pastors, "can only do very little to assist the spiritual growth of their faithful," whereas in the AICs "the small size of the communities permits the pastor to give needed spiritual counseling and attend to other needs of each individual member."[29] This is especially significant in urban areas, where immigrants from the countryside often feel alienated from the way of life to which they had become accustomed. The AICs have made a special effort to serve such persons: "They concern themselves with unemployment and family separation and take up the questions of social and political liberation, even though in a different way from political parties."[30] In this respect, these churches complement the work for social, economic, and political liberation championed by such visible leaders of the historic churches as Archbishops Tutu and Ilunga. All of these likewise foster on the African continent the kind of liberation theology and spirituality that for many persons is most readily associated with Latin America, where the term "theology of liberation" first arose. It is to this that we will turn at the beginning of our next and final chapter.

QUESTIONS FOR REFLECTION

1. Two of the special characteristics of African Traditional Religion are the veneration of ancestors and the use of dance and vibrant music in religious ritual. Is either or both of these practices simply to be wondered at (and perhaps admired) by persons in very different cultures, or do you think the African practices should in some way be appropriated by churches in other parts of the world?
2. This chapter's quotation from Chinua Achebe's novel *Things Fall Apart* depicts Westerners, including missionaries, in a very negative light as persons who "put a knife on the things that held us together." Do you consider this a fair judgment? What may have been some of the positive influences of the missionaries, even ones who were very critical of African Traditional Religion?
3. Scholars who write about liturgical inculturation regularly take pains to say that it involves more than mere "adaptation" of certain native practices. How would you yourself define inculturation? Could you give an example of how it is a kind of "two-way street," with the native culture influencing the modes of

29. E. Ikenga-Metuh, "The Revival of African Christian Spirituality: The Experience of African Independent Churches," *Mission Studies* 7 (1990): 166.

30. Hans-Jürgen Becken, "African Independent Churches," in *Dictionary of Mission*, 8.

Christian belief and practice even as the Christian proclamation impacts that culture?

4. From this chapter's description of the Zairean Mass, which element(s) of the Mass might lend vitality to the liturgical practice of churches that have traditionally been more reserved in their rituals? Do you share Raymond Moloney's concern that liturgical dance might get out of hand?
5. Archbishop Bakole wa Ilunga may have sounded unduly harsh in telling his fellow citizens of Zaire that "if our ancestors could return and see what is going on in our society . . . they would not recognize their descendants." How effective do you judge such stinging criticism to be? Are you personally convinced that church leaders like Archbishops Ilunga and Tutu have a responsibility to speak out forcefully on social and political issues? If so, how would their approach ideally differ from that of a professional politician?

SUGGESTIONS FOR FURTHER READING AND STUDY

On African Traditional Religion

Egbulem, Chris Nwaka, O.P. "African Spirituality." In *The New Dictionary of Catholic Spirituality*, edited by Michael Downey, 17-21. Collegeville, Minn.: Liturgical Press, 1993.

Mbiti, John S. *Introduction to African Religion*. 2nd rev. ed. London: Heinemann, 1991. See especially chap. 1, "The African Heritage" (pp. 2-10), chap. 2, "What Is African Religion?" (pp. 11-19), and chap. 6, "How God Is Approached by People" (pp. 60-69).

On Liturgical Spirituality and Inculturation in Africa

Egbulem, Chris Nwaka, O.P. "An African Interpretation of Liturgical Inculturation: The *Rite Zairois*." In *A Promise of Presence: Studies in Honor of David N. Power, O.M.I.*, edited by Michael Downey and Richard Fragomeni, 227-50. Washington, D.C.: Pastoral Press, 1992.

Éla, Jean-Marc. *My Faith as an African*. Translated by John Pairman Brown and Susan Perry. Maryknoll, N.Y.: Orbis Books; London: Geoffrey Chapman, 1988. See especially chap. 2, "The Ancestors and Christian Faith" (pp. 13-32).

Moloney, Raymond. "The Zairean Mass and Inculturation." *Worship* 62 (1988): 433-42.

Obeng, Pashington. "Asante Catholicism: An African Appropriation of the Roman Catholic Religion." In *African Spirituality: Forms, Meanings, and Expressions*, edited by Jacob K. Olupona, 372-400. World Spirituality 3. New York: Crossroad, 2000.

Uzukwu, Elochukwu E., C.S.Sp. *Worship as Body Language: Introduction to Christian Worship: An African Orientation.* Collegeville, Minn.: Liturgical Press, 1997. See especially chap. 1, "Human Gestural Behavior as Ritual and Symbolic" (pp. 1-40), and chap. 5, "Emergent Creative Liturgies in Africa" (pp. 265-321).

On the Struggle for Justice as Part of African Christian Spirituality

Ilunga, Bakole wa. *Paths of Liberation: A Third World Spirituality.* Translated by Matthew J. O'Connell. Maryknoll, N.Y.: Orbis Books, 1984. See especially chap. 4, "A Bleak Picture" (pp. 16-19), chap. 5, "Looking for the Causes" (pp. 20-34), and chap. 33, "Ecclesial Communities in the Service of Liberation" (pp. 171-83).

Tutu, Desmond. *Hope and Suffering: Sermons and Speeches.* Compiled by Mothobi Mutloatse. Grand Rapids: Eerdmans, 1984. See especially chap. 2, "Liberation as a Biblical Theme" (pp. 48-87).

———. *The Rainbow People of God.* Edited by John Allen. New York: Doubleday, 1994. See especially chap. 6, "The Divine Imperative" (pp. 53-79), and chap. 32, "A Miracle Unfolding" (pp. 259-69).

On the Spirituality of the African Independent Churches

Becken, Hans-Jürgen. "African Independent Churches." In *Dictionary of Mission: Theology, History, Perspectives*, edited by Karl Müller, S.V.D., Theo Sundermeier, Stephen B. Bevans, S.V.D., and Richard H. Bliese, 6-9. Maryknoll, N.Y.: Orbis Books, 1997.

Ikenga-Metuh, E. "The Revival of African Christian Spirituality: The Experience of African Independent Churches." *Mission Studies* 7 (1990): 151-71.

Isichei, Elizabeth. *A History of Christianity in Africa: From Antiquity to the Present.* Grand Rapids: Eerdmans; Lawrenceville, N.J.: Africa World Press, 1995. See especially chap. 10, "West Africa *c.* 1900 to *c.* 1960" (pp. 264-98).

10

Christian Spirituality in the Americas

EACH OF THE TWO previous chapters discussed, in a very selective way, movements and figures in Christian spirituality on a particular continent. This final chapter will have to be even more selective since it will be considering spirituality on two quite diverse continents, South and North America. Over the past century, one of the most significant movements in Latin America (including Mexico and the countries of Central America, which are, strictly speaking, part of North America) has been liberation theology, so we will begin by discussing the spirituality characteristic of it, above all as represented in the works of the man generally considered the leader of the movement, Gustavo Gutiérrez. Even though people usually associate liberation theology and spirituality with the situation of those millions of persons whose lives are constricted by the bonds of severe material poverty, the liberation movement has come to be understood as referring to other kinds of bonds as well. Feminist spirituality, which seeks the flourishing of women both in the churches and in civil society, will therefore be considered next, as represented by authors from the white, black, and Latina communities. The third section of the chapter will turn to what could broadly be called "affective spirituality," as found both in the works of the man often called the greatest of all the theologians of North America, Jonathan Edwards, and in the Pentecostal movement, which has spread rapidly not only in the Americas but throughout the world. The fourth and final section will focus on one particular aspect of the spirituality of the very prolific and versatile twentieth-century writer Thomas Merton.

LIBERATION SPIRITUALITY: GUSTAVO GUTIÉRREZ

To help order this presentation of the influential and controversial movement of liberation theology and the spirituality that characterizes it, it will be useful to recall what we said in our first chapter about the value of Bernard Lonergan's works for the study of spirituality. That Canadian philosopher and theologian noted that in any endeavor we regularly and necessarily move through various operations that correspond to four levels of consciousness, which he called the experiential, the intellectual, the rational, and the responsible. On the intellectual level we seek to understand what we have experienced; on the rational level we judge whether or not our understanding was correct; and on the responsible level we make decisions about possible courses of action and then carry these out.

Lonergan insisted that we perform these interrelated operations whether or not we are aware of doing so. An indication that he was correct about this may be seen in the fact that independently of Lonergan a prominent twentieth-century physicist, Harold Schilling, came up with a similar pattern, although one that is somewhat simpler in the sense that he conflated the intellectual and the rational operations into one. In several books and articles, Professor Schilling advanced the position that both in the natural sciences and in religion we find the same threefold and circular pattern of activity.[1] In his terminology, the first "circle" is empirically descriptive and experiential. For the scientist, this represents the activities of observation, experimentation, and the gathering of data, while in the realm of religion this is the circle of faith experience, not just of an individual but of an entire religious community. Schilling's second circle is the theoretical. Here scientists formulate particular laws and theories on the basis of their experiments, such as Boyle's Law, which expresses mathematically how the pressure of a confined gas varies with its volume, and the Kinetic Theory of gases, which not only helps explain specific laws but also sheds light on the principles of thermodynamics, the more general science of heat. The corresponding activity in the religious realm is that of theology, which interprets and explains the faith experience of the religious community through the formulation of appropriate concepts, doctrines, and patterns of thought. Schilling called the third circle the transformative, where scientists and engineers apply their experimental data and their laws and theories to particular situations for the purpose of controlling or transforming the physical world. Similarly, religious activity elaborates the implications of faith and belief for the way one lives, not just as an individual concerned for one's personal salvation but as a member of a community with responsibilities for transforming the world along the paths of justice and love.

---

1. A concise presentation of Schilling's position may be found in his article "The Threefold and Circular Nature of Science and Religion," in *Religion and the Natural Sciences: The Range of Engagement,* ed. James E. Huchingson (Fort Worth, Tex.: Harcourt Brace Jovanovich College Publishers, 1993), 40-46.

In all of this, one of Schilling's main points was that the movement is not one-directional, as though we move simply from the first circle to the second and then from the second to the third. Instead, there is an interdependence marked by reciprocal influence in all directions: In scientific work, theory (circle *b*) not only depends on observation and experimentation (circle *a*) but also influences and even guides the kinds of experiments that are conducted in that first circle. So too, theory is crucial for assaying the possibility of useful applications of a theory (circle *c*), but on the other hand theory is enlarged and enriched as one struggles with new problems in the attempt to apply a theory usefully. Similar interdependence is true of the relationship between the first and third circles, and all of this no less in the realm of religion than in that of science.

Despite the risk of some oversimplification, Schilling's scheme seems decidedly helpful for understanding liberation theology, whose three main components are experiencing the lot of the poor and oppressed (circle *a*), developing theological positions on the basis of what Scripture, church teaching, and the social sciences tell us about the causes of and remedies for the situation of such persons (circle *b*), and taking effective action to free them for a more fully human life (circle *c*). Precisely because of the interdependent nature of these three kinds of activity, one can better understand how and why liberation theologians often speak of *praxis* (a Greek term that could be translated as "action" or "activity") as giving rise to theology; in Schilling's scheme, this would be a matter of circle *c* influencing circle *b*. Against this background, we turn now to the work of the man who coined the term "theology of liberation."

Gustavo Gutiérrez was born in 1928 in a poor section of Lima, Peru. At the age of twelve he was stricken with the disease of osteomyelitis, which confined him to bed and to a wheelchair for the next six years, but during that time he read extensively and became well enough educated to gain admission to a local university. His preliminary studies were in medicine, but he soon switched to the study of philosophy and theology, which he continued at Catholic universities in Belgium, France, and Rome. Ordained a diocesan priest in 1959, Gutiérrez gained a part-time appointment at the Catholic Pontifical University in Lima the following year, simultaneously spending much time with the poor in the parish to which he was assigned and coming more and more to identify with their needs and hopes. He became increasingly convinced of the need for the church to "enter the world of the poor" and to understand its theology as "a reflection—that is, a second act . . . that comes after action," as he phrased it in a talk given to a meeting of priests and laity in July 1968 and entitled "Toward a Theology of

Liberation."[2] The following month saw the opening of the Second General Conference of Latin American Bishops, held at Medellín, Colombia, on the theme of "The Church in the Present-Day Transformation of Latin America in the Light of the [Second Vatican] Council." Gutiérrez was a *peritus* (theological expert) at this conference and so had a hand in the drafting of some of its most important documents, especially the ones on "Peace" and "Justice."

After the Medellín conference, Gutiérrez continued to clarify and refine his thought and in 1971 published in Spanish what has become his best-known book, which appeared in English two years later under the title *A Theology of Liberation*.[3] That work included a six-page section entitled "A Spirituality of Liberation," but even then Gutiérrez was aware of the brevity of that section and had the intention of eventually writing a fuller treatment of liberation spirituality. He carried out this intention a decade later with the publication of *We Drink from Our Own Wells*.[4] This book has three main divisions, the first part being Gutiérrez's attempt to describe the "matrix" of the spirituality that was coming to birth in Latin America, the second being his description of the main aspects of *every* Christian spirituality (understood as the following of Jesus), and the third being his outline of five features of the *particular* kind of spirituality he saw developing in Latin America, these five being conversion, gratuitousness, joy, spiritual childhood, and community. This third part of the book is enhanced by what Henri Nouwen, in his foreword, called "deeply moving texts written by Christian men and women who have experienced persecution and suffering but have been witnesses to the living and hope-giving God in the midst of their sufferings."[5]

As moving as those texts are, Gutiérrez himself noted the relatively unsatisfactory nature of his treatment of these five features, calling them "a series of rapid and rather rough strokes of the brush to sketch a profile that even now is only barely emerging" and admitting that "the subject deserves a more comprehensive and detailed book that is presently beyond my abilities."[6] For this reason, it would not be helpful to rely too heavily on *We Drink from Our Own Wells* for an understanding of what Gutiérrez means by "liberation spirituality." In fact, perhaps the most pertinent sentences in the entire book

---

2. Gustavo Gutiérrez, "Toward a Theology of Liberation," in *Liberation Theology: A Documentary History*, ed. Alfred T. Hennelly, S.J. (Maryknoll, N.Y.: Orbis Books, 1990), 63.

3. Gustavo Gutiérrez, *A Theology of Liberation: History, Politics, and Salvation*, trans. Caridad Inda and John Eagleson (Maryknoll, N.Y.: Orbis Books; London: SCM Press, 1973).

4. Gustavo Gutiérrez, *We Drink from Our Own Wells: The Spiritual Journey of a People*, trans. Matthew J. O'Connell (Maryknoll, N.Y.: Orbis Books, 1984).

5. Henri Nouwen, foreword to *We Drink from Our Own Wells*, xix.

6. Gutiérrez, *We Drink from Our Own Wells*, 4 and 94.

come near the end, where he writes: "As a matter of fact, *our methodology is our spirituality*. There is nothing surprising about this. After all, the word 'method' comes from *hodos*, 'way.' Reflection on the mystery of God (for that is what a theology is) is possible only in the context of the following of Jesus."[7] Since the following of Jesus necessarily includes the kinds of activity that he himself performed—bringing good news to the poor, proclaiming release to captives and recovery of sight to the blind, and letting the oppressed go free (Lk 4:18)—spirituality for the liberation theologians must include, and even give priority to, a "love of preference for the poor." Our presentation of liberation spirituality will accordingly be organized around the basic methodology of liberation theology, namely, the interplay among the principal and mutually conditioning components of the movement that we mentioned above: the "circles" of (1) experience, (2) theological reflection on this experience in the light of faith, and (3) praxis, the kinds of activity that foster liberation.

The experience that is so foundational for liberation spirituality is the reality endured each day by millions of people in Latin America, including in a special way those who live lives of destitution in the *favelas* and shantytowns that surround the large cities. But experience is never a matter of what could be called "just taking a look." There is always a context, and for an advocate of liberation spirituality this is the context of faith, which means seeing these persons as children of God, as one's brothers and sisters in Christ. Apart from that context, the poor might be regarded simply as nuisances, to be ignored as much as possible.

Because this faith context has been present in some persons since the earliest days of Spanish and Portuguese colonization, it would be altogether correct to say that liberation theology and spirituality did not arise only in the 1960s or even in the twentieth century. One of Gutiérrez's most important and passionately written books is about the sixteenth-century Dominican friar Bartolomé de Las Casas, who came as a missionary to the New World and, together with some of his fellow friars, was appalled by what he saw. In 1510 a group of them arrived at the Caribbean island of Hispaniola, where the natives of the island had already been suffering foreign occupation for nineteen years, being treated as useless animals and having their deaths mourned only because they would now no longer be able to work the gold mines and plantations for their overlords. That year Las Casas and the other Dominicans decided to draft a sermon to be preached on the Fourth Sunday of Advent in the presence of all the notables of the island, including the

7. Gutiérrez, *We Drink from Our Own Wells*, 136; emphasis mine.

Spanish admiral. The sermon has come down to us in Las Casas's version and includes the following words:

> You are all in mortal sin! You live in it and you die in it! Why? Because of the cruelty and tyranny you use with these innocent people. Tell me, with what right, with what justice, do you hold these Indians in such cruel and horrible servitude? On what authority have you waged such detestable wars on these people, in their mild, peaceful lands, where you have consumed such infinitudes of them, wreaking upon them this death and unheard-of havoc? How is it that you hold them so crushed and exhausted, giving them nothing to eat, nor any treatment for their diseases, which you cause them to be infected with through the surfeit of their toils, so that they "die on you" [as you say]—you mean, you kill them—mining gold for you day after day? . . . Are they not human beings? Have they no rational souls? Are you not obligated to love them as you love yourselves? Do you not understand this? Do you not grasp this? How is it that you sleep so soundly, so lethargically?[8]

It was in such words that the theology of liberation was first formed, even as it was through Gutiérrez's own living with and among the poor of his parish in Lima that he came to develop the main lines of his own theology. Like so many of his fellow theologians in Latin America, he regularly insists that it is not sufficient, even for a person of faith, merely to read about the plight of those who live on the edge of destitution. It is crucial to experience it firsthand, to be "inserted" among the people. One sees this in what could be called the conversion of Bishop Oscar Romero, who as a young priest was quite suspicious of liberation theology and would hardly ever quote from the Medellín documents in his homilies. But once he was made bishop of San Salvador in the Central American country of El Salvador and came to experience more directly and with increasing frequency the suffering of his people and—an especially telling incident—the murder of one of his first priests along with two parishioners, he changed. In a talk he gave less than two months before his own murder in March 1980, he said explicitly that "experiencing these realities and letting ourselves be affected by them . . . moved us, as a first, basic step, to take the world of the poor upon ourselves." He then specified the kinds of experience he had met in this "world of the poor":

8. Bartolomé de Las Casas, *Historia de las Indias*, bk. 3, ch. 4, quoted by Gustavo Gutiérrez, *Las Casas: In Search of the Poor of Christ*, trans. Robert R. Barr (Maryknoll, N.Y.: Orbis Books, 1993), 29.

> There we have met [agricultural] workers without land and without steady employment, without running water or electricity in their homes, without medical assistance when mothers give birth, and without schools for their children. There we have met factory workers who have no labor rights, and who get fired from their jobs if they demand such rights; human beings who are at the mercy of cold economic calculations. There we have met the mothers and the wives of those who have disappeared, or who are political prisoners. There we have met the shantytown dwellers, whose wretchedness defies imagination, suffering the permanent mockery of the mansions nearby.[9]

Gutiérrez spoke in a similar vein when once asked in an interview what it meant to be a priest in a country like Peru. He replied: "It means not becoming accustomed to seeing the newspapers filled day after day with pictures of mutilated corpses, of mass graves, of innocent people mowed down. It means not getting used to the fact that fellow human beings must search the garbage to find something to eat, that they must trick their stomachs by eating dirt . . . It means maintaining a permanent attitude of shock and rejection in the face of all these indignities."[10]

This starting point in personal experience no doubt has much to do with the fact that the theology of liberation has a very different tone or "feel" from much of the theology produced in the first world. Even when the latter theology deals with the theme of liberation, it will tend to start with the topic as such, will search the Bible, tradition, church teaching, and the writings of other theologians in order to establish a critical grounding for the topic, and will then deduce consequences for the guidance of action. Legitimate though this approach may be, its different starting point means that critiques of liberation theology from those quarters often appear to miss the mark.

There is, however, one criticism on which there is room for genuine debate, and this concerns what we have called the second "circle," the attempt of a theologian like Gutiérrez to reflect on his experience in the light of faith and with the help of the social sciences. Many liberation theologians, to one degree or another, make use of categories and concepts from the writings of Karl Marx to help explain the plight of those who live in dire poverty. One of Gutiérrez's most forceful critics in this regard has been Joseph Ratzinger, who was head of the Vatican's Congregation for the Doctrine of the Faith

---

9. Archbishop Oscar Romero, "The Political Dimension of the Faith from the Perspective of the Option for the Poor," in *Liberaton Theology*, 295.

10. Gutiérriez, "Criticism Will Deepen, Clarify Liberation Theology," in *Liberation Theology*, 420.

before he was elected pope and took the name of Benedict XVI. In addition to issuing two documents about liberation theology that emanated from that congregation in the mid-1980s over his signature, Cardinal Ratzinger had also begun a direct investigation of Gutiérrez's theology in 1980 and four years later published an article in an Italian journal that criticized the Peruvian theologian by name. One of the cardinal's major objections was that it is not possible to take only part of Marx's thought and declare that this could be used to analyze societal problems without inevitably becoming enmeshed in the entire Marxist ideology, with its avowed atheism and its virulent critique of religion. In Ratzinger's words, "The ideological principles come prior to the study of the social reality and are presupposed in it. Thus no separation of the parts of this epistemologically unique complex is possible. If one tries to take only one part, say, the analysis, one ends up having to accept the entire ideology."[11]

Gutiérrez does not find this criticism of his work convincing. In his most thorough treatment of the issue, he writes:

> Elements of analysis which come from Marxism play a part in the contemporary social sciences that serve as a tool for studying social reality . . . The question of how closely connected the ideological aspects of Marxism are with Marxist social analysis is a question much discussed in the social sciences. The same is true even within Marxism itself . . . I must make it clear, however, that in the context of my own theological writings, this question is a secondary one. In fact, given the situation in which Latin America was living, it seemed to me more urgently necessary to turn to more clearly theological questions.[12]

This kind of reply did not and will not satisfy his critics, not least because the issue is more than the theoretical one of whether Marxist social analysis can be separated from Marx's atheistic ideology, or whether the way in which theologians like Gutiérrez refer to Israel's exodus from Egypt places too much emphasis on that as a political liberation over against its leading to the religious covenant with God that gave the event its deeper meaning. The German journalist Heinz-Joachim Fischer, who has long been a personal friend of Joseph Ratzinger and who published one of the first books about him after his election to the papacy, claims that it was the actual conse-

---

11. Congregation for the Doctrine of the Faith, "Instruction on Certain Aspects of the 'Theology of Liberation'" (Vatican City, August 6, 1984), in *Liberation Theology*, 402.

12. Gustavo Gutiérrez, "Theology and the Social Sciences," in idem, *The Truth Shall Make You Free: Confrontations*, trans. Matthew J. O'Connell (Maryknoll, N.Y.: Orbis Books, 1990), 60 and 62.

quences of liberation theologians' calling upon the poor to struggle for release from their wretched living conditions that gave a number of church leaders pause:

> More and more bishops took the view that the status quo was the lesser evil, even when governments were decreasing their commitment to the liberation of the people from misery, ignorance, and exploitation, and necessary reform measures were dying on the vine. The violence employed in the struggle for liberation in some Latin American countries usually claimed even more victims among the people and caused more oppression than an imperfect form of government.[13]

Fischer's reference to the consequences of liberation theology brings us to the third "circle" or component of the movement, the way in which it fosters practical results. For the most part, this does not mean the advocacy of specific courses of action but rather the work of consciousness raising, fostering in the people of Latin America an understanding of what could be called "integral salvation." This means that salvation is not understood as beginning only after death, in what St. Paul called a "face-to-face" meeting with the Lord that is promised to all faithful disciples. Although it does include that, salvation also entails the many aspects of life here and now that Pope Paul VI spoke about in his encyclical *Populorum Progressio*, a document often alluded to by liberation theologians. There, after noting "less human" conditions such as the deprivation of minimum living conditions and the exploitation of workers, the pope began listing "more human" conditions, such as the broadening of knowledge, the acquisition of cultural values, and cooperation for the common good. He concluded with ones "more human still," namely, acknowledgment of God as the source and term of all genuine values and, above all, "faith, the gift of God accepted by humans of good will, and unity in the charity of Christ, who calls us all to participation as sons and daughters in the life of the living God, who is the father of all human beings" (no. 21). The Latin American bishops quoted those words from Paul VI's encyclical at their Medellín conference in 1968, at which they also summarized the kind of praxis that is generally characteristic of liberation theology. As noted above, it is not a matter of taking over the role proper to politicians and other government officials but is rather a matter of encouragement and education for freedom. In the words of the bishops:

---

13. Heinz-Joachim Fischer, *Pope Benedict XVI: A Personal Portrait*, trans. Brian McNeil (New York: Crossroad, 2005), 17.

> Our contribution does not pretend to compete with the attempts for solution made by other national, Latin American, and world bodies; much less do we disregard or refuse to recognize them. Our purpose is to encourage these efforts, accelerate their results, deepen their content, and permeate all the process of change with the values of the gospel. We would like to offer the collaboration of all Christians, compelled by their baptismal responsibilities and by the gravity of this moment. It is our responsibility to dramatize the strength of the gospel, which is the power of God.[14]

The aim expressed by the Latin American bishops in that paragraph is similar to that enunciated by Gutiérrez in the opening words of the introduction to the first edition of *A Theology of Liberation*, where he said that the movement's aim is "reflection, based on the Gospel and the experiences of men and women committed to the process of liberation in the oppressed and exploited land of Latin America." Since the time he wrote those words the movement has expanded, as he notes in the introduction to the revised edition of the work, written some fifteen years later. There he noted that the expansion was not only temporal, in the sense that some earlier formulations by himself and others had been refined, improved, and at times corrected as part of a process of maturation; the expansion was also spatial, in that thinkers on other continents and in other cultures have adopted the liberation perspective. We have already seen something of this in the work of the Filipina Benedictine sister Mary John Mananzan and the Zairean archbishop Bakole wa Ilunga. We will see it next in what Gutiérrez has called "the especially fruitful thinking of those who have adopted the feminist perspective."[15]

FEMINIST SPIRITUALITY: SANDRA SCHNEIDERS, JACQUELYN GRANT, AND ADA MARÍA ISASI-DÍAZ

Already in the first chapter of this book we mentioned the North American theologian Sandra Schneiders as being in the forefront of those who have written about the relatively new academic discipline of spirituality. In addition to that work and her publications in the fields of Scripture and canonical religious life in the Catholic Church (she herself joined a congregation of religious sisters in 1955), Schneiders has also written lucidly about feminism,

---

14. Second General Conference of Latin American Bishops, "Message to the Peoples of Latin America" (Medellín, September 6, 1968), in *Liberation Theology*, 91.

15. Gustavo Gutiérrez, *A Theology of Liberation: History, Politics, and Salvation*, trans. Caridad Inda and John Eagleson, rev. ed. (Maryknoll, N.Y.: Orbis Books, 1988), xix.

especially what she calls "Gospel feminism" as distinct from the secular version of this movement. The same threefold methodology that we saw in Latin American liberation theology likewise characterizes this kind of feminism, namely, the experience of oppression, reflection on this in the light of Christian faith and with the help of the social sciences, and working actively for liberation.

The experience to which Schneiders refers is that of women's being disadvantaged in relation to men in almost every conceivable setting—familial, cultural, social, and religious—resulting in women's relative powerlessness and inability to be self-determining. When discussing the root cause of this situation, feminists regularly say that "the personal is the political," meaning that the oppression experienced by women is not incidental but is generated by the social systems in which they live. The overarching term for all such systems is patriarchy, which Schneiders defines as "the social system of father-rule, which is the basic form of social organization in every historical society we know anything about, at least in the west."[16] As a result of this arrangement, in which the role of head of the social unit belonged to the husband-father, "there was an evident and intrinsic connection established between maleness, property, and power on the one hand and femaleness, economic dependence and powerlessness on the other" (23). The long-term goal of radical feminists (where "radical" means not "fanatical" but "going to the root, *radix*, of the problem") is accordingly a society in which all persons, regardless of their sex, can be self-determining, that is, able to attain "the effective recognition of their full humanity as persons and the freedom to exercise that personhood in every sphere" (9).

With regard to the question of how this relates to specifically Christian spirituality, Schneiders notes that some women have given up on the churches as being irredeemably patriarchal and have turned to other kinds of religious practice, including Wicca, a nature religion originating in pre-Christian Europe. Many others, however, including Schneiders herself, have remained in the church and are living in the hope that the gifts they can bring to the church will eventually be fully recognized. Such women, she writes, "bring a spiritual strength tempered in intense suffering and a loyalty that has survived twenty centuries of exclusion and oppression. To this vision of faith and this strength of hope they add a love of Christ, of the church itself, and of the world that has fueled a burning commitment to ministry since the earliest days of the church's history and which is still unquenched despite what raised consciousness has enabled them to see" (111).

---

16. Sandra M. Schneiders, *Beyond Patching: Faith and Feminism in the Catholic Church*, rev. ed. (New York: Paulist, 2004), 22. Subsequent parenthetical references to this book indicate the page number.

Certain features characterize the spirituality of these women, including five that Schneiders singles out and on which she briefly comments. First, and in accord with the fact that feminist spirituality is rooted in women's experience, there is much emphasis on narrating their stories, this being both a technique for consciousness raising and a source of mutual support: "By telling their own stories women appropriate as significant their own experience, which they have been taught to view as trivial" (87). Second, they seek to overcome traditional dichotomies of body and spirit by celebrating as holy and spiritually powerful precisely those aspects of bodiliness that are often associated with shame and silence (such as menstruation, which is to be regarded not as a taboo but as a sign of women's connectedness with the life cycle). This emphasis on human bodiliness is related to a third feature, the recognition that nonhuman nature, too, is to be revered and protected from exploitative violence: "Feminists are convinced that only a spirituality which values both women and all those elements of the universe that have been 'feminized,' including nature, children, the poor, the disabled, the aged, and the infirm, can contribute to a renewed and livable world" (88). Fourth, there is much emphasis on ritual that is joyful and fully participative as against the unemotional and overly verbal liturgical practice often found in mainline churches. The feature that Schneiders considers fifth and last is, she says, also perhaps the most important: the intrinsic relationship between personal growth and transformation on the one hand and the struggle for social justice on the other, since "the changes and growth which must happen in women if they are to be and to experience themselves as fully human . . . are the same changes that must occur in society, namely, the reintegration of what has been dichotomized, the empowerment of that which has been marginalized and abused, [and] the liberation of that which has been enslaved" (89).

In the preface to the revised edition of her book, Schneiders makes a point that had not seemed necessary at the time she published the first edition but that in fact has become widely acknowledged: there are many feminisms, even of the "Gospel" variety, meaning among other things that "white scholars cannot speak for women of color" (xiv). White feminists have undergone severe criticism for not recognizing this sooner, some of the criticism coming from black women, some from Latinas. Of the former, Jacquelyn Grant (b. 1948) has been among the most outspoken. An ordained minister in the African Methodist Episcopal Church, Grant insists that even though legal slavery in the United States was abolished at the time of the Civil War, the residue of many of its oppressive practices can still be detected in racist attitudes, which she finds even in well-meaning white feminists: "White women have defined the movement and presumed to do so not only for themselves but also for non-White women . . . [This is] to do what oppressors always do;

it is to define the rules and then solicit others to play the game . . . They have simply accepted and participated in the racism of the larger American society when they have done so."[17]

To emphasize the difference, Grant and other black women have generally avoided the term "feminism" and instead opted for a term coined by Alice Walker, "womanist," referring to such qualities as audaciousness, courage, willful behavior, responsibility, and being in charge.[18] Where womanism differs from white feminism is in its emphasis on three interconnected types of oppression: not only sexism but also racism and classism. As regards racism, "For many Black people, emancipation [from legal slavery] meant slavery without chains . . . The image that Blacks were inferior and that they were intended to service white America remained intact" (197). In turn, this brought with it the reality that blacks were largely members of the poorest class in the United States, "relegated in the labor market to the same service jobs and menial work which had been forced upon them during slavery . . . Blacks were servants and Whites were masters and never were the two to be changed" (197). By experiencing all three dynamics of oppression—those due to their sex, race, and class—"Black women share in the reality of a broader community. They share race suffering with Black men; with White women and other Third World women, they are victims of sexism; and with poor Blacks and Whites, and other Third World peoples, especially women, they are disproportionately poor" (216-17).

The points made in the preceding paragraph could be affirmed by black women of any religion or none. Grant does, however, also point to some specifically Christian aspects of womanist spirituality, above all the use of the Bible and the role of Jesus in this tradition. For black women the Bible was a major source for religious validation in their lives, but they were able to read or hear it critically, approaching the text in the light both of its own major concerns (for example, liberation for a covenanted life with God) and of their own experience as oppressed women. A former slave recalled that when the slave-master's minister would hold services for the slaves, he would regularly quote from the Letter to Titus: "Tell slaves to be submissive to their masters" (2:9), but this woman told her grandson, "I promised my Maker that if I ever learned to read and if freedom ever came, I would not read that part of the Bible."[19]

---

17. Jacquelyn Grant, *White Women's Christ and Black Women's Jesus: Feminist Christology and Womanist Response,* American Academy of Religion Academy Series 64 (Atlanta: Scholars Press, 1989), 200. Subsequent parenthetical references to this book indicate the page number.

18. Alice Walker, *In Search of Our Mother's Garden* (New York: Harcourt, Brace, Jovanovich, 1983), xi.

19. Howard Thurman, *Jesus and the Disinherited* (Nashville: Abingdon, 1949), 30-31, quoted by Grant, *White Women's Christ,* 212.

For many black women, the role of Jesus has been still more important than the Bible. Sojourner Truth, a former slave who became a religious missionary and gained national fame as a preacher for women's suffrage, was once asked if the source of her preaching was the Bible, to which she replied: "No, honey, can't preach from de Bible—can't read a letter. When I preaches, I has jest one text to preach from, an' I always preaches from this one. My text is, 'When I found Jesus.'"[20] For her and for countless black women, Jesus has been encountered as one who empowers them, one with whom they can identify because they believe that he identifies with them. Long before the term "womanist" was coined, and continuing up to today, what Grant calls this "tough, active love" of Jesus has been central to the spirituality of countless black women.

The kind of criticism that Jacquelyn Grant and other blacks have directed at white feminists has also been voiced by women in the Hispanic/Latina community, most forcefully perhaps by Ada María Isasi-Díaz, who came to the United States as an exile from Fidel Castro's Cuba while she was still in her teens. She writes:

> Euro-American feminists, being part of the dominant culture, deal with Hispanic women—and other racial/ethnic women—differently from the way they deal with each other. They take for granted that feminism in the USA is *their* garden, and therefore they will decide what manner of work racial/ethnic women will do there . . . Euro-American feminists need to understand that as long as they refuse to recognize that oppressive power-over is an intrinsic element of their racism/ethnic prejudice, they will continue to do violence to feminism.[21]

Just as black feminists sought a term that would symbolize the distinctive characteristics of their movement, so too did Isasi-Díaz and some of her companions. They found it in their music, where women are simply called *mujer*, so they decided to call their particular form of feminist theology *mujerista* theology. Like the womanists, *mujeristas* focus not only on sexism but also on racism and classism. Although Isasi-Díaz herself tends to avoid the term "spiritual" because of the anti-corporeal connotations it has acquired in some circles, she does at times use such terminology, as when writing that "spirituality is measured by our ability and willingness to immerse ourselves

---

20. Olive Gilbert, *Sojourner Truth: Narrative and Book of Life* (Chicago: Johnson Pub. Co., 1970), 83, quoted by Grant, *White Women's Christ,* 214.

21. Ada María Isasi-Díaz, *Mujerista Theology: A Theology for the Twenty-First Century* (Maryknoll, N.Y.: Orbis Books, 1996), 18-19.

in personal relationships and in struggles for justice."[22] This concern for justice is one of the most important aspects of her *mujerista* spirituality, another being the importance of popular religion. We will briefly consider each.

Many of Isasi-Díaz's essays are autobiographical, and in these she frequently mentions the transformative impact of the three years she spent as a missionary in Peru. At that time she was a newly professed member of the Ursuline order of religious sisters and was living in one of the poorest sections of Lima. She writes: "I often talk about those years as an 'exodus' experience—an experience that radically changed my life. Those three years gave me the opportunity of being reborn; they made me understand what the gospel message of justice and preferential option for the poor was all about."[23] Although she later left the Ursulines, she continued her deep concern for issues of justice. In another autobiographical essay she recounts a time some years later when she was walking a picket line on a cold winter day outside the South African embassy in Washington, D.C., to protest that government's policy of apartheid. To her surprise, she found herself undergoing what she later called a mystical experience:

> Little by little I became aware of an immense peace washing over me. I felt myself to be where I was and in many other places at the same time. I felt I was being cared for by God, that the divine was with me and in me in a way different from my usual experience. This sense of the divine in me and I in the divine was a bodily one: I could feel, sense God, and I could wrap my arms around the divine in an unmediated way, unmediated by understanding or even faith. The intensity did not last long, and yet this sense of participating in the divine filled me in such a way that it remains with me today. The experience left me with an immediate sense of joy beyond anything of my own willing.[24]

Isasi-Díaz certainly does not claim that such an experience is the reason why she continues to struggle against injustice, whether it be what is suffered by Latina women or by other groups, but what she experienced that day on a sidewalk in Washington is surely in the background of what she has written elsewhere: "As the years have gone by I have accepted that for me to strive to live to the fullest by struggling against injustice is to draw nearer and nearer to the divine. Drawing closer to God and struggling for justice have become for me one and the same thing."[25]

22. Isasi-Díaz, *La Lucha Continues: Mujerista Theology* (Maryknoll, N.Y.: Orbis Books, 2004), 29.
23. Isasi-Díaz, *Mujerista Theology*, 24.
24. Isasi-Díaz, *La Lucha Continues*, 24-25.
25. Isasi-Díaz, *Mujerista Theology*, 33.

A second key aspect of *mujerista* spirituality, at least as found in the writings of Isasi-Díaz, is an emphasis on popular religion. Here, too, she regularly develops the theme in an autobiographical manner, as when she recalls the time when she was invited to walk in the place of honor in a procession on the outskirts of Lima in honor of Jesus Christ under the title of El Señor de los Milagros, the principal popular devotion in Peru. Hundreds of thousands participate each year in the main procession, while many parishes also have their own processions. Isasi-Díaz saw barefooted women walking next to her in fulfillment of promises, little children being lifted high to touch the statue of Christ, and elaborate altars decorated with flowers at various places along the route of the procession. She later reflected on what this had meant to her:

> As I walked home after the procession, I realized how privileged I was to have been part of such an outpouring of faith—the faith of the poor and the oppressed that maintains them, that is their sustenance in the most trying of situations. I felt that my well-reasoned faith, a so-called sophisticated faith illumined by the "right" kind of theology, was not any deeper or any more pleasing to God than the faith of the poor people I had seen expressed for two days . . . But perhaps the most important learning from the experience was the fact that I came to trust the religious understandings and practices of the poor and oppressed. I have ever since accepted their religiosity as part of the ongoing revelation of God in our world—in my life.[26]

Isasi-Díaz turns to another expression of Hispanic popular religion when she describes the *fiesta* honoring Our Lady of Guadalupe at the parish where she often worships in East Harlem, with the church blanketed with roses and the parishioners singing devotional songs with great fervor. She concludes: "The religious practices of these 'minoritized' people enable them to resist the negative feelings society projects on them . . . Living in a society that does not value them, their conviction that Guadalupe and her divine son love them satisfies the need we all have to be precious for someone. Just as we are giving ourselves to Jesus and Mary, they are giving themselves to us without reserve. This is all that these grassroot folk need to know. This is what gives us strength to carry on in very difficult circumstances."[27]

Strange as it may sound at first hearing, the highly affective nature of these Hispanic fiestas is generically similar to the exuberance of religious feeling that was expressed in the Great Awakening that occurred in New England in

26. Isasi-Díaz, *Mujerista Theology*, 30.
27. Isasi-Díaz, *La Lucha Continues*, 27-28.

the early 1740s. Its principal defender was the man often called North America's greatest theologian, to whose spirituality we now turn.

AFFECTIVE SPIRITUALITY: JONATHAN EDWARDS AND PENTECOSTALISM

Jonathan Edwards (1703-1758) was born in East Windsor, Connecticut, into a devout Congregationalist family, his father and his maternal grandfather, the renowned Solomon Stoddard, both being ministers in that denomination. He himself was ordained in 1727 in Northampton, Massachusetts, where he shared the pulpit with his grandfather for two years and then was on his own after Stoddard's death in 1729. Slightly more than a decade later a wave of religious revivals peaked throughout many of the American colonies in conjunction with the preaching tour of England's famed revivalist George Whitefield, a wave that historians call the Great Awakening, usually dated from 1740-1742.

Inspired by the visiting English revivalist, many uneducated itinerant preachers surfaced at this time, and with many of them came controversy. The most notorious instance of discord took place when an itinerant preacher named James Davenport led a group of men and women out of the precincts of the established church in New London, Connecticut, and onto the town wharf, where they placed all the great works of the Puritan authors on a bonfire and incinerated them. Such instances of misplaced zeal led to a deep split among the American clergy. Some, led by Charles Chauncey of Boston, were convinced that the revivals were simply the work of the devil, while others, with Edwards at their head, felt that there had indeed been excesses (such as the book burnings) but that the revivals as such reflected what Edwards called "a divine and supernatural light" at work in the community.

Although Edwards is notorious for the sermon "Sinners in the Hands of an Angry God," which he preached during those very years and which so terrified some of his hearers that they would fall into frantic sobbing, screaming, and fainting right in the pews, the content of that sermon is not at all representative of the bulk of his preaching or of the way he wrote about "true religion." Such religion, he said, "in great part consists in holy affections," and the greatest of them all is love, the "fountain of all other affections."[28] Accordingly,

---

28. Jonathan Edwards, *A Treatise Concerning Religious Affections*, in *Selected Writings of Jonathan Edwards*, ed. Harold P. Simonson, 2nd ed. (Long Grove, Ill.: Waveland Press, 2004), 125, 128.

> from a vigorous, affectionate, and fervent love to God will necessarily arise other religious affections; hence will arise an intense hatred and abhorrence of sin, fear of sin, and a dread of God's displeasure; gratitude to God for his goodness, complacence and joy in God when God is graciously and sensibly present, and grief when he is absent, and a joyful hope when a future enjoyment of God is expected, and fervent zeal for the glory of God. And in like manner, from a fervent love to men, will arise all other virtuous affections towards men.[29]

There is no doubt that Edwards himself was here writing from his own experience. Even though he delivered his sermons without the histrionics that have sometimes characterized famous preachers, the deep emotion with which he spoke was evident to all. Of Edwards's speaking style, his younger friend and associate Samuel Hopkins wrote: "His words often discovered a great degree of inward fervor, without much noise or external emotion, and fell with great weight on the minds of his hearers. He made but little motion of his head or hands . . . but spake so as to discover the motion of his own heart, which tended in the most natural and effectual manner to move and affect others."[30] Edwards himself gives us a glimpse into this "motion of his own heart" in his autobiographical *Personal Narrative*, which is among the most beautiful pieces of spiritual literature ever written. Just as earlier writers like Origen and Bernard of Clairvaux had turned to the Song of Songs to help express their love of Christ, so too did Edwards in his narrative, even as he also turned to that other great book—the book of nature—to give voice to such love. Looking back on a time of his life some twenty years earlier, he wrote:

> My mind was greatly engaged to spend my time in reading and meditating on Christ, on the beauty and excellency of his person, and the lovely way of salvation by free grace in him. I found no books so delightful to me, as those that treat of these subjects. Those words ... used to be abundantly with me, "I am the Rose of Sharon, and the Lily of the valleys" [Sg 2:1]. The words seemed to me sweetly to represent the loveliness and beauty of Jesus Christ ... The sense I had of divine things would often of a sudden kindle up, as it were, a sweet burning in my heart, an ardor of soul that I know not how to express ...

---

29. Edwards, *Treatise,* in *Selected Writings,* 129-30.

30. Samuel Hopkins, *The Life and Character of the Late Reverend Mr. Jonathan Edwards* (Boston, 1765), quoted by George M. Marsden, *Jonathan Edwards: A Life* (New Haven/London: Yale University Press, 2003), 220.

> After this my sense of divine things gradually increased, and became more lively, and had more of that inward sweetness. The appearance of every thing was altered; there seemed to be, as it were, a calm, sweet cast, or appearance of divine glory, in almost every thing. God's excellency, his wisdom, his purity and love, seemed to appear in every thing; in the sun, and moon, and stars; in the clouds and blue sky; in the grass, flowers, trees; in the water, and all nature.[31]

It would be difficult to read those words and not think back to Francis of Assisi and his "Canticle of Brother Sun," just as in another sense one finds in Edwards's reflections on the centrality of affections a foreshadowing not only of later revivals in Baptist and Methodist churches but also of another powerful movement in Christianity in recent centuries, the Pentecostal movement.

Pentecostal-like revivals, with their emphasis on "baptism in the Holy Spirit" and speaking in tongues, sprang up in various parts of the world throughout the nineteenth century, but a particularly influential event occurred in the first decade of the twentieth century in Los Angeles, California. A young black preacher named William Seymour began teaching that God had a third blessing in addition to the traditional two of conversion and sanctification. This third was "the baptism of the Holy Spirit," paralleling the experience that came upon the disciples at the first Christian Pentecost, as described in the second chapter of the Acts of the Apostles. Excommunicated by his pastor from the Church of the Nazarene for teaching this alleged heresy, Seymour and his followers rented an old church on Azusa Street. There, in the spring of 1906, members of his congregation began speaking in tongues and manifesting other signs of deep religious fervor. In the words of one historian of the movement, "They shouted three days and three nights. It was the Easter season. The people came from everywhere . . . As the people came in, they would fall under God's power; and the whole city was stirred. They shouted there until the foundation of the house gave way, but no one was hurt."[32] Soon, Protestants from several other countries came to see what was happening and then took the movement back to their own lands, where it flourished to such a degree that by the beginning of the twenty-first century it has been estimated that Pentecostal and charismatic Christians represent more than 27 percent of global Christianity.[33]

---

31. Edwards, *Personal Narrative*, in *Selected Writings*, 21-22.

32. Walter Hollenweger, *The Pentecostals* (Peabody, Mass.: Hendrickson, 1988), 23.

33. Christopher Cocksworth, "Charismatic Spirituality," in *The New Westminster Dictionary of Christian Spirituality*, ed. Philip Sheldrake (Louisville, Ky.: Westminster John Knox, 2005), 186.

In Latin American countries, Pentecostal Christians are sometimes called *evangélicos*, thereby indicating the central role that the Bible plays in their lives. After noting that a hand-held Bible is a badge of participation in many Pentecostal churches, the sociologist of religion David Lehmann goes on to discuss the immediacy of the link between the persons in the scriptural text (such as Moses or the people of Israel) and the listener or reader: The former are "exemplary personages . . . whose histories are worthy of imitation, not saints to whom votive offerings or petitions are made. The personages may be heroic, or virtuous, but they are not super-human: on the contrary, their humanity is emphasized so that the listener can identify with them, and the moral has to be explicated every time the story is told."[34]

We mentioned above the exuberant nature of the services at the Azusa Street Mission in the first decade of the twentieth century. Such exuberance continues to characterize Pentecostal worship everywhere in the world. This is manifested in such phenomena as the experience of being filled with or overpowered by the Holy Spirit ("the baptism of the Holy Spirit"), speaking in tongues, proclaiming prophetic words, giving evidence of miraculous healings through expectant prayer and the laying on of hands, and an increased recognition of the presence of evil in the world. Although some persons find their first exposure to such forms of worship frightening or even repulsive, they often feel drawn to return and eventually become full participants. In an interview with a sociologist, one Brazilian woman described her conversion in the following way:

> At the beginning . . . I didn't like it because there was a lot of screaming, people falling on the floor, and I was scared . . . But later I got used to it and I liked it. I plan to continue in this religion until the end . . . Before going to church I had many problems. I was very nervous, so I would get upset about anything. At church they do a cleansing. It seems like we change . . . I got many things in life that I didn't have.[35]

That woman's emphasis on the way her life was changed for the better is reflected time and time again in the statements of others. Richard Shaull, who has studied the Pentecostal movement in Brazil for many years, has summed up its transformative effect in the following words:

---

34. David Lehmann, *Struggle for the Spirit: Religious Transformation and Popular Culture in Brazil and Latin America* (Cambridge, U.K.: Polity Press, 1996), 179.

35. "Interview with Leila," in Richard Shaull and Waldo Cesar, *Pentecostalism and the Future of the Christian Churches: Promises, Limitations, Challenges* (Grand Rapids/Cambridge, U.K.: Eerdmans, 2000), 17.

> Especially among women, who constitute the majority in most Pentecostal churches, this spiritual experience produces an extraordinary new quality of life, which has a decisive impact on the family and also on the church and society . . .
>
> When they are welcomed in Pentecostal churches, they find "communities of healing" where sisterly love helps them to recover from the fierce individualism characteristic of the society in which they live. In this atmosphere of support and solidarity women experience great changes in their lives and feel the compelling need to witness to others about what God and the brothers and sisters of the churches, their "extended family," have done to bring about the complete transformation of their lives.[36]

The Roman Catholic counterpart of this Protestant Pentecostal spirituality is usually called the Catholic Charismatic renewal, which began after the Second Vatican Council on several university campuses in the midwestern United States and rapidly spread throughout the country and abroad. A leading Belgian cardinal, Leon Joseph Suenens, became a guide and mentor for this movement. In his many writings about the Charismatic renewal he regularly used phrases that could just as easily have come from the pen of Jonathan Edwards as the latter defended the religious fervor of his day against the criticism of opponents like Charles Chauncey. Thus, of the early participants in the Catholic movement, Cardinal Suenens wrote: "They spoke of a new awareness of the love of God such as they had not experienced before; of a desire to pray and glorify God; of an insatiable thirst for Scripture. Moreover they felt a power within them to bear witness to the risen Christ."[37]

Charismatic prayer, however, is not the only kind that has become prominent in recent times, for there are also numerous practitioners of one or another form of contemplative prayer, many of whom have been inspired and instructed by the writings of a prolific monastic author who became the most widely read monk in Christian history. Thomas Merton's willingness, indeed eagerness, to learn not only from the tradition of the Eastern and Western churches but also from the other great world religions made him, along with Abhishiktananda and Bede Griffiths, one of the leading pioneers in what is sometimes called interfaith spirituality.

---

36. Shaull, in Shaull and Cesar, *Pentecostalism,* 228.
37. Leon Joseph Cardinal Suenens, *A New Pentecost?*, trans. Francis Martin (New York: Seabury, 1974), 74.

CONTEMPLATIVE PRAYER: THOMAS MERTON

Thomas Merton began his best-known book in these words: "On the last day of January 1915, under the sign of the Water Bearer, in a year of a great war, and down in the shadow of some French mountains on the borders of Spain, I came into the world. Free by nature, in the image of God, I was nevertheless the prisoner of my own violence and my own selfishness, in the image of the world into which I was born."[38] The rest of that book, and in some respects the rest of his eighty or more other books, can be seen as a series of reflections on how he or any other human being can surmount such selfishness and so come to what he often called "the true self," the deep center of our being where we are invited to union with God.

The number of topics addressed in Merton's many books, articles, and poems is staggering, but there is no subject about which he wrote more frequently or passionately than that of contemplation. One of his earliest publications was a short book entitled *What Is Contemplation?*, written in response to a college student's request for an answer to that very question. Later books by him bear such titles as *Seeds of Contemplation*, *New Seeds of Contemplation*, *Contemplation in a World of Action*, and *Contemplative Prayer*, while just a few weeks before his accidental death while on a trip to Asia in 1968 he wrote a circular letter to his friends in which he commented positively on the scholarship and training of the Tibetan Buddhist monks he had met and then immediately added: "But they are also specialists in meditation and contemplation. This is what appeals to me most."[39] Since a person could not possibly come to an awareness of what Merton called one's true self apart from a contemplative stance, the best way to appreciate Merton's importance for Christian spirituality is to see what he said about contemplation.

For one thing, Merton saw contemplation as something to which all Christians, and indeed all human beings, can and should aspire. Even though he himself lived the final twenty-seven years of his life as a Trappist monk, he came more and more to the realization that one need not live in a monastery in order to be genuinely contemplative. Persons living very active lives in the world may well be "hidden" or "masked" contemplatives. Such persons "may reach a higher degree of sanctity than others who have been apparently favored with a deeper interior life," for "the 'masked contemplative' is

38. Thomas Merton, *The Seven Storey Mountain* (New York: Harcourt, Brace, 1948), 1.

39. Thomas Merton, *The Asian Journal*, ed. Naomi Burton et al. (New York: New Directions, 1975), 324.

one whose contemplation is hidden from no one so much as from himself," and "it is a strange and deep truth that the grace of contemplation is . . . in a sense most pure when it is barely known."[40] It is in part because of such statements that the prominent Merton scholar William H. Shannon has claimed that "Merton's unique contribution to American spirituality was to make contemplation an 'in' subject for all who were willing to undergo the spiritual discipline it called for."[41]

If Merton made contemplation an "in" subject, this was not because he was inclined to give precise definitions of what he meant by the term. Perhaps the closest he came was in an early book where he spoke of it as that "by which we know and love God as He is in Himself, apprehending Him in a deep and vital experience which is beyond the reach of any natural understanding."[42] He never disowned this quasi definition, but one finds in his later works a more personal kind of language, primarily couched in terms of "awareness" and "attentiveness." He was not especially interested in fine distinctions of the sort common in scholarly literature about the subject. He sought instead to focus on continuities in Christian experience, as when he wrote in one of his later essays: "To reach a true awareness of [God] as well as ourselves, we have to renounce our selfish and limited self and enter into a whole new kind of existence, discovering an inner center of motivation and love which makes us see ourselves and everything else in an entirely new light. Call it faith, call it (at a more advanced stage) contemplative illumination, call it the sense of God or even mystical union: all these are different aspects and levels of the same kind of realization: the awakening to a new awareness of ourselves in Christ, created in Him, redeemed by Him, to be transformed and glorified in and with Him."[43] It is important to note the terminology here: "awareness" (twice), "realization," "awakening." To the extent that one has this awareness of oneself "in Christ" or "in God," to that extent one is leading a contemplative way of life, regardless of where one lives.

As a simple illustration of that kind of awareness in Merton himself, let us consider a passage from *The Sign of Jonas*, based on journals that he kept from the winter of 1946 until the summer of 1952. On a February day in 1950 he had gone up to the garden house attic after dinner to meditate and pray, as was his custom, when suddenly he became aware of great excitement in the

40. Merton, *The Inner Experience: Notes on Contemplation*, ed. William H. Shannon (San Francisco: Harper, 2003), 64-65.

41. William H. Shannon, "Contemplation," in *The Thomas Merton Encyclopedia*, ed. William H. Shannon et al. (Maryknoll, N.Y.: Orbis Books, 2002), 81.

42. Thomas Merton, *Seeds of Contemplation* (New York: New Directions, 1949), 144.

43. Thomas Merton, "Contemplation in a World of Action," in idem, *Contemplation in a World of Action* (Garden City, N.Y.: Doubleday, Image Books, 1973), 175-76.

pasture below, which was full of starlings. At one point an eagle attacked them but the starlings flew off before any of them could be caught. Soon they had all again alighted on the ground. "Then, like lightning, it happened. I saw a scare go into the cloud of birds . . . and, in that split second, from behind the house and from over my roof a hawk came down like a bullet and shot straight into the middle of the starlings just as they were getting off the ground. They rose into the air and there was a slight scuffle on the ground as the hawk got his talons into the one bird he had nailed." Up to this point, one might compliment Merton on his ability to put into vivid language a scene from what Tennyson called "nature red in tooth and claw," but many nature writers have done that just as well, if not better. Merton, however, apparently as the most natural thing in the world, moves immediately to what could truly be called a contemplative response to the episode, the response of someone who is "aware" or "awake" to what it means to be "in Christ." In the final paragraph of the entry he addresses the hawk directly: "I wonder if my admiration for you gives me an affinity for you, artist! I wonder if there will ever be something connatural between us, between your flight and my heart stirred in hiding to serve Christ, as you, soldier, serve your nature. And God's love a thousand times more terrible!"[44]

There are countless passages in Merton that could illustrate the same point, some of them much more celebrated, such as the poignant reflection "Fire Watch, July 4, 1952," which serves as the epilogue to *The Sign of Jonas*, or the frequently quoted passage in *Conjectures of a Guilty Bystander* where Merton, while standing on a street corner in Louisville, Kentucky, "was suddenly overwhelmed with the realization that I loved all those people, that they were mine and I theirs, that we could not be alien to one another even though we were total strangers. It was like waking from a dream of separateness, of spurious self-isolation in a special world, the world of renunciation and supposed holiness."[45] The value of the account of the hawk and starlings, however, lies precisely in its still more mundane character, which allows it to exemplify how a contemplative stance will color practically anything we experience.

This also helps clarify Merton's increasing interest in Zen meditation as he grew older. The terms that characterized his understanding of Christian contemplation—awareness, awakening, realization—are the very ones that are also emphasized in Zen. In one of his essays on that tradition, Merton wrote: "Buddhist meditation, but above all that of Zen, seeks not to *explain* but to *pay attention*, to *become aware*, to *be mindful*, in other words to develop a certain *kind of consciousness that is above and beyond deception* by verbal formu-

---

44. Merton, *The Sign of Jonas* (New York: Harcourt, Brace, 1953), 274-75.
45. Merton, *Conjectures of a Guilty Bystander* (Garden City, N.Y.: Doubleday, Image Books, 1968), 156.

las."[46] Those who knew Merton best knew that there was no danger of his abandoning his Christian faith, but he was certainly convinced that his life as a Christian contemplative could be enhanced by drawing on the wisdom of other religious traditions, including Judaism, Sufism, and Zen and Tibetan Buddhism, to name only a few. He did not at all disdain the conceptual formulations that are found in the Christian creeds and theology, but he was also aware of the danger of stopping at these "instead of entering fully into the life of hope and love consummated by union with the invisible God 'in Christ and in the Spirit,' thus fully sharing in the Divine Nature."[47] This is one reason why his works continue to be read avidly by persons all over the world, for he modeled in his own writings and behavior the openness to the spiritual and moral truths in *all* the world's major religious traditions that was encouraged, even mandated, by the Second Vatican Council's decree *Nostra Aetate* on the relationship of the Catholic Church to other religions.

Another reason for the abiding interest in Merton's works is the forceful way in which he insisted that an authentic contemplative life necessarily includes an effective concern for all the great issues that confront people throughout the world in our time, including ones raised by Evelyn Underhill in Europe, by Mary John Mananzan in Asia, by Bakole wa Ilunga in Africa, by Gustavo Gutiérrez in Latin America, and by Sandra Schneiders, Jacquelyn Grant, and Ada María Isasi-Díaz in North America. Merton summed up some of the most important of these in a journal entry on June 6, 1963, when he wrote of the need for "sensitivity on the issues of peace, racial justice, but also technology and the great spiritual problem of the profound disturbances of ecology all over the world, the tragic waste and spoilage of natural resources, etc."[48] Because his vision knew no national or racial boundaries, it is fitting that this section on Thomas Merton should conclude our book's presentation of Christian spirituality in *global* perspective.

QUESTIONS FOR REFLECTION

1. Does Harold Schilling's threefold schema of experience, reflection on experience, and praxis make sense to you as a way of better understanding the work of liberation theologians? If so, how crucial is it to experience the lot of the poor directly, as distinct from reading about it?
2. Assuming that Gutiérrez is correct in saying that "our methodology is our spirituality," what is it about the methodology of liberation theologians that makes

46. Merton, "A Christian Looks at Zen," in idem, *Zen and the Birds of Appetite* (New York: New Directions, 1968), 38.
47. Ibid., 40.
48. Merton, *Turning Toward the World: The Pivotal Years*, ed. Victor A. Kramer (San Francisco: Harper, 1996), 330.

them so controversial in some quarters? What do you yourself consider to be the major strengths and weaknesses of their approach?

3. Some men are feminists, while some women are very critical of the feminist movement, claiming that they themselves do not feel at all oppressed. How pervasive (if present at all) do you find the oppression of women to be in your own society? If you judge that it does exist there, what do you consider the most effective ways to overcome it?
4. Some members of mainline Christian churches feel that the Pentecostal movement is characterized by excessive displays of emotion, while others judge it to be a healthy reaction to an overly cerebral way of being Christian. What is your own position regarding the place of affectivity or heartfelt emotion in Christian living?
5. Much more could have been said about Thomas Merton, including details about his vigorous protests against racism and against the U.S. military involvement in Vietnam during the final decade of his life. Do you think that his contemplative practice actually increased his concern for issues of justice and peace, or do you believe that these were just two relatively unrelated aspects of his life and work? If you think there was a connection, how would you describe the way contemplation would lead a person to become engaged in societal issues?

SUGGESTIONS FOR FURTHER READING AND STUDY

On Liberation Spirituality

Ashley, Matthew. "Liberation Spirituality." In *The New Westminster Dictionary of Christian Spirituality*, edited by Philip Sheldrake, 406-7. Louisville, Ky.: Westminster John Knox, 2005. This volume was simultaneously published in London, England, under the title *The New SCM Dictionary of Christian Spirituality*.

Goizueta, Roberto S. "Liberation Theology, Influence on Spirituality." In *The New Dictionary of Catholic Spirituality*, edited by Michael Downey, 597-600. Collegeville, Minn.: Liturgical Press, 1993.

Gutiérrez, Gustavo. *A Theology of Liberation: History, Politics, and Salvation*. Translated and edited by Sister Caridad Inda and John Eagleson. Rev. ed. Maryknoll, N.Y.: Orbis Books, 1988. See especially the introductions to the original edition and to the revised edition (pp. xiii-xlvi), and chap. 10, "Encountering God in History" (pp. 106-20).

Hennelly, Alfred T., S.J., ed. *Liberation Theology: A Documentary History*. Maryknoll, N.Y.: Orbis Books, 1990.

On Feminist Spirituality

Grant, Jacquelyn. *White Women's Christ and Black Women's Jesus: Feminist Christology and Womanist Response*. American Academy of Religion Academy Series 64.

Atlanta: Scholars Press, 1989. See especially chap. 7, "Women's Experience Revisited: The Challenge of the Darker Sister" (pp. 195-230).

Isasi-Díaz, Ada María. *La Lucha Continues: Mujerista Theology*. Maryknoll, N.Y.: Orbis, 2004. See especially chap. 1, "*La Lucha*: My Story" (pp. 11-23), and chap. 2, "Spirituality of the Picket Line" (pp. 24-36).

Purvis, Sally B. "Christian Feminist Spirituality." In *Christian Spirituality: Post-Reformation and Modern*, edited by Louis Dupré and Don E. Saliers, 500-19. World Spirituality 18. New York: Crossroad, 1989.

Schneiders, Sandra M. *Beyond Patching: Faith and Feminism in the Catholic Church*. Rev. ed. New York: Paulist, 2004. See especially chap. 3, "Feminist Spirituality: Christian Alternative or Alternative to Christianity?" (pp. 72-112).

On Affective Spirituality

Agnew, Mary Barbara, C.PP.S. "Charismatic Renewal." In *The New Dictionary of Catholic Spirituality*, edited by Michael Downey, 143-46. Collegeville, Minn.: Liturgical Press, 1993.

Edwards, Jonathan. *Selected Writings of Jonathan Edwards*. Edited by Harold P. Simonson. 2nd ed. Long Grove, Ill.: Waveland, 2004. See especially the excerpts from Edwards's *Personal Narrative* (pp. 19-31), the sermon entitled "A Divine and Supernatural Light" (pp. 49-65), and the excerpts from his *Treatise on Religious Affections* (pp. 123-30).

Land, Steven J. "Pentecostal Spirituality: Living in the Spirit." In *Christian Spirituality: Post-Reformation and Modern*, edited by Louis Dupré and Don E. Saliers, 479-99. World Spirituality 18. New York: Crossroad, 1989.

On Contemplation and Contemplative Prayer

Merton, Thomas. "Contemplation in a World of Action." In idem, *Contemplation in a World of Action*, 172-79. Garden City, N.Y.: Doubleday, Image Books, 1973.

———. *The Inner Experience: Notes on Contemplation*. Edited by William H. Shannon. San Francisco: Harper, 2003. See especially chap. 2, "The Awakening of the Inner Self" (pp. 6-18), and chap. 5, "Kinds of Contemplation" (pp. 57-70).

———. "A Letter on the Contemplative Life." In idem, *The Monastic Journey*, edited by Brother Patrick Hart, 218-23. Garden City, N.Y.: Doubleday, Image Books, 1978.

Shannon, William H. "Contemplation." In *The Thomas Merton Encyclopedia*, edited by William H. Shannon, Christine M. Bochen, and Patrick F. O'Connell, 79-84. Maryknoll, N.Y.: Orbis, 2002.

Selected Annotated Bibliography

ANTHOLOGIES OF PRIMARY SOURCES

Dupré, Louis, and James A. Wiseman, O.S.B., eds. *Light from Light: An Anthology of Christian Mysticism.* 2nd ed., rev. New York: Paulist, 2001. Contains extensive selections from twenty-three authors from the third century to the twentieth, including fifteen who are discussed in the present volume.

Egan, Harvey, S.J., ed. *An Anthology of Christian Mysticism.* Collegeville, Minn.: Liturgical Press, 1991. Includes selections from fifty-five authors plus some from the Bible; the selections are generally much shorter than those in the preceding anthology.

DICTIONARIES AND ENCYCLOPEDIAS

Downey, Michael, ed. *The New Dictionary of Catholic Spirituality.* Collegeville, Minn.: Liturgical Press, A Michael Glazier Book, 1993. Its 1,083 pages contain articles by 160 scholars, the articles being arranged according to ten topics: The Christian Mysteries, The Human Person, The Moral Life, The Person in Relation to the World, Growth and Development in the Spiritual Life, Prayer, Liturgy and Devotion, Discipline(s), History, and Types and Schools of Spirituality.

Dupré, Louis, and Don E. Saliers, eds. *Christian Spirituality: Post-Reformation and Modern.* World Spirituality 18. New York: Crossroad, 1981. This volume has four main parts: Roman Catholic Schools and Movements (e.g., Early Jesuit Spirituality), Post-Reformation Protestant and Anglican Spirituality (e.g., The Spirituality of the Afro-American Traditions), Orthodox Spirituality (e.g., Theosis in the Eastern Christian Tradition), and Twentieth-Century Trajectories (e.g., Christian Spirituality in an Ecumenical Age).

McGinn, Bernard, John Meyendorff, and Jean Leclercq, eds. *Christian Spirituality: Origins to the Twelfth Century.* World Spirituality 16. New York: Crossroad, 1985. This is the first of three volumes devoted to Christian spirituality in Crossroad's twenty-five-volume series World Spirituality: An Encyclopedic History of the Religious Quest. The nineteen chapters are divided into two main parts: Periods and Movements (e.g., The Early Christian Community), and Themes and Values (e.g., Liturgy and Spirituality).

Raitt, Jill, ed., in collaboration with Bernard McGinn and John Meyendorff. *Christian Spirituality: High Middle Ages and Reformation.* World Spirituality 17. New York: Crossroad, 1987. Similar in format to the preceding volume, here the twenty chapters are divided into two main parts: Schools and Movements (e.g, Religious

Women in the Later Middle Ages), and Themes (e.g, Marian Devotion in the Western Church).

Sheldrake, Philip, ed. *The New Westminster Dictionary of Christian Spirituality.* Louisville, Ky.: Westminster John Knox, 2005. At 680 pages, this dictionary is shorter than Michael Downey's, but its coverage is broader in that it includes many articles relating to the Eastern and Protestant churches as well as the Catholic Church. The first seventy-nine pages contain thirteen essays on basic topics, such as Spirituality and Culture, Spirituality and the Dialogue of Religions, and Contemporary Spirituality. A total of 180 scholars contributed to this work. It was published simultaneously in London under the title *The New SCM Dictionary of Christian Spirituality.*

SOME COLLECTIONS OF ESSAYS ON BROAD TOPICS

Abraham, K.C., and Bernadette Mbuy-Beya, eds. *Spirituality of the Third World: A Cry for Life.* Maryknoll, N.Y.: Orbis Books, 1994. This is a collection of papers from the Third General Assembly of the Ecumenical Association of Third World Theologians, held in 1992 in Nairobi, Kenya. Among the fifteen papers are ones on "The Spirituality of the Brazilian Base Communities" and "The Jesus of Faith: A Christological Contribution to an Ecumenical Third-World Spirituality."

Maas, Robin, and Gabriel O'Donnell, O.P., eds. *Spiritual Traditions for the Contemporary Church.* Nashville, Tenn.: Abingdon, 1990. The fourteen chapters of this book are divided into three main parts: The Roots of Contemporary Western Spirituality, Distinctive Spiritual Traditions, and The Feminine Dimension in Christian Spirituality. A unique feature of the volume is the placement of a "practicum" after each chapter; the practicum is intended to enable the reader to assimilate into his or her own devotional life the practice described in that particular chapter.

Senn, Frank C. *Protestant Spiritual Traditions.* New York: Paulist, 1986. Contains clearly written essays about the spirituality of the Lutheran, Reformed, Anabaptist, Anglican, Puritan, Pietist, and Methodist Churches.

Shorter, Aylward, W. F., ed. *African Christian Spirituality.* London: Geoffrey Chapman, 1978; Maryknoll, N.Y.: Orbis Books, 1980. The thirty-one short pieces in this volume are divided into two main parts: African Christian Spirituality (e.g., "A World of the Spirit"), and Readings in African Christian Spirituality (e.g., "The Religious Phenomenon of African-ness," "Jesus Christ—Universal Brother," and "African Culture and Spontaneous Prayer").

Index